THE LIFE OF JOHN RASTRICK, 1650–1727

THE LIFE OF JOHN RASTRICK, 1650–1727

edited by
ANDREW CAMBERS

CAMDEN FIFTH SERIES
Volume 36

CAMBRIDGE
UNIVERSITY PRESS

FOR THE ROYAL HISTORICAL SOCIETY
University College London, Gower Street, London WC1 6BT
2010

Published by the Press Syndicate of the University of Cambridge
The Edinburgh Building, Cambridge CB2 8RU, United Kingdom
32 Avenue of the Americas, New York, NY 10013-2473, USA
477 Williamstown Road, Port Melbourne, VIC 3207, Australia
C/Orense, 4, Planta 13, 28020 Madrid, Spain
Lower Ground Floor, Nautica Building, The Water Club,
Beach Road, Granger Bay, 8005 Cape Town, South Africa

First published 2010

A catalogue record for this book is available from the British Library

ISBN 9781107007703 hardback

SUBSCRIPTIONS. The serial publications of the Royal Historical Society, *Royal Historical Society Transactions* (ISSN 0080–4401) and Camden Fifth Series (ISSN 0960–1163) volumes, may be purchased together on annual subscription. The 2010 subscription price, which includes print and electronic access (but not VAT), is £113 (US $190 in the USA, Canada, and Mexico) and includes Camden Fifth Series, volumes 36 and 37 (published in July and December) and Transactions Sixth Series, volume 20 (published in December). Japanese prices are available from Kinokuniya Company Ltd, P.O. Box 55, Chitose, Tokyo 156, Japan. EU subscribers (outside the UK) who are not registered for VAT should add VAT at their country's rate. VAT registered subscribers should provide their VAT registration number. Prices include delivery by air.

Subscription orders, which must be accompanied by payment, may be sent to a bookseller, subscription agent, or direct to the publisher: Cambridge University Press, The Edinburgh Building, Shaftesbury Road, Cambridge CB2 8RU, UK; or in the USA, Canada, and Mexico: Cambridge University Press, Journals Fulfillment Department, 100 Brook Hill Drive, West Nyack, New York, 10994–2133, USA.

SINGLE VOLUMES AND BACK VOLUMES. A list of Royal Historical Society volumes available from Cambridge University Press may be obtained from the Humanities Marketing Department at the address above.

Printed and bound in the United Kingdom at the University Press, Cambridge

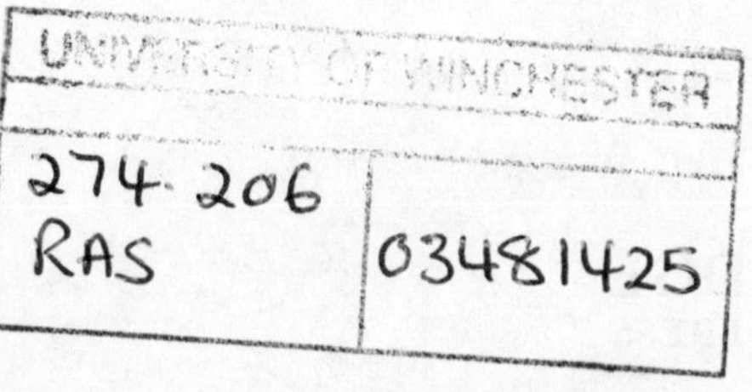

CONTENTS

LIST OF ILLUSTRATIONS

ACKNOWLEDGEMENTS

I have been working on John Rastrick on and off since 2002 and it is a pleasure finally to be able to acknowledge the help of those who have helped me to produce this edition of his manuscript autobiography, a book that Rastrick hoped was destined for wider circulation but that has been largely forgotten for almost three hundred years.

Blowing the dust from the manuscript – metaphorically rather than literally, since it appears to have been treasured throughout this time – I was startled to read what is not only a stylish and accomplished piece of early autobiographical writing but also one that illuminates many issues in the half-century or so after the Restoration. To have rediscovered such a source was immediately thrilling; working through its detail brought further revelations that convinced me that an edition was needed. Rastrick's autobiography tells us much about religion and politics in these years, offering a uniquely personal perspective upon both national and local events from within and without the Church of England. Along the way, we can see a distinctly individual account of a minister's understanding of science and the natural world; education, reading practices, and intellectual culture; marriage, family life, feuds, and friendships. I hope that those with interests in any of these fields will find Rastrick's narrative as interesting and enlightening as I have done.

My greatest debt is to Michelle Wolfe, who brought the manuscript to my attention and suggested that we work on it together. We planned to co-write an article and jointly to edit Rastrick's manuscript. It is my misfortune that circumstances dictated that I edit this book alone: it should have been her book too.

A number of librarians and archivists have been especially helpful throughout this project. Above all, the staff at the Huntington Library dealt patiently with my enquiries. Mary Robertson has been especially generous with her time and pointed me in the right direction just when I ran out of ideas. I must also thank the staff of the Heinz Archive and Library at the National Portrait Gallery; Magdalen College Library, Oxford; Dr Williams's Library; the John Hay Library at Brown University; Lincolnshire Archives; and the Norfolk Record Office. Particular thanks are due to those who sent me copies of manuscripts and special collections: J. Fernando Peña at the Grolier Club, New York; Jeffrey Makala of University of South Carolina Libraries; Jane

Ruddell, the Archivist of the Mercers' Company; Laetitia Yeandle at the Folger Shakespeare Library; and Jay Gaidmore at Brown University Archives.

I am grateful for the financial support provided by a Fletcher Jones Foundation fellowship at the Huntington Library in 2003, which allowed me to transcribe the manuscript, and to that of the University of Exeter in 2007, which allowed me to check it. A Bibliographical Society Major Grant in 2009 also enabled me to undertake related research at Brown University.

I would also like to thank those who helped with last-minute queries, supplied references and unpublished material and support, or listened politely to my retelling of Rastrick's life story during my visits to the Huntington, especially Ian Archer, Mike Braddick, David Como, David Cressy, Lori Anne Ferrell, Ken Fincham, Henry French, Mark Goldie, Alex Lumbers, Catherine Molineux, Joyce Ransome, Bill Sheils, Bill Sherman, and Alex Walsham.

Finally, Alice has provided love and support and welcomed John Rastrick as a troublesome houseguest for so long that she could be forgiven for thinking that he would never leave. I think we are both glad that he is finally moving on.

London
February 2010

ABBREVIATIONS

Calamy Revised	A.G. Matthews (ed.), *Calamy Revised: being a revision of Edmund Calamy's account of the ministers and others ejected and silenced 1660–2* (Oxford, 1934)
CCEd	The Clergy of the Church of England Database 1540–1835 (http://www.theclergydatabase.org.uk)
ESTC	The English Short Title Catalogue (http://estc.bl.uk)
Foster	J. Foster (ed.), *Alumni Oxoniensis: the members of the University of Oxford, 1500–1714: their parentage, birthplace, and year of birth, with a record of their degrees*, 4 vols (Oxford, 1891)
Lincolnshire Pedigrees	Arthur Roland Maddison (ed.), *Lincolnshire Pedigrees*, 4 vols (London, 1902–1906)
ODNB	H.C.G. Matthew and Brian Harrison (eds), *The Oxford Dictionary of National Biography*, 60 vols (Oxford, 2004) (http://www.oxforddnb.com)
OED	*The Oxford English Dictionary* (http://www.oed.com)
PRO	Public Record Office
TNA	The National Archives
Venn	John Venn and J.A. Venn (eds), *Alumni Cantabrigienses: a biographical list of all known students, graduates and holders of office at the University of Cambridge, from the earliest times to 1900. Part I: from the earliest times to 1751*, 4 vols (Cambridge, 1922)

ABBREVIATIONS

INTRODUCTION

John Rastrick: fragments of a life

In the Huntington Library in San Marino, California is a small, closely written, manuscript autobiography. MS HM 6131 carries an elaborate title-page, inscribed in a hand so neat and uniform that it almost looks as if it has been printed, bearing the title:

> A NARRATIVE; OR AN Historicall Account Of The most Materiall passages In the Life of John Rastrick: An Unworthy Minister of Jesus Christ At Kirkton in Holland in Lincolnshire. And afterwards Preacher to a Private Congregation at Spalding in the same County, & at Rotheram in Yorkshire, and at Lynn-Regis in Norfolk. Conteining chiefly God's Providences And His own experiences. Written by himself.

As will be discussed below, the whereabouts of Rastrick's manuscript between the middle of the eighteenth and the early twentieth centuries remain a mystery, but, even after it arrived at the Huntington, the manuscript was overlooked by scholars.[1] Although much of the excitement of history lies in the potential discovery of something 'new', it was surprising to come upon such a remarkable autobiography. Its author was known for leaving his position in the Church of England at the strikingly late date of 1687; what was not known, however, was that John Rastrick's autobiography is a distinguished piece of writing, among the most stylish, detailed, and entertaining examples of its kind. It is at once a pearl of nonconformist writing and a treasure trove of information about religion, politics, and culture in the half-century after the Restoration.

So much of what is known about the life of John Rastrick is included in his autobiography that no attempt will be made to supply a full biography here. Instead, this outline provides a brief sketch of the major events of his life and career, using the manuscript narrative and related materials. Although, as with other autobiographies, it should

[1]For the first detailed engagement with the manuscript, see Andrew Cambers and Michelle Wolfe, 'Reading, family religion, and evangelical identity in late Stuart England', *Historical Journal*, 47 (2004), pp. 875–896.

not be taken at face value, Rastrick's full and frank life story largely speaks for itself.[2]

Early years and education

John Rastrick was born at Heckington near Sleaford in Lincolnshire on 26 March 1650, the youngest and only surviving child of John and Ellen Rastrick.[3] Rastrick described his father as 'of the middle rank of Husbandmen' but he certainly rose in social status, particularly after the death of his wife in 1668 and his remarriage to a prosperous local widow, and he claimed the title of yeoman in his will.[4]

The 1650s were not the easiest decade in which to get an education and Rastrick's schooling was disrupted as schoolmasters died, moved on, or were removed. That, combined with a mother who was unhappy for her son to board out, meant that Rastrick was educated by no fewer than eight masters, from relatively informal education by the local minister to a year and a half at the Grammar School (now the King's School) at Grantham, a prestigious institution whose old boys included Henry More and Isaac Newton. Rastrick eventually settled under the tuition of Mr Walker, the minister of Great Hale, and delighted in the freedom that he was given to pursue his studies. In 1667, he went up to Trinity College, Cambridge, where his tutor was Thomas Bainbrigg, who was later vice-master of the college and would gain some notoriety as a religious controversialist.[5] Although he made social connections there that would serve him well throughout his career, Cambridge proved both a spiritual and an educational disappointment to Rastrick. He was plagued by melancholy and somewhat bewildered at the lack of direction in his studies. Nevertheless, it was at Cambridge that he developed his lifelong love of the works of Richard Baxter, an affinity for works of puritan practical divinity, and a continuing interest in the physical workings of the universe, notably through the works of Descartes.

[2]The following is based on Huntington Library, MS HM 6131, 'A NARRATIVE; OR AN Historicall Account Of The most Materiall passages In the Life of John Rastrick'. I have not provided references for each passage in this biographical sketch, since in large part it follows the sequence of events in the manuscript. References to other sources are provided where they occur.

[3]W.P.W. Phillimore, Ashley K. Maples, R.E.G. Cole, Thomas M. Blagg, and Reginald C. Dudding (eds), *Lincolnshire Parish Registers: marriages*, 11 vols (London, 1905–1921), IV, p. 89.

[4]Lincolnshire Archives, Lincoln, LCC Wills 1618/1/169.

[5]Thomas Bainbrigg (1636–1703), *ODNB*.

Church of England clergyman

By the time he took his BA in January 1671, Rastrick's life had changed. His mother had died and his father had remarried, and Rastrick returned to Heckington in eager anticipation of a life in the Church. In May 1671, he gained his first job, as curate to Basil Berridg, the rector of Algarkirk and Fosdyke. Serving as curate to Berridg, whom he thought 'a high, Austere and Lordly man', was a singular disappointment, and Rastrick moved in May 1672 to become curate at Wyberton, a post that offered scant financial reward but greater spiritual opportunities. A month later he married Jane Wilson, the daughter of a rector and prebendary of Lincoln cathedral. Rastrick was going up in the world. He was ordained priest in 1673 and, after he preached in a vacancy at Kirton in Holland, the parishioners put his name forward to the patrons of the living, the Mercers' Company of London. On 23 June 1673, Rastrick, who had just become a father, was presented to the living where he would remain for fourteen years.

When they recommended Rastrick's appointment to the Mercers' Company, the parishioners of Kirton seemed impressed by his 'exemplary life and conversation' and the good they received from his 'painefull preaching'.[6] But in time his intense and uncompromising religiosity drove a wedge between the priest and his parishioners. Rastrick thought he made too little progress in improving the spirituality of his parishioners. They, in turn, did not like his rigid stance on baptism any more than his tinkering with the wording of the burial and marriage services. They were bewildered that their clergyman would excommunicate ungodly parishioners but gladly pay the fines of local anabaptists out of his own pocket. These and other characteristics earned him a string of enemies, who met together at the King's Head tavern at Kirton. Indeed, Rastrick had a gift for stirring up personal animosity: one William Hunt threatened 'to sheath his Sword' in Rastrick's blood; while the steward of Magdalen College, Oxford, collecting rents in a neighbouring parish, declared that he would have stabbed Rastrick if he had not been a clergyman.[7]

Rastrick fared little better with the ecclesiastical authorities. He would always argue his case, even quoting the prayer-book rubric at Bishop White of Peterborough when he raised objections to Rastrick's

[6] Mercers' Company, London, Acts of Court, 23 June 1673.

[7] Rastrick's conflict with William Hunt was long-standing and wide-ranging. In addition to the incidents mentioned in the manuscript, in 1699 Hunt was sued by Rastrick and the overseers of the poor for Kirton for failing to pay back any of the equity or interest on £50 that he had borrowed in 1687 from a trust (established in the will of Jane Adamson) that had been set up to assist the poor of Kirton. See TNA, PRO C5/626/32. For Jane Adamson's will (1637), see TNA, PRO, PROB 11/176/415.

interpretation of altar policy. In 1687, he was finally cited to appear at the ecclesiastical court for his refusal to wear the surplice, his refusal to baptise children born out of wedlock, and his friendship with the nonconformist John Richardson, but a fortunate coincidence with James II's Declaration of Indulgence meant that no action was taken against him. Rastrick gave his answers to the charges in writing and heard no more of the matter. But, while others continued through these trying times, Rastrick decided that he could not in good conscience stay within the Church and resigned his cure on 27 November 1687.[8]

Meanwhile, his personal life was as strained as his professional life. Rastrick's marriage disintegrated as he tired of his wife's intellectual shortcomings and she in turn grew jealous of his spiritual intimacy with their maidservants and religiously inclined local women. Things came to a head when the young Mary Harrison started visiting the house: her attentions proved 'a Snare' to Rastrick, who admitted that his feelings for her were like those he had felt for his wife before they married. Rastrick was released from the snare by his wife's death from an autumnal fever on 27 September 1684. In twelve years of marriage, they had had eight children, four of whom – Abigail, Elizabeth, John, and Samuel – were still living when their mother died. Just six months later, after seeking God's approval regarding the legitimacy of his affections, Rastrick married Mary Harrison. They were married for six years and had four children, all of whom died within fourteen months of birth. A stillbirth followed in August 1691, and two weeks later Mary Rastrick died.

Nonconformist minister of Spalding, Rotherham, and King's Lynn

After a brief period of unemployment, Rastrick returned to work early in 1688, when he accepted the invitation to become the nonconformist minister to a congregation at Spalding in Lincolnshire who were alarmed at the spread of Thomas Grantham's Baptists in the area. He stayed for nine years, preaching his way through the Bible, but he was uneasy and increasingly frustrated by the divisions of the people and their unwillingness to accept his occasional conformity. When they withheld their contributions towards his maintenance, he accepted a call to remove to Rotherham in 1697. Although this

[8] There were also local tensions. In late October 1687, one Richard Stevenson, tenant to the Rectory of Kirton, had written to the Mercers' Company to complain 'of some Irregularityes practiced by the present Vicar'. Although the Mercers' Company resolved that they could take no notice of Stevenson's complaint, Rastrick was increasingly aware of the hostility provoked by his ministry. See Mercers' Company, London, Acts of Court, 24 October 1687.

position enabled Rastrick to cultivate strong links with Yorkshire's nonconformist ministers and gentry and occasioned a remarkable description of the natural history of the Peak District, he was again frustrated at the lack of serious spirituality in the area and disheartened at his lack of progress.

In 1692, Rastrick had married Elizabeth Horn, the daughter of James Horn of Long Sutton in Lincolnshire, the nephew of John Horn, the ejected minister of King's Lynn. Feeling isolated in Yorkshire, in May 1701 John and Elizabeth Rastrick set out to visit family and friends in Spalding, Wisbech, and King's Lynn. They never came back. At King's Lynn, Rastrick's old friend Anthony Williamson (who had succeeded John Horn as Presbyterian minister there) came into what must have been a fairly significant sum of money upon the death of his father-in-law, Mr Blithe, and used the money to offer Rastrick a position as his assistant.

For three years, their joint ministry appears to have progressed smoothly but, after Williamson's death in August 1704, Rastrick became embroiled in a series of escalating conflicts with a small but vocal and well-connected hyper-Calvinist faction among his congregation. The story of their enmity to Rastrick's ministry has a familiar ring to it. They objected to Rastrick's occasional conformity, his high-handed insistence on discipline, and the bluntness of his preaching. They were not amused at his publication of his decision to go out, in *An Account of the Nonconformity of John Rastrick* in 1705. And they were enraged at what they saw as his 'Baxterian doctrine' and his Arminianism.[9]

To be fair to Rastrick, the charge of Arminianism seems unjust – his position was one of hypothetical universalism – but it stuck in the minds of his opponents. It was over his theology of salvation that matters came to a head in 1707, as the enmity towards him crystallized into 'formal and formed opposition'. Rastrick's opponents could suffer him no longer: they left the meeting and withdrew their financial support. Meanwhile, they charged the man who paid Rastrick his salary – the aptly named Mr Money – with fraud and injustice. Although they put their differences aside in 1708, fearing the ramifications of the Jacobite invasion of Scotland, tensions boiled

[9]They would presumably have been bewildered by some of Rastrick's actions that are not mentioned in the manuscript, such as his gift of fifty shillings to the Dean and Chapter of Lincoln to purchase books for the library there. See Lincoln Cathedral Library, Lincoln MS 256, p. 10: '1707 Mem. that Mr Rastrick formerly Vicar of Kirton in Holland having some years ago subscribed fifty shillings for the use of the Library hath paid the said fifty shill. which is to be laid out in such books as the Dean and Chapter think fit'. Cited in Naomi Linnell, 'The catalogues of Lincoln Cathedral Library', *Library History*, 7 (1985), p. 6.

over once more in the following year. The leader of the faction, Seal Peast, petitioned Daniel Williams and Edmund Calamy, before finally shutting up the meeting-house in a desperate attempt to get rid of their minister. The exclusion was actually short-lived – some of the faction sided with Rastrick and he was readmitted – but only the deaths of two of Rastrick's most important enemies in 1713 effectively drew a line under the affair.[10]

Later life

After 1713, the chronology of the narrative ends and it is probable that it was at this time that Rastrick wrote his autobiography. Thereafter, although he served as the Presbyterian minister of Spinner Lane for another fourteen years, information about his life and career is more thinly spread. Certainly, affairs in his personal life appear to have been calmer than they once were. When she married the forty-two-year-old John Rastrick in 1692, Elizabeth was just twenty, barely older than her husband's eldest surviving daughter. But they appear to have got along well, spiritually and socially. Between November 1693 and April 1710, they had eleven children: four died within their first year; a fifth died aged twelve; and six more outlived their parents. By 1710, Rastrick, at sixty, had fathered twenty-three children, of whom at least nine were still living – a tenth (his eldest son, John) had gone to Carolina, and Rastrick appears not to have known whether he was dead or alive.

Little is known about Rastrick's ministry after 1713, though it seems reasonable to assume that any conflicts were less public. In April 1714, he preached a well-received sermon at the ordination of Samuel Savage at Bury St Edmunds in Suffolk, and shortly afterwards *A Sermon Preach'd at the Ordination of Mr. Samuel Savage, At St. Edmund's-Bury* appeared in print.[11] Beside repeating once more how the meeting-house at King's Lynn had been shut up against him – the lesson of which Rastrick appears to have interpreted as stick to your guns and providence will see things right – the sermon reveals how little his outlook on the duties of the minister had changed: Savage was to make discipline his watchword; he was not to admit all promiscuously

[10]The shutting up of the meeting-house appears to have had little lasting effect upon Rastrick's diplomacy. Intriguingly, in 1712 he appears to have met up with Daniel Defoe, who was travelling incognito, and to have agreed to put the people of King's Lynn straight regarding some of the wilder delusions of Whig propaganda. See George Harris Healey (ed.), *The Letters of Daniel Defoe* (Oxford, 1955), pp. 385–386 (letter to Robert Harley, Earl of Oxford, 20 September 1712).

[11]John Rastrick, *A Sermon Preach'd at the Ordination of Mr. Samuel Savage, at St. Edmund's-Bury, in the County of Suffolk, Apr. 22. 1714* (London, 1714).

to baptism; he was to reprove those whose conduct was disorderly; and he was to suspend the scandalous from the Lord's Supper. It was, Rastrick wrote, 'a Feast for Reconciliation and Friendship; and therefore, for Enemies to approach it, is intollerable, abominable, and Confusion'.[12] As well as this uncompromising disciplinary strain, the sermon once again shows Rastrick's theological moderation, asserting his belief in free will and reasserting his position on grace, whereby he upheld the General Grace of the Arminians and the Special Grace of the Calvinists, 'because there is no Contradiction betwixt these two'.[13] Perhaps most revealing are his comments on what the people should do to support their minister: accept his reproofs; inform him of those of loose behaviour; and encourage him by providing for him financially. The need to be bountiful is made at some length and the sermon concludes 'Why then should Believers grudge their Cost for Truth? for the Gospel and Interest of our Lord Jesus Christ?'[14]

This was Rastrick's last venture in print, but he maintained his intellectual curiosity and kept writing until the end of his life. He composed poetry and a short catechism and, after 1719, a more substantial volume entitled 'Plain and Easy Principles of Christian Religion and Obedience; or the necessity of keeping Christ's Commandments, in order to our preserving an interest in his favour, demonstrated from John xv. 10.' The manuscript is now missing, but it was written as a response to the Salters' Hall dispute – the meeting of London ministers in 1719 that was designed to settle the question of whether the Dissenters should have a subscription on the Trinity (to distance themselves from Arianism) but that, in the end, served only to shatter any doctrinal unity that Presbyterians, Independents, and Baptists still shared.[15] Rastrick's manuscript was informed by a careful reading of the vitriolic printed exchanges between the Arian-leaning Samuel Clarke (1675–1729) and his follower John Jackson (1686–1763) and the orthodox Whig Daniel Waterland (1683–1740) over the doctrine of the Trinity, which had preceded and precipitated the Salters' Hall dispute. Rastrick apparently agreed with the Presbyterian minister James Peirce (1674–1726) in the debate – and so presumably denied that he was an Arian but argued that Christ was subordinate in the Trinity. He left instructions for his son to publish the book – 'I leave it to you to tell the world' – along with the letters that he had received from Samuel Wright (1683–1746) and an appendix of

[12] Ibid., p. 58.

[13] Ibid., pp. 67–68.

[14] Ibid., pp. 71–75.

[15] On the Salters' Hall dispute, see Michael. R. Watts, *The Dissenters*, 2 vols (Oxford, 1978–1995), I, pp. 371–382.

'last Thoughts about the Trinity and Son of God'. This appendix apparently contained some thoughts on the nature of the universe and in particular upon comets, which he thought were 'worlds in a state of conflagration and dissolution', spinning through space, burning for the sins of their inhabitants. Rastrick's space odyssey was not published, perhaps unsurprisingly given the unorthodox nature of his belief: he thought that after the sun had been extinguished the earth would become a comet, just as other comets had once been occupied with 'rational inhabitants', each comet having its own saviour.[16]

Although he wrote of a modest life in a 'poor Smoky Cottage', the wills of John and Elizabeth Rastrick suggest that they enjoyed a fairly comfortable lifestyle.[17] Rastrick's portrait, which hung in his study, had been painted by Daniel de Koninck, an artist of some standing, who had moved to England in 1690. He kept up correspondence with old friends such as William Scoffin.[18] And he continued to receive donations right up until his death: some of those who had been touched by his ministry remembered him many years later. In 1757, for example, Samuel Brookes of Dorchester, Massachusetts, who had met Rastrick in 1727, left £20 to his heirs.[19] Elizabeth Rastrick's will also testifies to a family confident of displaying their status within King's Lynn society – the portrait of her cousin John Horn, the schoolmaster of King's Lynn, hung in the household hall together with a Dutch painting. There was a large clock, and the house was furnished with fashionable cane furniture. Rastrick's study included not only drawers, chests, and shelves full of books and manuscripts, but also mathematical instruments, telescopes, and a double barometer. Elizabeth's will made mention of jewellery, silver spoons, and carefully furnished bedrooms. Clearly helped by bequests from family and

[16]See the description of the manuscript in William Richards, *The History of Lynn*, 2 vols (King's Lynn, 1812), II, pp. 1063–1064.

[17]For the complaint, see Dr Williams's Library, London, MS 24.115, letter from John Rastrick to Mr William Steevens, factor at Queen-Hithe, London (14 December 1721), p. 41. Copies of the wills can be found at Norfolk Record Office, Norwich, Will Register, Kirke, 82–84 (Will of John Rastrick of King's Lynn, 1727); Will Register, Goats, 289–291 (Will of Elizabeth Rastrick, 1740). These are transcribed in the appendix on pp. 203–207 below.

[18]William Scoffin (1654/5–1732) had known Rastrick since at least 1681, when he became curate of Brothertoft, Lincs., and the pair stayed friends after they had both left the Church of England: 'they continued their intimacy by letter till Mr. Rastrick's death'. See Edmund Calamy, *The Nonconformist's Memorial*, ed. Samuel Palmer, 2nd edn, 3 vols (London, 1802), II, p. 438; and W[illiam] S[coffin], *An Help To the Singing Psalm-Tunes, By The Book. In a method more easy than is generally taught. With directions for making an instrument with one string, by which any tune may be easily learn'd* (London, 1725), p. iv.

[19]TNA, PRO, PROB 11/840/287 (Will of Samuel Brookes of Dorchester, Mass., 20 August 1757). See Peter Wilson Coldham, *American Wills Proved in London* (Baltimore, MD, 1992), p. 212.

friends, the Rastricks also had several holdings of property besides their house and gardens in Spinner Lane in King's Lynn, including in Heckington, Sutton St Mary (now Long Sutton), and Kirton in Lincolnshire.

Death

John Rastrick died on 18 August 1727 and was buried on 21 August at St Nicholas's Chapel, King's Lynn. His funeral sermon was preached on Matthew 25:21 by John Ford, who had succeeded Ishmael Burroughs as Presbyterian minister of Wisbech in 1724 and who would move to Sudbury in 1729. Rastrick's epitaph was apparently drawn up by his son William and revised by the Presbyterian minister of Boston, George Ault (d. 1733), and a Presbyterian minister at Cambridge, James Duchal (d. 1761). It read:

> Here lies buried, John Rastrick M.A. born at Heckington, near Sleaford, in the county of Lincoln, and educated at Trinity College in Cambridge. He was formerly Vicar of Kirkton, in the same county. And afterwards, as he could not with a safe conscience comply with certain requirements of the church of England, was an indefatigable preacher of the gospel to a christian church in this town, in separation from it.
>
> He was a man of eminent piety, charity, and modesty: of approved integrity; of remarkable study and industry; and well versed in almost every part of learning, but especially the mathematics. A truly christian divine: an eloquent and striking preacher; a faithful and vigilant pastor: an intrepid reprover of vice, and a most zealous encourager of virtue.
>
> Having finished his course, imbittered alas! with various trials, he joyfully yielded up his soul to God, August 18, 1727. Aged 78.[20]

In addition to his epitaph, Rastrick's will demonstrates his steadfast religious moderation. Even after forty years outside it, Rastrick's religious and cultural identity still owed as much to the established

[20] I follow the abbreviated translation in Calamy, *The Nonconformist's Memorial*, II, pp. 476–477, with some obvious mistakes corrected. The Latin text, printed on p. 437, reads: 'H. S. E. Johannes Rastrick, A.M. Heckingtoniae, juxta Sleaford, in agro Licoln natus; et in Coll. SS^{tae} Trin. apud Cantab. educatus. Olim annos 14 Vicarius de Kirkton in Hollandia in agro jam dicto: et denique (quoniam Ecclesiae Anglicanae, praeceptis quibusdam, conscientia illaesa, obtemperare nequibat) Gregi Christiano, ab Ecclesia publica separato, in hoc oppido, annos 26 Evangelii praeco indefessus. Vir eximiae pietatis, charitatis, ac modestiae; spectatae integritatis, studii et industriae, singularis, omnique fere doctrinae genere instructus; mathematica vero imprimis peritus Comes audivit facetus, theologus vere Christianus, concionator facundus et acer, pastor vigilans et fidelis, vitii reprehensor intrepidus, atque virtutis fautor amicissimus. Peracto demum vitae cursu, aerumnis eheu! non paucis obsito, spiritum Deo laetus reddit, Aug. 18, 1727, aetat 78.'

church as it did to nonconformity. In his will, he left his books and manuscripts to his son William on condition that he remain a minister. If, however, neither William nor any of his sons-in-law were a minister, whether conformist or nonconformist, Rastrick willed that his books should form the core of a new public library for the use of the dissenting ministers of Norwich, which was to be managed by the dissenting clergy and an equal number of conforming clergy of their choice. Likewise, he willed that, if William Rastrick died without heir, his four acres of land in Kirton should be given as an augmentation to the vicarage there, in part remembering a legacy once left to him when he was minister there. William Rastrick did continue a minister, although he was never ordained and had to exchange with the minister of Wisbech at communion times. Nevertheless, he was regarded as a cultivated intellectual, who drew up an important plan of King's Lynn and compiled a significant index of the ejected ministers of 1662, which he appears to have circulated in manuscript and which was used by Samuel Palmer in his updated edition of Calamy's *The Nonconformist's Memorial*.[21]

Little is known of what became of Rastrick's other children, beyond that which can be extracted from the volume of family letters and verse that is now in the Lincolnshire Archives.[22] When John Rastrick died, Samuel Rastrick was a silk dyer in London; he died in 1750. Rastrick's eldest daughter, Elizabeth, had married Edmund Burton of Wisbech at Spalding in 1695. In 1727, as mentioned above, Rastrick did not know if his eldest son, John (b. 1675), a stocking weaver who had gone to Carolina, was still alive. The five daughters of Rastrick's third marriage outlived both their parents. It seems likely that the continuation of the account of Rastrick's children was kept up to date by either his daughter Sarah (b. 1698) or Deborah (b. 1709). The last death recorded in the manuscript is that of Martha Rastrick in 1756. John Rastrick's immediate family line came to an end with the death of Deborah in 1779. As her inscription in St Nicholas's Chapel, King's Lynn testified, it was the end of an era: she was, it stated, 'the last of the Rev^{d}. Mr. John RASTRICK'S Family'.[23]

[21] William Rastrick (1697–1752), *ODNB*; Calamy, *The Nonconformist's Memorial*.

[22] Lincolnshire Archives, Lincoln, MS 2 Cragg 4/7 (Letters and Verse of the Rastrick Family). This volume contains copies of many letters and meditations written by Rastrick's daughter Elizabeth, as well as scattered items from other family members.

[23] E.L. Grange and J.C. Hudson (eds), *Lincolnshire Notes and Queries: volume 1* (Horncastle, 1889), pp. 228–229, records the inscription for Deborah Bayley (née Rastrick) (1709–1779).

John Rastrick's publications and manuscripts

Works printed

1. *An Account of the Nonconformity of John Rastrick, M.A. Sometime Vicar of Kirkton, near Boston, in Lincolnshire; containing the occasions and circumstances of his secession from that place. In a letter to a friend* (London, 1705).

   Printed separately and, with separate title-page, in the third volume of Edmund Calamy, *A Defence of Moderate Non-conformity*, 3 vols (London, 1703–1705).

2. *A Sermon Preach'd at the Ordination of Mr. Samuel Savage, at St. Edmund's-Bury, in the county of Suffolk, Apr. 22. 1714* (London, 1714).
3. Letter (unattributed) in *Philosophical Transactions of the Royal Society*, 23 (1702), pp. 1156–1158; concerning Roman coins found at Fleet in Lincolnshire and other discoveries.[24]

Surviving manuscripts, letters, etc.

1. Huntington Library, MS HM 6131, 'A NARRATIVE; OR AN Historicall Account Of The most Materiall passages In the Life of John Rastrick'.
2. Marginalia in John Rastrick, *An Account of the Nonconformity of John Rastrick, M.A.* (London, 1705). British Library, shelfmark 698.g.23.1–8, pp. [2], 38, 44.

   This marginalia, in Rastrick's distinctive hand, is a transcription on p. 2 (the blank reverse of the title-page) of the part of the preface to the third volume of Calamy's *A Defence of Moderate Non-conformity* that related to Calamy's publication of Rastrick's work. It explains how Calamy had come to know about Lincolnshire's after-dissenters and had written to Rastrick at King's Lynn to find out more, receiving the *Account* in reply, which Rastrick permitted Calamy to publish. As well as minor typographical corrections on p. 44, Rastrick inserted an extra paragraph relating to his removal to Spalding as a marginal note on p. 38.

3. Dr Williams's Library, London, MS 24.115, letters from John Rastrick to Mr William Steevens, factor at Queen-Hithe, London (24 December 1721; 1 August 1724; 21 July 1725), pp. 44–46 (irregular pagination).

[24] The subsequent letter of Ralph Thoresby (*Philosophical Transactions of the Royal Society*, 23 (1702), pp. 1158–1160) continued to cite Rastrick's account without attribution. See also the further letter of Thoresby (*Philosophical Transactions of the Royal Society*, 32 (1722), pp. 344–346). For Rastrick's authorship, see [Nathaniel Kinderley, the younger], *The Ancient and Present State of the Navigation of the Towns of Lyn, Wisbeach, Spalding, and Boston* (London, 1751), pp. 8–9.

Three autograph letters from John Rastrick to William Steevens, all written at King's Lynn. Steevens had evidently been brought up in Spalding, at the time when Rastrick was a minister there. By 1721, Steevens was a corn factor at Queenhithe, London and the letters show that he was also acting as a banker for Rastrick and other Norfolk nonconformists. Among other things, the letters concern Steevens sending Rastrick pictures, the close links between Rastrick and the elder Nathaniel Kinderley, Rastrick's financial dealings, and the distribution of charitable bequests among nonconformist ministers.

4. Lincolnshire Archives, Lincoln, MS 2 Cragg 4/7 (Letters and Verse of the Rastrick Family, early eighteenth century).

A composite volume of Rastrick family papers, consisting mainly of letters and verse, from the early to mid-eighteenth century. Includes a long autograph letter of John Rastrick to his cousin Elizabeth Ayre, fos 24r–25r.

A separate gathering of pages at the end of the manuscript, which are separately foliated, appear to have originated from one of John Rastrick's cousins. They include: a copy of a poem by John Rastrick, beginning 'Lord, if Thou but hide thy Face', fo. 1v; 'The Advice of a Minister to his Daughter', probably by John Rastrick, fos 3v–4r; and a copy of William Pell's Table and Directions for reading the Scriptures, written out for his cousin by John Rastrick, fos 4v–5r.

Missing manuscripts

1. 'Plain and Easy Principles of Christian Religion and Obedience; or the necessity of keeping Christ's Commandments, in order to our preserving an interest in his favour, demonstrated from John xv. 10. By John Rastrick, M.A. sometime Vicar of Kirkton, near Boston, and now Minister of the Gospel at King's Lynn, Norfolk.'

Described in *The Gentleman's Magazine: And Historical Chronicle*, 59 (1789), p. 977, and in William Richards, *The History of Lynn* (1812), pp. 1063–1064, who was in possession of the manuscript. Richards remarks that it would make duodecimo of 250–300 pages. It included a letter, pinned to the manuscript, instructing William Rastrick to publish it after his father's death. Apparently written in response to the Salters' Hall dispute of 1719, the manuscript included letters from Samuel Wright and an appendix detailing Rastrick's 'last Thoughts about the Trinity and Son of God'.

2. 'A Short Catechism; containing the chief heads of the Christian religion, and faith of Christ. By John Rastrick.'

Brief description in *The Gentleman's Magazine*, 59 (1789), p. 977, and in Richards, *History of Lynn*, p. 1064.

3. 'The Dissolution'.

Poem, apparently attached to 'A Short Catechism', and reproduced, with some variations, in Richards, *History of Lynn*, pp. 1065–1066; *The Gentleman's Magazine*,

59 (1789), pp. 1033–1034; and John Evans, *Memoirs of the Life and Writings of the Rev. William Richards* (Chiswick, 1819), pp. 160–163.

4. 'An Evening Hymn'.

Poem, apparently attached to 'A Short Catechism', and reproduced in Evans, *Memoirs*, p. 163.

Further writings mentioned in the 'Narrative'

fo. 1v 'Two bundles of loose papers', one containing further passages from his life
'Adminiculum Concionatorium'
fo. 2v Diary
fo. 69r 'A Disswasive from Church Merchandize'

'A NARRATIVE; OR AN Historicall Account Of The most Materiall passages In the Life of John Rastrick'

Date of the manuscript

Rastrick's manuscript is undated, and internal evidence provides the best clues as to the date of composition. It is possible that the surviving manuscript is an autograph copy and/or that certain sections of the manuscript, notably the prefatory letter to William Rastrick (fo. 1v) and the account of his children (fo. 89r), were written at different times.

The earliest date at which the main body of the manuscript can have been written, assuming that it was written continuously, is around the summer of 1713. Within the narrative, Rastrick recorded the deaths of Seal Peast in February 1713 and of Mr Waters 'three or four Months' later (fo. 73r). The only later date mentioned within the body of the text is a marginal note that refers to Rastrick's acquisition of Stephanus's Greek Concordance in 1714, when he was aged sixty-four (fo. 76v). There is therefore a good case for accepting a date around the latter end of 1713. This would mean that the narrative of events of his ministry in King's Lynn was brought up to date and that the note on Stephanus was added in 1714, since the text stated that he had not been able to acquire the volume. Such a date is not complicated by any of Rastrick's references to printed books. None of these were published after 1713 and the vast majority were published (at least for the first time) well before 1700.

Further circumstantial evidence for this date concerns the ages of his children. In his prefatory letter to his children, Rastrick expressed his concern that he might die while many of them were still young and that his passing might prompt in them a desire 'to know what your Poor Father was' (fo. 2v). His youngest child, Jeremiah, was born in 1710, while Deborah was born in 1709, Ann in 1704, Hannah in 1700, Martha in 1699, Sarah in 1698, and William in 1697. A date significantly after 1713 would not seem to fit with this desire for vicarious immortality. For a number of other reasons, a later date than around 1713 is unlikely, not least the lack of any narrative relating to this period and the absence of any mention of his publication of his sermon at the ordination of Samuel Savage in 1714.[25]

Such a date is, however, complicated by Rastrick's 'An Account of my Children', a table of the dates of the births and deaths of his children by each of his three wives. This table (fo. 89r, and see Figure 2) appears at the end of the manuscript and includes an entry in Rastrick's hand recording the death of his son Jeremiah in April 1722 and his burial early in May of that year. The entries relating to the period after 1727, recording the deaths of Rastrick's children until 1756, are written in two different hands. It seems likely that Rastrick kept this list up to date long after he wrote the rest of the manuscript and that additions were made after his death, perhaps by his daughter Deborah.

A Comparison of 'A NARRATIVE; OR AN Historicall Account Of The most Materiall passages In the Life of John Rastrick' and An Account of the Nonconformity of John Rastrick

'Hearing of Some Ministers in and about Lincolnshire who formerly had Livings in the Church of England', Edmund Calamy wrote to John Rastrick at King's Lynn, 'desiring him to favour me with the History of his Treatment in the Church and the Grounds of quitting his Living'. The result was what he thought an 'instructive Narrative', made all the more remarkable in Calamy's mind because 'had he not been urg'd to it, his Case would hardly ever have fallen under general Notice'.[26] This narrative, *An Account of the Nonconformity of John Rastrick, M.A. Sometime Vicar of Kirkton, near Boston, in Lincolnshire; containing the occasions and circumstances of his secession from that place. In a letter to a friend*, was published in 1705. It appears to have been printed, with its own title-page, both as part of the third volume of Edmund Calamy's *A*

[25]Rastrick, *A Sermon Preach'd at the Ordination of Mr. Samuel Savage*. The style of Rastrick's description of the shutting up of his meeting-house in this sermon mirrored that in his manuscript 'Narrative'.

[26]Edmund Calamy, *A Defence of Moderate Non-conformity. In answer to the reflections of Mr. Ollyffe and Mr. Hoadly, on the tenth chapter of the Abridgment of the life of the Reverend Mr. Rich. Baxter*, 3 vols (London, 1703–1705), III, pp. xiii–xiv.

Defence of Moderate Non-conformity (London, 1703–1705) and as a stand-alone work.[27]

Much of Rastrick's *Account* is recycled and adapted in his manuscript narrative. He clearly had recourse to either a printed copy of the *Account* or a copy of the manuscript that he had sent to Edmund Calamy when he wrote his manuscript narrative. The overlap between the *Account* and the narrative is not described in the footnotes to the main transcription, but a brief description is provided here. Of the fifty-two pages of the *Account*, pages 4–40 are reused in large part in the manuscript between folios 39r and 51v. In general, the manuscript provides a slightly fuller version of Rastrick's decision to leave the Church of England, adding the names of his problematic parishioners, the names and positions of the Lincolnshire conforming clergy whom he admired (fo. 42r), and an account of the Popish Plot (fos 42v–43r). Occasionally the printed account includes a little material not included in the manuscript, but the differences are mainly minor variations of phrasing, style, and punctuation.

Description of the manuscript

HM 6131 is bound in vellum, contains eighty-nine folios, and measures approximately 15.5 × 9.5 cm. Rastrick wrote on loose sheets of different types of paper of varying quality. He probably sewed the volume himself. The tightness of the binding renders it impossible that the volume was bound before the narrative was written.

The narrative was and remains a beautiful *thing*, a bespoke object crafted with considerable patience, care, and effort. As can be seen in Figure 1, the title-page was crafted to mirror the aesthetics of print. It includes a hand-drawn border, a title that mimics those of printed books, and a biblical quotation beneath a ruled line. Facing it, and also resembling the conventions of printed publications, a letter to Rastrick's son William has been pasted into the manuscript. The narrative was, above all, designed to be read and cherished in the Rastrick family.

There is no contemporary pagination or foliation; at a later date the manuscript was foliated in pencil, and these folio numbers are followed in this edition. Both the flyleaf and the endpaper have been glued to the cover. Each is a letter to John Rastrick, pasted so that only part of the side bearing the address now remains visible. The visible portion of the flyleaf reads 'astrick att' and, below, 'in'. The endpaper

[27] For an example of the work as a stand-alone publication, see John Rastrick, *An Account of the Nonconformity of John Rastrick, M.A.* (London, 1705), British Library, shelfmark 698.g.23.1–8.

is torn but the visible portion reads 'To Mr R [...] his House [...] Kirkton [...]'.

Although a printed clipping attached to the inside cover of the manuscript describes the volume as a duodecimo, its composition is in fact irregular. Rastrick numbered the first page of eighteen sheets with an arabic numeral centred at the bottom of the recto of the sheet. Many of them have been written heavily as if to indicate that they were to be printed in bold type. These numbers have not been reproduced in the edited text but are positioned as follows:

1 – fo. 2r	7 – fo. 38r	13 – fo. 54r
2 – fo. 10r	8 – fo. 40r	14 – fo. 56r
3 – fo. 18r	9 – fo. 42r	15 – fo. 58r
4 – fo. 20r	10 – fo. 46r	16 – fo. 62r
5 – fo. 28r	11 – fo. 50r	17 – fo. 66r
6 – fo. 36r	12 – fo. 52r	18 – fo. 70r

The volume is thus a composite of sheets folded as if folios, quartos, and octavos.

Both the tightness of the volume and the quality of the paper, which has resulted in considerable show-through on some sheets, make reading the manuscript difficult in places and this problem is exacerbated by Rastrick's pathologically small and closely packed writing. As will be discussed in the editorial conventions below, the size of the writing makes determining some capital letters particularly difficult. Despite this, with a magnifying glass the narrative reads well and Rastrick's writing is exceptionally even and consistent. The main body of the manuscript is written with wide margins and in clear paragraphs with centred headings at the start of titled sections, while in other places a change of tack in the narrative is indicated by writing the first word of a passage in a slightly larger hand. Rastrick uses a smaller hand for full passages of quotation and at times slants his hand slightly to indicate short passages of quotation, presumably to specify that they were to be printed in italics. There is very little underlining, only a few words of reported speech to which Rastrick draws attention and which he presumably intended to be printed with such underlining. There are a considerable number of marginal notes throughout the manuscript, from short references to longer discursive comments. In some cases, Rastrick simply wrote his comment in the margin. In others, he indicated the position in the text to which a note referred with a marginal note with an asterisk and began the note itself with the asterisk (or other symbol). These features of the manuscript are identified in the footnotes.

Rastrick wrote on both sides of each folio of the manuscript in a fair-quality black ink. In places, particularly those written on poor-quality paper, the ink has spread somewhat, making reading more difficult. In these places there is considerable show-through, although little that means that doubtful readings occur. The consistency of the colour of the ink suggests that the manuscript was written up onto these sheets in long stretches. Such consistency makes it quite obvious when Rastrick has changed or re-cut his pen. Some sections of the manuscript are written in an ink that has faded to a more brownish colour. The use of brown ink on pages otherwise written in black ink clearly shows Rastrick reading over and checking the manuscript, adding missing words and marginal notes. Where changes of ink give clues to revisions, they are remarked in the footnotes. The quality of the hand and the relatively small number of cancellations and interlineations make it very likely that the manuscript was a fair copy, written from loose papers or perhaps a rough draft.

Provenance

Little is known with certainty about the provenance of Rastrick's manuscript. As we have seen, his will stipulated that his books and manuscripts were to go to his son William 'provided and upon condition that he continue a minister and preacher of the Gospell whether in a Conforming or nonConforming Capacity'. William Rastrick succeeded his father as Presbyterian minister at Spinner Lane and so fulfilled the condition of the will. That he received the manuscript on his father's death is suggested by the character of the prefatory letter that is pasted into the volume.

In his *History of Lynn*, William Richards noted that he possessed Rastrick's 'Plain and easy principles of Christian religion' and 'A short catechism', together with some of his poetry. He also suggested that Rastrick's manuscripts were dispersed after the death of his son William:

> His unprinted, or unpublished works appear to have been much more numerous and considerable; but they got into different hands after the son's death, and most of them perhaps have been since lost. Some of them were in the possession of the son's successors Messrs. *Mayhew* and *Warner*, and some in that of the late Dr. *Lloyd*. What became of them we know not.[28]

[28]Richards, *The History of Lynn*, II, p. 1063. William Rastrick's successors were Anthony Mayhew (d. 1783) and William Warner (d. 1802); David Lloyd (d. 1794) was master of King's Lynn Grammar School.

There is no reason to doubt Richards's account of the dispersal of Rastrick's manuscripts and it is very unlikely that he had seen the narrative: he would surely have commented upon and used the manuscript. In any case, the volume was certainly not among those of his printed books and manuscripts that were sent to Brown University after his death in 1818.[29]

At some stage, however, the manuscript did indeed cross the Atlantic. Although the Huntington Library has no record of the acquisition of the manuscript, a small printed clipping describing the manuscript, with the pencilled date '9 F[ebruary] [19]20' pinned to it, provides some clues. On the clipping is stamped in very small letters 'Anderson'. It transpires that the manuscript had come up for sale as lot number 805 in a general sale at the Anderson Galleries in New York on the evening of Tuesday 10 February 1920. The sale catalogue described it as:

AN INTERESTING UNPUBLISHED MANUSCRIPT

805. RASTRICK (REV. JOHN). A Narrative; or an Historical Account of the most Materiall passages in the Life of John Rastrick; An Unworthy Minister of Jesus Christ at Kirkton in Holland in Lincolnshire. And Afterwards Preacher to a private Congregation at Spalding in ye same Country, & Rotheram in Yorkshire, and at Lyme-Regis [*sic*] in Norfolk. 12mo, original vellum. In half morocco slip case. Circa 1692

THE ORIGINAL MANUSCRIPT ENTIRELY IN HIS AUTOGRAPH, closely, but beautifully written on 174 pages. Facing the title is a memorandum of the narrator to his son William, in which he states that his desire was that each of his children should have one narrative of the passages of his life, 'yet I desire and charge you that it be not wrote as you find it, here in my name or first person singular; but, that you compose a Narrative out of it yo'self in the third person.'

At the end is an account of Rastrick's children. He married three times, and had in all 24 sons and daughters. There is a long account of Rastrick in the Dictionary of National Biography.[30]

[29] For the bequest of Richards's library to Brown University, see John Evans, *Memoirs of the Life and Writings of the Rev. William Richards* (Chiswick, 1819), pp. 262–263; Charles Coffin Jewett (ed.), *A Catalogue of the Library of Brown University, in Providence, Rhode-Island. With an index of subjects* (Providence, RI, 1843), pp. viii–x. I am grateful to Jay Gaidmore for providing copies of correspondence and catalogues from Brown University Archives.

[30] Anderson Galleries, *English, French and American literature in original manuscripts, first editions, handsome bindings and standard sets from the libraries of Mr Roland R. Conklin of Huntington, Long Island, Mrs Mary E. Plummer of New York, the late Hon. Henry H. Peck of Waterbury, Conn. and other owners and estates: Order of Sale, Monday afternoon, February 9, lots 1–213, Monday evening, February 9,*

It is almost certain that Henry Huntington acquired the manuscript at this sale. Unfortunately, the other items in the sale do not shed light on the whereabouts of Rastrick's manuscript before this date: it was a truly general sale, with items from over fifty consignees, of whom just three were named in the catalogue, and with material arranged alphabetically and offered for sale in four sessions.

*lots 214–427, Tuesday afternoon, February 10, lots 428–641, Tuesday evening, February 10, lots 642–855, Wednesday afternoon, Feburary 11, lots 856–1010 [*sic, *for 1070]* (New York: Anderson Galleries, 1920), sale number 1462, p. 171 (lot number 805). I thank Mary Robertson for her help with deciphering the clipping.

EDITORIAL RATIONALE AND CONVENTIONS

John Rastrick hoped that his narrative would be published, but he was also aware that doing so would inevitably change the nature and appearance of his life story. While I have not followed his instructions to change the account into a third-person narrative and to remove his prayers, devotions, letters, and 'whatsoever may be thought indecent, and of no use' (fo. 1v), some changes have been made in preparing this printed edition. These are worth describing both in terms of overall strategy and in matters of detail.

The purpose of this book is to provide an *edition* of John Rastrick's manuscript. It does *not* seek to replicate the exact form of the manuscript in printed form. Such an ambition seems to me to be misplaced, for two main reasons. First, print is a different technology from manuscript and, although this edition will remain faithful to the manuscript's spelling, punctuation, and capitalization, scholars particularly interested in technical aspects of the manuscript will always be best served by recourse to the original. Second, this edition aims to be readable. So I have avoided, where possible, scattering the text with all sorts of different types of brackets or designating the expansion of abbreviations with the use of italics. As a general rule, the text has been expanded but not modernized. Particular issues are addressed below.

Abbreviations

Abbreviations have been silently expanded as a matter of course; this includes abbreviations of proper names and books of the Bible. This edition does not retain the superscript of the original, since such usage is closely associated with the technology of writing. There are two exceptions to this rule, regarding numbers, where superscript has been retained because its usage is customary, convenient, and not liable to misinterpretation: the use of '8°' for octavo on one occasion (fo. 5r); and the retention of ordinal numbers expressed as '1st', '2nd', etc. where they have been rendered this way in the manuscript. For the same reason '&' and '&c.' have been retained and not expanded to 'and' and 'et cetera'. Common abbreviations such as 'Dr' have been retained, excepting those instances where an abbreviation was clearly signalled through the use of superscript, and the abbreviation thus expanded. Hence, ‘S^r’ has been expanded to ‘Sir’, but not ‘Mr’ to ‘Mister’.

Spelling, punctuation, and capitalization

Original spelling, punctuation, and capitalization have been retained. Like so many early modern writers, Rastrick was no lover of unnecessary punctuation. He did not routinely start sentences with capital letters or finish them with full stops, or any other form of punctuation. To render the text more readable without inserting extra punctuation, an extra space has been inserted at the end of the sentence, regardless of whether Rastrick indicated the end of the sentence with punctuation. In many (but not all) cases, such a decision is not an editorial intervention but merely following the manuscript, where the spaces between sentences are longer than those between individual words. However, Rastrick did write in paragraphs, in which he indented the first word, and the paragraphing of the edited text replicates that of the manuscript.

Although original capitalization has been retained, there is one particular problem with the manuscript that is not easily resolved: the initial letter ‘s’. In part because of the exceptionally small hand, deciding without doubt in which instances the manuscript employed a capital ‘s’ is problematic. Although there are clear instances of the use of the capital and lower-case ‘s’ as an initial letter in the manuscript, a very large proportion might be interpreted as either. Such issues are frequently in the eye of the beholder. To that end, I have taken the uncomfortable decision of using the capital ‘s’ (as a rule) for the initial letter of nouns and words at the beginning of sentences. This means that many of the most obviously capitalized s-words retain their initial capitalized letter, while avoiding the capitalization of adjectives, conjunctions, etc., where the ‘s’ might be rendered as a capital or a lower-case letter, and ensuring a degree of consistency.

Rastrick used ‘i’ and ‘j’ and ‘u’ and ‘v’ much as they would be used today and his use has been retained. He did not use archaic letter-forms such as the long ‘s’ or ‘ss’. For the titles of books in the footnotes, ‘w’ has been used in place of ‘vv’; ‘i’ and ‘u’ are always used for vowels and ‘j’ and v’ for consonants.

Additions and deletions

Interlineations are placed within < >. All other sets of brackets follow those used in the original manuscript, except in those instances where ‘[*sic*]’ denotes a spelling or formulation that might otherwise be taken as a mistake in transcription. Footnotes indicate where text has been deleted. The use of the formulation 'replacing [...] above the line' indicates that the original text has been cancelled. Where a word has been written above the text as a revision to the original but the original word has not been cancelled, this has been indicated in the notes.

Illegible words in the text (only at fo. 23r) are represented by ellipses. Words rendered illegible through cancellation, and illegible words in marginal notes, are described in footnotes.

Foliation and gatherings

Folio numbers are recorded without breaking the text, in the manner '/fo. 17r/'. Catchwords have not been reproduced. Rastrick's irregular numbered gatherings have not been reproduced in the edited text but are described in the introduction on p. 16 above.

The appearance of the text

Rastrick was not only an elegant writer but also, to adopt Robert Darnton's phrase, possessed of a developed typographical consciousness. His manuscript is obsessively neat and small. Rastrick deliberately used variations in the size and style of his hand to indicate how a published text might look. Such variations are recorded in the footnotes, along with variations in ink and pens. Rastrick's section headings have been retained.

The account of the births and deaths in the Rastrick family (fo. 89r) has been reproduced as a table, imposing an orderliness that is less evident in the manuscript. The aesthetics of this page, and of the title page and dedicatory epistle, can be seen in Figures 1 and 2.

It has not been practical to reproduce Rastrick's marginal notes as marginal notes in this edition, even though it is likely that he would have intended a printed edition to carry such notes, as was customary in the early eighteenth century. Instead, these marginal notes have been reproduced as a second layer of footnotes, with the marginalia signalled in the body of the text by an asterisk. In the many instances where Rastrick himself used an asterisk (or other symbol) to denote a marginal note, these are indicated at the start of the marginal note itself.

Dates

For the most part, Rastrick gives both years for dates between 1 January and 24 March, with the final two digits one above the other, resembling a fraction. They are reproduced here as, for example, 1708/9. In a very few cases, where the year is taken to finish on 24 March, the notes record the date in the style 1708/9 as above.

For dates in the footnotes, I have taken the year to begin on January 1.

Annotation

Where necessary and possible, footnotes identify places, individuals, and editions of printed books. Footnotes on relatively well-known individuals include a short reference to a standard source, frequently the *Oxford Dictionary of National Biography*. For those not included in such resources, the identification is often slightly fuller, including more detailed relevant material such as the dates that a clergyman was in post. Annotation is brief and not intended to be extensive or comprehensive. Although Rastrick's narrative throws light on a wide range of subjects, I have not attempted to provide references to current scholarly literature or debates.

Those books cited in the narrative and its marginal notes have been identified in the footnotes, using short bibliographical references but including, where possible, details of the precise edition to which Rastrick referred. Where he cites precise passages of particular works, these references have been verified and any discrepancies noted.

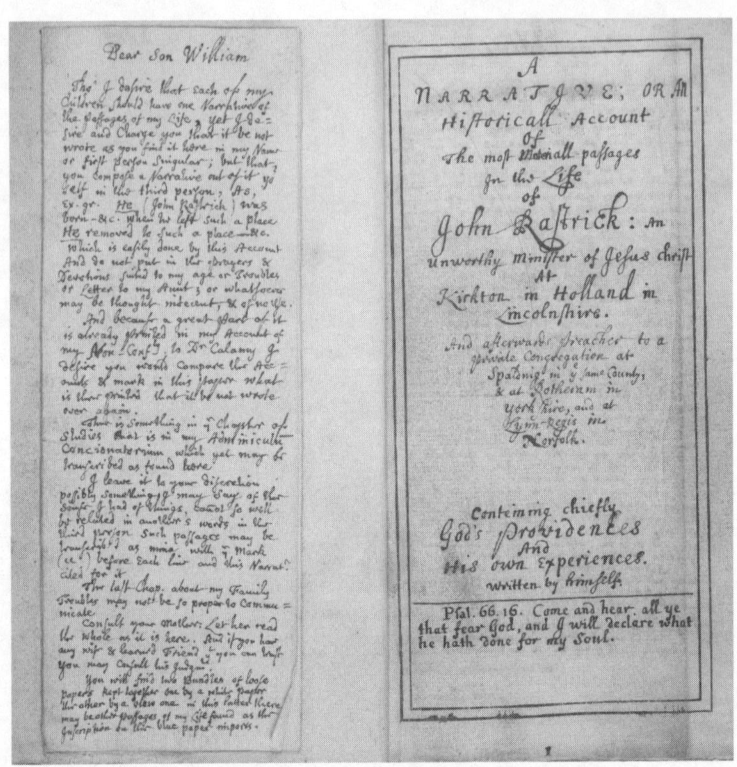

Dear Son William

Tho' I desire that each of my Children should have one Narrative of the Passages of my Life, yet I desire and Charge you that it be not wrote as you find it here in my Name or first Person Singular; but that you compose a Narrative out of it yo self in the third person; As, Ex. gr. He (John Rastrick) was born – &c. When he left such a place He removed to such a place – &c. Which is easily done by this Account. And do not put in the Prayers & Devotions suited to my age or Troubles or Letter to my Aunt; or whatsoever may be thought indecent, & of no use.

And because a great Part of it is already Printed in my Account of my Non-Conf[y] to D[r] Calamy I desire you would compare the Accounts & mark in this Paper what is there printed that it be not wrote over again.

There is something in y[e] Chapter of Studies that is in my Adminicula Concionatorium which yet may be transcribed as found here.

I leave it to your discretion possibly something I may say of the sense I had of things, cannot so well be related in another's words in the third person such passages may be transcribed as mine. with y[e] Mark (" ") before each line and this Narrat[ive] cited for it.

The last Chap. about my Family Troubles may not be so proper to Communicate.

Consult your Mother: Let her read the whole as it is here. And if you have any wise & learned Friend y[t] you can trust you may consult his judgm[t].

You will find two Bundles of loose papers kept together one by a white Paper the other by a blew one in this latter there may be other Passages of my Life found as the Inscription on the blue paper imports.

A
NARRATIVE; OR AN
Historicall Account
Of
The most Materiall passages
In the Life
of
John Rastrick: An
unworthy minister of Jesus Christ
At
Kirkton in Holland in
Lincolnshire.

And afterwards Preacher to a private Congregation at Spalding in y[e] same County, & at Rotherham in York shire, and at Lynn-Regis in Norfolk.

Conteining chiefly
God's Providences
And
His own Experiences.
Written by himself.

Psal. 66. 16. Come and hear, all ye that fear God, and I will declare what he hath done for my Soul.

1

Fig. 1 'A NARRATIVE; OR AN Historicall Account Of The most Materiall passages In the Life of John Rastrick', fos 1v–2r.

A NARRATIVE; OR AN HISTORICAL ACCOUNT OF THE MOST MATERIALL PASSAGES IN THE LIFE OF JOHN RASTRICK

/flyleaf/[1]

/fo. 1r/
[Blank page]

/fo. 1v/

Dear Son William

Although I desire that each of my children should have one Narrative of the passages of my Life, yet I desire and charge you that it be not wrote as you find it here in my Name or first person singular; but that, you compose a Narrative out of it your Self in the third person, As ex. gr. He (John Rastrick) was born – &c. when he left such a place He removed to such a place – &c. which is easily done by this Account And do not put in the Prayers and Devotions suited to my age or Troubles or Letter to my Aunt; or whatsoever may be thought indecent, and of no use.

And because a great part of it is already printed in my Account of my Non-Conformity. to Dr Calamy[2] I desire you would compare the Accounts and mark in this paper what is there printed that it be not wrote over again.

There is something in the Chapter of Studies that is in my Adminiculum Concionatorium[3] which yet may be transcribed as found here

[1]This sheet, which is glued to the cover, appears to be a letter addressed to John Rastrick. The visible side is that bearing his address, but the only visible letters are 'astrick att' and, below, 'in'.

[2]John Rastrick, *An Account of the Nonconformity of John Rastrick, M.A.* (London, 1705), which appears to have been printed both separately and as the final volume of Edmund Calamy, *A Defence of Moderate Non-conformity*, 3 vols (London, 1703–1705). The overlap between Rastrick's manuscript and printed accounts are described in the introduction above. For Edmund Calamy (1671–1732), Presbyterian minister and historian, see *ODNB*.

[3]Nothing further is known of this manuscript: see above, p. 13.

I leave it to your discretion possibly something I may say of the Sense I had of things, cannot so well be related in another's words in the third person Such passages may be transcribed as mine with the Mark (cc) before each line and this Narrative cited for it

The last Chapter about my Family Troubles may not be so proper to communicate.

Consult your mother. Let her read the whole as it is here. And if you know any wise and learned Friend that you can trust you may consult his Judgment.

You will find two Bundles of loose papers kept together one by a white paper the other by a blew one in this latter may be other passages of my Life found as the Inscription on the blue paper imports.

/fo. 2r/

A
NARRATIVE; OR AN
Historicall Account
Of
The most Materiall passages
In the Life
of
John Rastrick: An
Unworthy Minister of Jesus Christ
At
Kirkton in Holland in
Lincolnshire.
And afterwards Preacher to a
Private Congregation at
Spalding in the same County,
& at Rotheram in
Yorkshire, and at
Lynn-Regis in
Norfolk.

Conteining chiefly
God's Providences
And
His own experiences.
Written by himself.

Psalm 66.16. Come and hear, all ye
that fear God, and I will declare what
he hath done for my Soul.

/fo. 2v/

To my Children

Dear Children.

You are most of you the children of my Old Age, I may leave you young And when I am gone and you are grown up you may have a desire or not unwarrantable Curiosity to know what your Poor Father was, where he had lived and what he thought and did in the world, which in your younger years you were not capable of observing and minding; or did not think of enquiring after: But you may be informed in the following Sheets; to which purpose they may be of use to you. They were first begun in the Form of a Diary, from which the Devotional Passages and Meditations of my younger time are here transcribed. I wrote them for my own use but now they are here they may not be altogether unuseful for you. Come my children, hearken unto me and I will tell you what the Lord hath done for my Soul. Blessed be his Name that drew my Soul betimes unto himself: so that He has been the Support and Comfort not only of my youth but of my whole life. May He be the like to you. Its true, though (as Bishop Hall said of himself) what I have done be worthy of nothing but forgetfulness; yet, what God hath done for me is worthy of a written and grateful Memoriall.[4] What you find amiss in me take warning by and avoid: If in any thing I endevoured well, be you followers of me as I was of Christ. Some Wayes I took that were not very gratefull to the Flesh, nor made for my outward Interest in the World, and for which I was by many accounted a Fool; but the Lord never forsook me in them. What I have said about my Studies may be useful for you my younger Sons if either of you be Ministers as I have greatly desired if the Lord so pleased that one of my own might be. The Lord in Heaven be with you, and bless you; and be a God, a Father, and a Portion to you, both now and for ever.

And you my children know you the God of your father and serve him with a perfect heart and with a willing mind: for the Lord searcheth all hearts, and understandeth all the Imaginations of the Thoughts; if you seek Him He will be found of you; but if you forsake Him, He will cast you off for ever.

That he may be truly and sincerely sought and joyfully and happily Found of you all is the hearty Desire and Prayer of

your tender affectionate Father
John Rastrick

[4]Joseph Hall (1574–1656), 'Observations of some specialties of divine providence in the life of Jos. Hall, Bishop of Norwich', in *The Shaking of the Olive-tree* (London, 1660), pp. 1–2: 'What I have done is worthy of nothing, but silence and forgetfulness; but what God hath done for me, is worthy of everlasting and thankfull Memory.'

/fo. 3r/

I John Rastrick (an unworthy Minister* of Christ) was born at Heckington near Sleeford on March 26. Anno Domini 1650. My Father, of the middle rank of Husbandmen, of which that town consists. My parents had 5 children before me of whom 4 dyed infants: One lived almost 9 year, and dyed, about five months before I was born. The death of that child was a great grief to my indulgent, tender, passionate Mother, insomuch as she hath often said, she could have gone into the grave with him; but that (if I may use her own words, which I have often heard her speak) she <had such an impression on her Spirit as if she> heard (as it were)[5] a voyce, saying to her, Have a care of the child that is within Thee; Or, Take heed of that Thou art withall. This gave a check to her excessive grief. The Lord thereby as it were intimateing to her, that he had a greater Work for him to do, and as great a Comfort for her, if she would trust his mercifull Providence.

When I was born, (the last and now onely child they had) I did not suck of my Mother's Breasts, but was put out to nurse; where (had not the Lord (upon whom I was cast from the womb, and who is my God from my Mother's Belly) been wonderfully mercifull unto me) I had then perished as I have often heard them speak But my Father, haveing been at my nurse's with me, and going home and beginning to tell my Mother of my weakness and danger ([6]who apprehending the worst from his manner of breathing, before he

*Marginal note, written in an ink that has faded to brown, running down the length of the page:
Memorandum.
My father wrote his name Raistrigge; and others of our relations Raystrygge. But we had a kinsman of our Name at London, an occulist, who told us that we wrote our Name wrong; and that it should be as he wrote his; that is, Rastrick: for that the Family was originally of Rastrick of Yeland parish near Halifax in Yorkshire. And he sent us down our Coat of Arms, desiring it might be kept by the eldest of the Family, which is, A chevern betwixt three Roses Gulles on a Field Argent with a Mullet or Star Sable; the whole encircled with two green lawrell branches and a crest Or. Tradition told us, that the first Rastrick at Heckington came out of York-shire (which possibly he might do with packhorses to Norwich as they do at this day) and settled at a House on the North side of Heckington called Boston-garth. That he had four Sons, and each of them a Son, one of whom my great Uncle George, I knew. Tradition also told us, that one, the only one left, of the Family in Yorkshire marryed a Gentlewoman that would not have him except he changed his Name, which he did, and wrote himself by that new Name she imposed on him (which what it was I have forgot) with an alias Rastrick. Upon the

[5]These brackets have been inserted in the brown ink of the marginal notes, perhaps after the main body of the text was written.

[6]*and* deleted.

could get <out> his words[7], passionately cryed out, Alas! My child's dead;) she <therefore> suddenly in an anguish hasted away to me, and (almost despairing of my Life indeed when she saw me,) took me away, and put me to another nurse By whose breasts, (after I had vomited up the morsells the other nurse had /fo. 3v/ thrust down, which I personally did) I* was (by the concurrence of God's blessing restored and preserved. With luck I continued till I was almost a year old, and then my Parents took me home.

When I was at home and begun to go; God's Providence over me further appeared in a yet more wonderfull preservation. For (as I take it) in Hay or Harvest time, every body being employed abroad, and so Servants not at home, and my Mother (being buisie on a day brewing) <haveing> left me alone in the yard to play, now and then looking out after me. before she was aware, I was got to a pond that was in the yard and was fallen in; where I lay over head and ears. My Mother at her next looking out, (not presently seeing me) cast her ey upon the water where she espyed a red cloth swimming which was the Skirt of the Coat I wore, and ran and tooke me out of the water, to her thinking Deade; in which very great Fright she called in hastily a neighbour or two; who holding me for the water to run out, I was after some time, with very much difficulty, beyond all expectation recovered to life again: And my God (as he did his Servant Moses) preserved me from the water.

When I was 4 years old my Parents put me to School to our Mr Barnes an English Schoolmaster in that Town, who taught me to read. Here we had morning and evening prayers in use in the School, and a Psalm constantly sung every night before we left School, which one <of> the Schollers read; and when I began to read indifferently <well> my Master put me often to read the Psalm my Self. God wrought in my Soul a Tincture of Religion and godliness betimes; the Impressions of which (I bless his name) were deeply made when I was very young. My Father would shew me the Minister's Texts, and tell me some of the Historys of the Bible when I used to sit on his Knee, and before I /fo. 4r/ understood what belonged to such things, or what he meant by them. but I quickly grew very inquisitive after them; and would ask my Father the meaning of every word and thing that was hard to me, which possibly might the more prompt him to those endeavours. In my childhood I was of a simple nature,

*Marginal note, continued from previous page: Information & Advice of our London Relation before mentioned it was that I altered the writing of our Name: Besides also that as it was before, it seemed to me to be scarce consistent with any Orthography, and occasioned peoples miscalling us Rastridg. For which reason Mr Gataker changed his Name from Gatacre as may be seen in his Life published by Clark.

[7] *unto* deleted.

easie of Belief and soon imposed upon, but very angry with any that I understood lyed to me. and so, that which I understood to be vice, I hated and opposed with great eagerness.

Concerning my Understanding and Inclinations about spirituall things in my childhood; I remember this instance: When I was reading my Psalter (as I take it) the 2^{d} time over and my Father, (as I sat on his Knee) was watching me to understand the Figures that I might know how to <turn to>[8] any Psalm or verse in my Book; which we practised in Psalm 119. because there was numbers to 3 places or figures As I read vers 103. How sweet are Thy Words unto my Tast, yea sweeter than honey to my mouth I called to mind and told my Father of the like passage in Psalm: 19.10. and observed to him how fitly they agreed, and pointed to one another. To which he (I suppose to try me) replyed that the one was spoken of his words, the other of His Judgments: But I Answered, Father, don't you know, that there's his Words, and there's his Judgments, there's his Laws, and there's his Commandments. there's his Statutes, and his precepts, and His Testimonys, all used in the same Sense; Are they not all one Father? in both the Psalms? To which he Assented, and fell a weeping; For I was but a child sitting on his Knee.—— But however my Father haveing (as I said) with tears observed these things Resolved from that Time to continue me at School; not knowing what God might have designed to do with me; which Resolution he ever held notwithstanding the change, and my Mother's after aversness as follows in its place.

/fo. 4v/ Mr Barns my first Master dying I was destitute for a while of a Teacher and therefore exercised my Self in reading at Home; untill Mr Duckling (our then Minister[9]) taught School after him: whose Scholler I became He enterd me in Grammar and taught me to write which I remember I then earnestly desired; thinking what a fine thing it would be if I could set down any thing to read it again; though it was long before I could conquer <it or attain> any readyness and exactnese in it

Now it pleased God to visit me with the Small Pox a Disease which proved mortall to my brother about the same age: But it pleased God (tho I was very full of them, and very sick senseless and blind) to restore me. I fell sick November. 1. and after Christmas went to School again. When the violence of my distemper took away my Senses I was almost a whole night (as my Father who told me related) in Earnest Prayer to God to deliver me from such terrible Objects as were represented to my Fancy: which dream of mine (for so I call it differing nothing therefrom but that I spoke my thoughts, which in <common> dreams is not usually done) I can now distinctly

[8] Replacing illegible word (possibly *understand*), above the line.

[9] John Duckling, MA (died in or before 1672), ordained 1639; vicar of Heckington, Lincs. (1646–); and vicar of Helpringham, Lincs. CCEd; Venn, II, p. 71.

remember in most or all of the circumstances as I can any thing in all my youth.

At the Turn of the Times, Mr Sharp (an Episcopall Divine, and indeed a solid Learned and able one, but had not such a voyce and delivery as to take much with me then) returned to Heckington;[10] and Mr Duckling my <2d> Master went away; and we again wanted a School. In This Vacancy I kept my Self employed at Home (1) with my pen. (2) collecting and composing (according to my capacity) certain Prayers out of the Psalms and other parts of the Bible, and good books, writing them /fo. 5r/ down together in a little 8° book. (3) in Reading and conferring the Bible and other good Books. We had in our Family Dyke's Decietfulness of Man's Heart[11] and Dent's Plain man's path way to H.[12] —— Old books: These I delighted to reade and they much affected me. O what would I have given if I had had it that Dent's Plain Man's Pathway had been perfect, for it was torn and much of it gone and my Father bought no books except very small and cheap ones. I remember before this he had bought me the School of Vertue,[13] about youth's behaviour wher I was taught to put Lord Protector instead of King in one of the Prayers: and he brought me from Boston once a small catechism of Mr Cotton's called Milk for Boston Babes when I was so young and childish as to be troubled that it was not for Heckington babes, and thought it was not for me; but was <soon> satisfyed, and learned it.[14] But at Mr Dent's and Dyke's Books (when my understanding grew a little riper) I sat at night with great delight; 'Twas my grief to go to bed, especially so soon as 8 or 9 of the clock, the country hours. God blessed these means to work in my heart a quick Sense of Religious and divine things, which abode on my Spirit. As I walked in the Fields from our pasture abroad methought if I might but go to Heaven, I cared not whatever I did or underwent. And now I began to get some Prayers out of Books (by heart) to say at nights, when we were in Bed, (for we used not to pray before <we were in bed>, and we lay all in a room.) Whereas untill this time I used to answer my Father in repeating some part of Perkin's catechism, the 6 Principles; when we were in Bed.[15] For that

[10] Robert Sharpe, BD (died in or before 1670), was vicar of Heckington from 1635. CCEd. *Sketches, Illustrative of the Topography and History of New and Old Sleaford* (Sleaford, 1825), p. 249, notes that he was rector from 1636 to 1646 and again from 1660 to 1666.

[11] Daniel Dyke, *The Mystery of Selfe-deceiving. Or A discourse and discovery of the deceitfullnesse of mans heart* (London, 1614, and many later editions).

[12] Arthur Dent, *The Plaine Mans Path-way to Heaven* (London, 1601, and many later editions).

[13] F[rancis] S[egar], *The Schoole of Vertue* (London, 1557, and many later editions).

[14] Rastrick's reference is presumably to John Cotton, *Spiritual Milk for Boston Babes* (London, 1657) and not to the edition printed in Cambridge, Massachusetts in 1656, or to the earlier editions, which were entitled *Milk for Babes*.

[15] William Perkins, *The Foundation of Christian Religion Gathered into Sixe Principles* (London, 1590, and many later editions).

was the catechism our Masters taught us: The Assembly's I cannot remember I had yet known.[16] And thus after these Providences, and in these Employments was the first Decad of years of my age spent.

/fo. 5v/ About the beginning of the year 1661 (to the best of my rememberance my Father sent me to School to Great Hale a Town about half a mile from Heckington (whither I went every day) to Mr Woolmer Minister there (my third master) where I proceeded in my Grammar Learning.

Shortly after there came to Heckington from Lincoln one Thomas Grantham, a good Scholler, and well skilled in the Art of Teaching; to him my Father sent me to School, who was my 4th Master.[17] I remember he would encourage us to learn though never so dull; and tell us that the aptest to learn commonly soonest forgot it, but the hardest when they had once conquered it usually retained it best: For, (as he told us) the first Sort are like Free Stone, the other like Marble; 'tis easy to engrave in Free Stone, but the letters are also soon worn out again: but in Marble though it be hard to engrave, the writing remains Durable. This Similitude I was much taken with. He was inclined to the Quaker's ways, and opinions I remember Mr Sharp our Minister came one night to discourse with him, about the time of leaving School; I had a great mind to hear them Discourse, and therefore when they had begun, I stayed trifling in the School after the rest of the Schollers but was not suffered to stay long, and so heard not much, though I much desired it. He being not well settled in his mind sold his Books (some few of which my Father bought for me) and soon left the Town, and me once more destitute of a Teacher.

About this time Mr King, (the famous Minister of Okeham in Rutland now comeing (upon the turn of the time, and turning out of Ministers) to live at Lesingham by Sleeford,)[18] was procured to preach (betwixt his Ejection and the Silencing Act) once or twice at Heckington: But such a preacher had I never heard before in all my Life; for zeal and serious fervency O how I admired him! and how sorry was I when Prayer and Sermon was done. /fo. 6r/ Very great Impressions were hereby made in my mind. Chiefly now was the first time I can remember that ever I had any thoughts about the Ministry; and upon this it was that God first wrought in my heart a Complacency in, and Inclination towards that sacred Office which I now more than ever affected. For I was not only concerned about

[16] Rastrick does not distinguish between the Larger and Shorter versions of the Westminster Catechism, although his reference to the catechisms in the plural might suggest that he used a combined edition, *The Confession of Faith . . . Together with the Larger and Shorter Catechisms* (London, 1649, and many later editions).

[17] Not to be confused with the noted teacher Thomas Grantham (*c.*1610–1664). *ODNB*.

[18] Benjamin King (*c.*1612–1677), vicar of Oakham, Leics. (1647–1660); resigned; licensed at Oakham (1672). *Calamy Revised*, p. 308.

what he said and the Application of it to my Self as a christian, but as a Preacher my Self thinking with my Self, as I heard him, that if I were a Minister or when I were one after such a manner and with such a voyce would I preach as he did and I looked upon his preaching not only as one looks upon a fine house that is to live in it, or a fine Suit of clothes that is to wear it, but as a Carpenter or Tayler looks upon them that is to make such. Though it was then the most unlikely and improbable thing in the world (considering my Father's mean circumstance in the world &c.) that ever I should come to such a thing; nor had I the least Thought of it (for all this) as to any positive Intention or purpose of my own <, or any formed hope.>[19]

Being now at Home and from School as I said before I was kept employed much after the same manner as I had been in former vacancys: But my Father being desirous of my Learning and to continue me at School; would not suffer me to be longer away than he could well provide for me, and therefor was still thinking of some better master, or some publick Schoole for me. There was one Mr Read a newly Ejected Minister in Linsey coast (or presently to be ejected)[20] to whom a neighbour of ours (the same that procured Mr King to preach) sent his Son; to whom also my Father would have put me but, my Mother hindered that, not being able to endure that I should be so far from her; so that that design fell. But nothwithstanding shortly /fo. 6v/ after (Anno Domini 1662 I being then 12 years old gone) my Father sent me to the Free School of Grantham. where I was entered under my 5th Master. This was a School of very good note, and well governed.* Here was care taken for the training of us

*Marginal note: * One of my Schoolfellows at Grantham was the Son of one Peters an inhabitant of the part called Holland. His father sent him to Oxford, and purchased the next advowson of a great living, Hougham, not far from Grantham of some hundreds of pounds per annum: But at Oxford his Son dyed. When the living fell, he had a daughter that he designed to marry to one Mr Seccar, Minister of Bloxham, and so give her the living for her portion: But before he could be possessed, Mr Seccar fell sick and dyed. In his Sickness it was contrived and designed that if he dyed his Brother Mr Seccar a Physician should take Holy Orders and marry the Daughter But within a week or ten days (after Mr Sec. the Minister dyed,) this Brother of his, Mr Seccar the Physician dyed also! And I was at Sleeford when Mr Peters went weeping up the Angel yard for this disappointment: And all men were amazed that a three-fold cord should be so broken. Thus God declared against this corruption in the Church. Lord! when wilt thou cast the Buyers and Sellers out of thy Temple?[21]

[19] Inserted in smaller hand.

[20] Edmund Calamy, *A Continuation of the Account* (London, 1727), pp. 609–610 notes that Mr Christopher Read held out as a nonconformist for a short while but was persuaded to accept a living and died soon after. Perhaps the same Christopher Reade, BA who was vicar of Cloford, Somerset, in 1641 and was perhaps sequestered to the rectory of Bassingham, Lincs. in 1646. Foster, III, p. 1239.

[21] The elder Peters is William Peters, who was patron of Thomas Secker when instituted rector of Hougham in 1676. Thomas Secker, MA was chaplain to the earl of Shrewsbury;

up not only in humane learning but in Piety: On Saturdays in the afternoon we went to School an hour or more upon that pure account to learn our catechisms &c. All of us that could write were enjoyned to write Sermons in the church; and at or about the second ringing we went to School on the Lord's days where our Sermon notes were called for, or we to repeat them. And we always had prayers before we began School every morning. Here I greatly desired learning and was in love with it; and (as I remember) I often wished that I was as good a Scholler as those in the highest Seat of all; and it gave me in my mind I should be so, though I knew of nothing but leaving School and being at home to be employed and trained up in Husbandry and country buisness.

In this place being far from home (which I used not to be before) and seldom seeing my Parents; I was very melanchollly upon that account, which wrought me to a very serious frame and temper of Spirit; which every body took notice of. and this made me (according to my capacity) very fervent as well as very frequent in Prayer. Here somebody espying me on my knees in the garden told it there where I boarded, and they jeared me with Praying to the Walls. yet for all this to go to God in prayer was the onely comfort I had, which when I was disconsolate I usually met with by this means. And when at any time, I saw or thought of any grievous calamity or disease, wanting outward means of help or cure: I was sure (methought) if I were /fo. 7r/ in the like case, the Lord would help me if I prayed to him. Which Blessed be God, I have since found in a very great measure to be very true. God I hope (not in vain but) for very great purposes working that impression in my mind in my tender years.

At this School I stayed but one year, for Anno Domini 1663 being taken home against Whitsunday My Mother would not suffer me to go any more thither; nor did she desire me any whether else, or to any further learning, but that I should keep at Home under her ey and ear and learn to work for my Living &c. Upon this; not onely my Master at Grantham was concerned as loath that I should be spoyled, and my parts (which he it seems thought somewhat promising, though, for Reasons I have, I know not how he could think so) to be quite buryed: But there was also a Gentleman a Lawyer one Mr Perkins (whose daughter was afterwards wife to Dr How of Boston)[22] who lived near

rector of Bloxholm, Lincs. (1672–1676); and rector of Hougham with Marston, Lincs. (1676). He died in October 1676. CCEd; Venn, IV p. 39. Henry Stokes was Master of the Free Grammar School, Grantham (1650–1663); the ushers were Joseph Clarke (until 1662) and Edward Stokes (from 1662). See, S.J. Branson, *The History of the King's School, Grantham: 660 years of a grammar school* (Gloucester, 1988), p. 140.

[22]William Perkins of Grantham (bap. 1629–d. 1693), admitted to Inner Temple (1665). Venn, III, p. 347; Obadiah Howe (1615/16–1683), Church of England clergyman and author. *ODNB*. Howe succeeded Anthony Tuckney as vicar of Boston, Lincs. in 1660.

the Free-School; whom I cannot tell that ever I saw about once or twice that twelvemonth, much less could I think that he had at all known or at least regarded me (a very puny boy, of the meanest habit) and he was one that my Father (to the best of my remembrance) did never use to employ who yet wrote a Letter to my Mother to persuade her to keep me longer at School; which I have here inserted in his own words

Mistress Rastrick

I have taken notice of your Son's Ingenuity and pregnancy at Grantham School, and he is very hopeful to make an useful member in the common wealth if he may proceed in his learning a little longer time, and you and his Father may have the greater joy and comfort of him; I hearing that your Indulgency and tenderness over him is such that you are minded to take him home; if so /fo. 7v/ I concieve you will both wrong your child, and your Self, and mistrust God with him; for you know not what the Lord hath ordained him for. Let him have his reasonable time at School for that's his harvest. So desiring to be excused for my boldness with you I leave this to your Consideration, and commit you to the Protection of the Almighty, with my best respects to you, and your husband and Son, I rest

Grantham, Your affectionate
12 of June, friend to serve you
1663. Will: Perkins

This letter we had thought more stranger had we not conjectured that a friend and neighbour of my Father's had acquainted him with the case, and put him upon writing; Thus solicitous were both Friends and Strangers about me and my concerns (by God's Good providence) in my juvenile years. But this letter prevailed nothing at all with my Mother first in her Resolution to bring me up to work and get my living that way. yet for all this, long it was not before I went to another Free School, upon this occasion following.

On a day as I was looking in Ovid's book de Trist. in English[23] (which I used sometime to read to her,) she bad me read up, that she might hear; But as I delayed (turning up and down the book, for a place fitter for her to hear, than that where I was reading) in a very great passion she turned me out of the house, and set me to fill the Dung-cart that stood in the yard: to which I was fain to buckle[24] my Self as well as I could. This did not at all please my Father, who cared for no work of Husbandry of my doing at any time. And therefor (when the Cart was filled) He sitting in the Barn door called me over to him in a most Loveing manner (as I complained of my blistered fingers)

[23] Ovid, *De tristibus*. Individual parts had been printed in English translation since 1572; the first full translation was by Zachary Catlin in 1639.

[24] *buckle*: to gird oneself, apply oneself resolutely to a task. *OED*.

asking me if I would go to School again, and telling me I should. That day he and I went into the field to weed wheat wher we had a great deal of talk (pleasant enough to me) of /fo. 8r/ the Free School at Sleeford (which was but a mile off and our Market, and where my Parents might see me, and I them almost every week) and how I might do there; and that I might board at My Aunt's at Lesingham a mile off at a lesser charge and more pleasing to my Mother. This was soon agreed, and resolved upon. The next Munday (the Market day) my Father took me to Sleeford, spoke to, and agreed with the Master; and I was presently entered in that Free School, under Mr Masters (my sixt Schoolmaster).[25] I was boarded at Lesingham aforesaid (the first year) and walked daily to School in the pleasant and suitable company of Joseph and Benjamin two Sons of Famous Mr King the Non Conformist aforementioned:[26] afterwards I boarded for half a year in the Town. and thus (by God's Providence) I was again put into a way of Learning; and before I left that School was entered into the Greek tongue.

Hither I went in the Summer Anno Domini 1663. in the 13th year of my age gone. Here I thirsted after learning as eagerly as ever I had done; and had a persuasion in my mind that I should be a Scholler and sometime my mind would be firmly fixt, and I concluded within my Self that nothing so sure as I should be a Minister, notwithstanding all seeming Hindrances, and Impossibillitys. But when at other times this seemed improbable I thought I would see (if I must be of a Trade) if I could get to be Apprentice to a Bookbinder howsoever.

Here I lived (while at Lesingham) under the Ministry of Mr Justice an Excellent Preacher,[27] and begun to write Sermon notes from my memory after I came from church; according to my capacity at that time which I afterwards enterd into a Book. And for the Frame and temper of my Soul; I used to be often in secret Prayer and Meditation /fo. 8v/ in which I tooke the truest and most satisfactory delight; and from where I reaped the most solid comfort. Once as I went home from School I lost something by the way, and returning to seek it late at night (praying all the way to God; (for I was afraid of displeasing my father by the loss of it,) I found it where I had left it hard by the the way Side. About this time I espyed this fault in my Soul; I often found that after a blessing recieved I could not (methought as I desired) praise God, or give him thanks proportionably either to the mercy recieved,

[25] The master of the Free School, Sleaford, Lincs. in 1663 was Peter Stevens. See *Sketches . . . of New and Old Sleaford*, p. 86.

[26] Two of the three sons of Benjamin King. One was Benjamin King, apothecary of New Sleaford, Lincs., who died in 1703. *Calamy Revised*, p. 308.

[27] Jasper Justice, BA was instituted rector of Lessingham, Lincs. in 1660. CCEd. Perhaps the same as Jasper Justice (BA 1642–1643), who probably kept a school at Arksey, near Doncaster. Venn, II, p. 492.

or (which was the chief thing) to my importunity in Prayer for the same. When I read any good Book of judgment Hell, and Heaven, or that exhorted to repentance; I wondered at the hardness of my heart that I could not mourn for, nor bewail my Sins; and that I could be no more affected in so great a case!

At Christmas Anno Domini 1664 I was taken from School again after I had been at Sleeford's about a year and a half and was now at Home for about a quarter of a year. And now at this time as before (though the Schoolmaster at Sleeford did not throughly answer our expectations at the last, his School therefor lessening very much. My mother was chiefly blamed for my loosing of my time by all our Friends and Neighbours[28] who concerned themselves in my affairs about my welfare and proficiency as (to my great wonder since, at the Providence of God therein,) very many did. Indeed my Mother would fain have had me brought up as other her Neighbour's Sons were to Husbandry at the Plow and Cart, and now was the time she thought I was betwixt makeing and marring /fo. 9r/ and if I did not now begin to lay my bones to work and lay to live (as her phrase was) I should be more unfit afterwards; and she was afraid lest my Father should keep me so long at School until I were fit for nothing. Or if I were not fit for Husbandry, she was however for some honest Trade as Mercer or Baker &c. yet (see the Providence of God!) There were none she could move it to who knew her and me who were of these Trades that liked her purpose, or would take me; but told her she would wrong me to hinder me from learning. She could not abide I could always live Idely as I did; and asked me if I meant always to go to School a great boy; &c. I answered her, yes, till I repented (as Plato said) to be wiser, or better. And I used to tell her long before this, that work was not all of one kind; There is Mentall Labour as well as bodily, the Work of the Head, as well as of the hand. &c.

But as for my Father all his desire always was that I should be at School; And (seeing what was in me (as he said) and that I was fit for nothing else) he often protested, saying, he durst do no other (under God) but give me Learning; and bad my Mother Trust to Providence, and (as his usuall Speech was many a time) use the means, and commit the Success to God.

And as for my Self I was wholly enclined to learning; and indeed I could not endur to work. While I was at School I used to be taken home a week in wheat Harvest time, (otherwise my Mother would not be content) when being tyred with labour I heartily wished and longed for the week's end, that I might /fo. 9v/ be at School again; and thought with my Self, if I had but any Learning able to teach a School, I would follow any employment rather than work for my Living: and it

[28] Illegible word cancelled.

troubled me the more when I saw Mr Sharp (the Minister) sometimes (though rarely, for he was a studious man) walk, and ride about the field; and I lyed there all day sweltring in the Heat & Sun.

Things standing thus; my Mother (wearyed with accusations) to free her Self from all blame, went her Self (at Easter Anno Domini 1665) to Mr Sharp our Minister, partly to advise with him what to do with me and also to desire him to teach me, if it were but an hour or two in the day, when he could be at leisure; if it were but that I might keep what I had got. When she asked his counsell what to do with me, he desired to know of her what she thought I was most enclined to; She Answered, she thought to nothing at all; &c. But he yielded to her main request, and was willing to teach me, upon the conditions aforesaid when he could be at leisure. To him therefore I went the next day; and he was (for the time he continued) my seventh Master; and I for the most part his onely Scholler.

Once (I remember) I got a Sight of his Study; and seeing so many Books, and papers lying on the Table with pen and ink, Reading Glass, and other studying furniture and a Library so great (as I then thought it was) that took up one Side of a Wall: The Thoughts of his delightful Study and Pleasant Conversation among his Books so delighted me ever after and had such a pleasing relish in my mind, that I wished, and extremely desired that I might have but the <such> same, and (methought) could not but rejoyce in the Hopes thereof.

/fo. 10r/ About the latter end of this Summer (Anno Domini 1665.) Mr Sharp was called away; and removed from Heckington to Alford a Market Town in the parts of Linsey, in the same county to be their Pastor; and left me once more without a Teacher; and indeed without any thoughts or hopes of ever going to School more. and I was therefore employed in such Country buisness as I was fittest for. I kept our Cows in the Common Fields and Meadows of Heckington for 2 or 3 months All Studys and Concerns of Learning (as I remember) were now quite laid by; save only that I took a Book with me now and then into the Fields; which my Father would have me do. Though my mind could not but be very much wearied and alienated from such things; and while I was thus engaged, to hear of a School would now have been strange News to me indeed.

But after a few months, this strange News (by God's Wonderfull Providence) proved true. At the beginning of December (that same year) my Father haveing need of Advice about some Law buisness went upon this occasion to Swineshead to Counsellour Woolmer.[*29]

[*]Marginal note: Matthew Wolmer of Swineshead Esq.

[29]Matthew Woolmer (alias Consell) of Swineshead, Lincs.; matriculated Queen's College, Cambridge (1632); admitted to Lincoln's Inn (1635); called to the bar (1646); bencher (1670). Venn, IV, p. 462.

That Gentleman (haveing once seen me, and some Deed or Evidence of my drawing; and reading of my hand=writing,* which he liked.) inquired about me of my Father. John (said he) what dost thou do with thy Son? What a Scholler is he? My Father told him with what Masters I had been, and how I was then at home; adding withall that I minded nothing but my book; and would follow (or at least was fit to follow) nothing else; and the like. Mr Woolmer presently advised my Father to take Great Hale in his way Home, and see Mr Walker the Minister (newly come from Kyme thither, of whom Mr Woolmer gave my Father some character and I believe by his desire and recommendation, he influenced the buisness; for my Father was a perfect Stranger to him)[30] /fo. 10v/ and wished him to try whether he would teach me: and if he would not he desired him to try Mr Goodknap (a Worthy and Faithfull Minister of Christ at Burton)[31] either of these places would be within my daily reach on foot, and I need not board out at charge for to my Mother's trouble. My Father presently took his advice came home that same day by Hale, and called on Mr Walker, upon that account; who (though unwilling at first, yet) hearing how far I was learnt, was entreated to teach me on condition that he found me (upon tryall) ingenious, apt and capable; and therefore desired my Father to bring me the next day that he might see and try me, and resolve. I had not been long come out of the Field from my wonted Employment but my Father came home with this unexpected news. This was <Thursday>[32] and the next day (<Friday>[33]) according to appointment we went; and upon Tryall he Ordered that I should come the next [34]day, and so to continue: (though it was Saturday and but a fortnight before Christmas.[35] And so I was admitted under my Eighth and last master.

On[36] one of the Holydays (either my Father came when I was at School (for I learned all Christmas except 3 or 4 days) or else he and I went on purpose to see my Master Walker, where we were very Welcome and my Father had a great deal of serious discourse with him about me; and then made it his buisness to desire him to give him his best advice what to do with me; and what calling it were best for me to follow; and to that end related to him fully my Fashions

*Marginal note, in pencil and probably later: his handwriting in greek.

[30] John Walker, MA, curate of Great Hale. CCEd.

[31] Jeremy Goodknap, MA (died in or before 1681) was instituted rector of Burton Pedwarine, Lincs. in 1663. His patron was Thomas Orby. CCEd; Venn, II, p. 235.

[32] Replacing *Friday*, above the line.

[33] Replacing *Saturday*, above the line.

[34] The first part of this word has been scrubbed out, possibly *Mon*.

[35] Illegible sentence scrubbed out. The cancellation renders the text illegible.

[36] *e* at end of *on* cancelled.

and Inclinations from my Childhood; (particularly I remember that passage related about page 3.) My Master haveing now had about a fortnight's Tryall of me, urged /fo. 11r/ my Father above all things to put me to Cambridg in Order to the Ministry providing his utmost endeavours thereto and to fit me in a year, or a year and a half at the furthest, which accordingly he did: though when all was done I was but a Weak School Scholler in comparison of what I should have been, and onely entered in the Greek tongue. With this my Father then freely closed; and to me the Resolution was pleasing enough. There was but one Difficulty in view, and that was, whether my Father's Estate would be sufficient for this, to maintain me there a due time. But this he did the less fear, haveing hitherto plainly found, (which Observation he often mentioned;) that his Estate was always at the best, when my charge was at the Greatest; and he did always thrive the most, when my being at publick School put him to the most Expence. and a Wonderful Providence of God it was, by me to be ever admired magnified and praised. This was the first time that ever my Father and I thought (to any purpose) of <my> going to the University; or that I had leave to entertain any Positive Resolutions of Undertakeing that holy honourable and weighty Office of the Ministry.

How long it was before my Mother Understood all this I cannot now tell: But on a time (long after) when I was from School she took the opportunity to go to Hale on purpose to speak with my Master Walker about it; who was so resolved and spoke so plainly and roundly with her about it, that it put her into such a passion that either for weeping she could not see, or for perplexity and confusion of mind she could not know her plain way Home; but wandered into the fields far and wide; and much ado she had to recover her Selfe & her way home.

/fo. 11v/ This was the pleasantest time that ever I had at School in all my Life. My master was as free with me, as if I had been his companion; would often upon some speciall occasion set me to make English Verses and Theams as well as Latine. He lent me Books: (viz good English books of Piety, as well as learning;) and when he was out of the way; I would often be getting into his Study (which was at the end of the Chimney in the Hall, and always stood open) which was a great delight and help to me; and he was not angry that I should Pore amongst his Books. Here amongst others I met with Mr Bolton's Works which I extremely liked, and they wrought much upon me: amongst other things, looking (I remember) into Mr Bolton's Life[37]

[37]E. B[agshawe]., 'The life and death of the author', first published in *Mr Boltons Last and Learned Worke* (London, 1632), was reprinted in editions of Robert Bolton, *The Workes of the Reverend, Truly Pious, and Judiciously Learned Robert Bolton* (London, 1641).

(having never seen any Minister's Lives before) I was so taken with that little I could get time to read in it, that it mightily excited my endeavours and raised my desires after the Ministry; so that as I went home, there being a hill in a Pasture in my way like an old Mill Hill, I got into the hollow that was in the top of it, and O how zealously and earnestly did I pray to God that he would fit me for his Ministeriall Work. For now I begun to order my Studys and Thoughts with respect to this one main end which I had in mine ey; and which as I went home from School in the Evenings I often Meditated upon with abundance of affection and delight. the very remembrance of which Meditations and Prayers leave a pleasant relish in my mind to this day. I often fixed in my mind rules of Preaching and the /fo. 12r/ Pastorall Office, which I took from the best Examples I knewe.

Mr Goodknap's Ministry at Burton (whom I used to hear as often as conveniently I could) began to make great Impressions on my Spirit O how pleasant and savoury were his Sermons to me; and my Meditations thereon in my Walks Home! Now I made a Book wherein I wrote (in the faintest hand I had) all my Sermon Notes, and continued it untill I filled it, and after. and when I got more Divinity Books it was my manner when I had heard a good Sermon to consult all the Books I had on the Subject, partly from a desir I had to know whether Librarys and Books would help me to as excellent things as Pulpits and Preachers did; which was profitable to my Self, and I believe would be so to others. Though as yet I had but very few Books. a Gentleman giveing me 2 or 3 half Crowns enabled me to buy Quarles's Emblems;[38] Virel's Grounds of Religion,[39] the Assembly's Catechisms &c.[40]

In these, and such books as these was my delight out of School time, when I might read what I would: and when other's were at Play, I chose rather for the most part to be at my book, and should have been more if I had had more variety of Books. I envyed not my play fellows their Sports when I was well engaged amongst these more Pleasant Companions. When I was at Play amongst other boys (especially at evenings when I used for the most part to be better employd) my mind was not free, and at ease; I thought I was out of my Way and Duty: And I was often crossed by one correcting Providence or other; which (as so many hints given me) I soon knew how to Interpret, as if the Language of them had been; What dost thou here? Is this thy place?

[38] Francis Quarles, *Emblemes* (London, 1635, and many later editions).

[39] Matthieu Virel, *A Learned and Excellent Treatise Containing All the Principall Grounds of Christian Religion* (trans. London, 1594, and thirteen further editions until 1635).

[40] *The Confession of Faith.*

&c. whereby I became singled out from others of my rank and age. two or three of these I will instance.

/fo. 12v/ When I was very young, and coming from our Parents with the Maid that had been milking on the Lord's day I staid among some boys that were Playing at knur[41] (as we called it) only looking on them as they plaid; but long I had not staid before the knur took me on the ey, with so sharp a Stroke that it laid me in abundance of Torment for that night. I soon understood what this was for; and it made me more cautious about the Observance of the Lord's day afterwards.*

Another time when I went to Sleeford School and boarded at Lesingham the boys there having got a Bonefire, upon some such usuall day or occasion; in the night I would needs run out to them but before I came out at them one of their fire=sticks[42] met me in the teeth (as it were) and broke my face I could not certainly tell whether it was designedly thrown at me or no because I was so far off, and it was so dark that I knew not how they could see me. So I came no nearer them: but home again I went; humbled myself before God in Earnest Prayer, confessing the sinfulness of my carnall desires and curiosity; and took it as a call from such company.

Another Instance is; while I was now learning at Mr Walkers One Evening after School, instead of going home as I used, I stayed playing amongst other boys in the Church yard but presently One against his will hit me on the ey with a Dab So smart and sevre [*sic*] a blow that it spoyled my Sport, and gave me Warning not to spend my time in vain; and not to associate my Self with common or vilious or Playfull Comrades.

/fo. 13r/ This was the Judgment that I then past on these and such like corrections as these; I took them as Warnings and Calls out of a Profane World; and accordingly they sent me to my Prayers. Blessed be my God who hath called me from the vanitys of this world, to better things. from common to spiritual Society with Books, but chiefly with Himself.

While I learnt with Mr Walker my Father had once so great and dangerous a Swelling in his leg, as put us all in fears of him; and had he then dyed, all my hopes had been quite dashed: I went into the Barn; (as the most private place I could find) and in Prayer Earnestly Entreated and besought God for His Recovery; which was presently

*Marginal note: Add to these, that I never felt the weight of my Masters hand at Grantham but once, and that was for rambling out one Lord's Day 3 or 4 miles into the Country with two more of my own Towns boys in fruit time.

[41] *knur*: a wooden ball used in the north-country game of knur and spell, which resembled trap-ball. *OED*.

[42] *fire-sticks*: the sticks used to start a fire.

Granted; for my Father was speedily and safely cured, and restored. I note this to the Praise of my God and mine own Establishment.

On Munday June 3rd (Anno Domini 1667) I went to Cambridg, and my Mother parted with me (as to what appeared) with more freedome and Satisfaction than either she or I expected. And on Wednesday June 5. I was admitted in Trinity Colledg, under the Tuition of Mr Bainbridg, fellow there.[43] And indeed that I should be so was afterwards my great wonder being so weak a Scholler hindered by so many Vacancys and New Masters, and to whom the Tongues was always so insuperable a difficulty. This Summer my Tutor read Logick and Ethics to me all over: But my Understanding was not ripe enough, to encline me to fancy or enable me to fathome philosophicall Studys as I should have done. The use thereof did not so clearly appear to me as to beget in me that Love thereto, /fo. 13v/ and diligence therein that I should have had. But I earnestly prayed to God to give me such a competency of Humane Learning, as was necessary to the understanding of Divinity, and to my designed work. But my expectations were most frustrated about the Preachers of the Place; I most of all wondered and was troubled to find so little, and so indifferent preaching; for I could seldome hear any that I liked or that did me Good which I was forced to complain of to my Father in my first Letter to him of July 6. 1667. That the Nursery of Learning (and piety too it should be) should abound so little with that which I accounted the chief fruits thereof. Besides which also the Ceremonys and formalitys of (*) the Chappell Worship went much against me. Indeed I had not so much pleasure in being there as would have been necessary to have prevented and kept off that discomposure of mind that I found disposed me to dulness, recklessness and forgetfulness, (which now troubled me extremely) and so much Melancholy that I could not read, think, or hear of any eminent Minister of Christ in the Scriptures or other History (as particularly in reading once the story of Stephen's seperation therto in Acts 6.) but my mind would reflect upon itself with a kind of akeing regret (as I then expressed it) proceding from a strong and ardent desire I had to be but as one of the least of those Eminent Servants of Gods I read /fo. 14r/ or thought of. And oftentimes (methought, to use my expressions at that time) the Spirit of my God would witness together with mine, and certify me that as sure as I did sit, stand &c. I should be such a Minister of

*Marginal note: * particularly their Bowing: against which I entred a remark, in a notebook. pag. 25.

[43]Thomas Bainbrigg, DD (1636–1703), fellow of Trinity College, Cambridge (1656–1703); later vice-master of Trinity College, Cambridge and religious controversialist. *ODNB*.

that Sort, that I desired; which forced me with Prayers and Tears to the Throne of Grace upon that account; and (I bless God) with much Comfort.

About the middle of November following this same year, 1667. I returned into the Country to my Father's at Heckington partly because I had now spent all the money my Father could well provide for me for this year; and partly upon my Mother's earnest desire, and to see her, who was now brought very weak with the yellow jaundice a disease which she contracted within a week or fortnight after my going to Cambridg. Here I read over Mr Rob. Bolton's Works and such other Books as I had either bought at Cambridg, or were lent me by Mr Edward Whiston the then Minister of Heckington who was a pious man and a very Profitable Preacher; and whose Society (beyond what I had met with at the University) was as useful to me, as it was much frequented by me this winter.[44]

This winter it pleased God to take from me my dear and indulgent Mother who dyed on February 20. Anno Domini 1667/8 Ætatis, 63.

And now my former fears and troubles vanished, and my Hopes encreased and I had more peace and quiet in my mind and comfort in my Life this winter in the country than I had at Cambridg all that Summer before.

/fo. 14v/ May 21st (being Whitson week.) Anno Domini 1668. I went to Cambridg again where I begun to be extreamly Melancholy; chiefly tormented with Fears that I should dy before my age or before I had finished my course with Joy in the Work of the Ministry or had spent my Self in doing good in my Generation in that holy Calling. And the Temptations of Satan and my own Imagination suggested that almost every thing I saw were (methought) Signs thereof. These things much disturbed me in my Study.

In September following I fell into a Quartane Ague[45] which brought me down again into the Country the latter end of that Month. My Father was now marryed again to one Amy Dickinson of Silk= Willowby (a Town wher Famous Mr Lawrence who wrote the Treatise of Faith was once Minister[46]) a Widdow she was of good report and esteem, and without children; notable for huswifery and afterwards for Chirurgery: with whom my Father lived 10 years more comfortably than he had done before in that Relation. She was very kind and loving

[44] Edward Whiston, MA (died in or before 1678), vicar of Heckington (1666–1670); vicar of Moulton, Lincs. (1670–1678). CCEd; Venn, IV, p. 384; *Sketches . . . of New and Old Sleaford*, p. 249.

[45] *quartan ague*: a (malarial) fever recurring every fourth day (i.e. every seventy-two hours). *OED*.

[46] Matthew Laurence, MA, rector of Silk Willoughby, Lincs. (1627–1647); member of the Ipswich Classis; author of *The Use and Practice of Faith* (London, 1657). Venn, III, p. 53.

to me, and very carefull and tender over me. My Ague continuing all this following Winter my Melancholy also continued though (I bless God) not so tormentingly as at Cambridg: For in the country I was better pleased; and my New Mother bringing me many new Relations (for she had 5 sisters) gave me the Opportunity and Benefit of the Diversion of frequent Journeys to visit them; which was a great relief to me (two of them also being very pious) by one of whom I was first brought acquainted with that emminently Learned and Holy Divine Mr Richard Brocklesby Minister of Kirkby Super Bane not far from Horncastle a Person of so serious raised and heavenly a Spirit temper and conversation as I had never seen before in all my Life; exceedingly affected was I by his example.[47]

/fo. 15r/ My Ague and Melancholy together kept me under the frequent apprehensions of Death, and made me serious. My thoughts yea and my dreams ran upon this; and though I feared lest God should take me away in my youth, yet it troubled me that I could not prepare my Self to dy; and to think what a sad condition I was in as I was: These thoughts often forced me (twice more especially) before the Throne of Grace with tears complaining that I should have sinned against so infinitely gracious a God and yet I was afraid all was but Hypocriticall. It grieved me that my discourse was not gracious as beseemed a Christian; and what Fruits of my Faith (thought I) can I shew more than any other civill honest person.

Very earnestly did I pray to God to be delivered from this Disease, and that with such comfort and Assurance that God in due time would restore me to my former estate of Health again to His glory and my own Comfort Establishment and Confirmation in the experience of his Mercys and Promises for the Future. notwithstanding the relucting troublous conciets of my mind and the Temptations of Satan) which (thought I) when I shall see! —— And accordingly (to the Praise and Glory of my God I here note it) in February following my Ague left me, and some good Degree of health was restored to me.

When I was recovered I remembered a sinfull Folly which I was guilty of at Cunsby, when I had my ague and now more considerably reflected upon; which was this I was persuaded to a foolish diabolicall medicine (of which kind there are many for that disease amongst the Vulgar) to see if I could get it away; but (Blessed be God; (for so in this case I may well;) it left me not: I was sensible of the Folly, though not then so sensible of /fo. 15v/ the Sin that was in it, till I spoke with

[47]Richard Brocklesby, MA (1634/5–1714), theologian and nonjuring Church of England clergyman; ordained 1658; rector of Kirkby on Bane, Lincs. from 1661; later rector of Folkingham, Lincs.; deprived 1702; retired to Stamford, Lincs. *ODNB*; CCEd; Venn, I, p. 223.

Mr Brocklesby and asked his Judgment of such like tricks who was with the same mind with Bishop Hall (Cases of Consc. Dec^{d}3^{d} Case 2^{d} pag. (oper.) 820.[48]) who there clearly decided such things. But I was glad I was not cured by it, and entred a thankfull memoriall of it in these following words

[49]What shall I render to my God for his wonderfull mercifull providences towards me a foolish creature, that he would not suffer Satan to cure mee, but did afterwards graciously heal me himself in a far more fit convenient time! (Being the time about which I concluded (in my Sickness) that he would hear my prayer, and deliver me.) To the Glory of thy Grace and mercy (Lord) let me speak it and to the comfort and establishment of me thy unworthy Servant in the experience of thy goodness towards me. How might it have troubled me, and justly too had it been otherwise, and had I then been cured. Foolish simple Children see not what dangers they run into: but their Father carrys a watchfull ey over them.

O what a loving mercifull Father is my God Lord, I desire to thank Thee, I desire to bless and praise Thee, but Oh (methinks) how far do I come short. Help me (holy Father) rightly to improve all thy providences and mercys and all my experiences of both Help me to shew forth Thy praise in my life, as well as speak it forth to thee with my lips. How true is that, Romans 8. 28.

Holy Father for thy Son my Saviour Jesus Christ's Sake deliver me from Satan, and all his Temptations, particularly from those monstrous horrid, blasphemous, execrable injections with which he vexes me: The lord rebuke him. Deliver me from Melancholy and from Fantasticall conciets, and let me set myself free about my buisness without fear of Satan's approaches. Deliver me from pride and make me an humble holy serious sincere and confirmed Christian Let nothing at any time occurr that may damp or disturb my peace, or shake my confidence in Thee my God, but confirm me, and keep me close to Thee. Let all things work together for my Good, for I desire to love Thee.

These were the poor Breathings of my Soul towards God at that time; upon which Occasion I begged deliverance also from those Blasphemous Injections wherewith Satan begun to hurry me before my writing this memoriall.

/fo. 16r/ But this preceeding errour was not the onely thing of this nature wherewith Satan befooled and deluded me; For I was got to that pass that I begun to be a great Observer of Signs, and to mark in

[48]Joseph Hall, *Divers Treatises Written upon Severall Occasions by Joseph Hall* (London, 1662).

[49]The following three paragraphs, ending *to love Thee*, are distinguished by being written in a narrower hand.

the Kalender of my Common Prayer book all the criticall or unlucky days that I could meet with in all such Foolish Astrologicall Books as came to my hands: and if at any time any thing befell me, or I begun any thing on any of these days, or if any bad Sign happned, I used to be extreamely troubled, and that for a considerable time; and to conciet formidable things from such idle reasons: And indeed these (thus occasioned) were no finall part of my troubles and Melancholy both this and the following year. But out of these Snares The Lord did cleerly and graciously extricate me by two speciall Providences in the two following years (to be mentioned (God willing) in their place) that I blotted out all the marks in my Kalendar and (blessed be God) became a more confirmed Resolved Enemy to all such heathenish, diabolicall and Astrologicall whimsys and fancys ever since.

At the Beginning of June and in whitsun=week Anno Domini 1669 I went to Cambridg again where I was this Summer more furiously assaulted with the Temptations and injections of Satan; and more deeply Melancholly than ever I had been before almost overcome with conciets. One trouble or melancholly thought occur upon the neck of another, and almost drown or extinguish it; And then I thought O if I were but free from this, no matter for the other I could deal with the former trouble well enough. and then either the former would return and make me think so of the present or a third matter of trouble would come and make me think the same of both And though they were irrationall troubles about foolish Trifles (many of them) which my Reason did frequently contradict yet could not I keep my mind from akeing /fo. 16v/ nor look upon any thing with delight nor enjoy my Self, nor mind my Studys.

The most materiall or considerable of all my troubles were about my future Ministry (as is mentioned before) either lest I should not live to it, or be so fit or able for it as I desired; And it was often chiefly with relation to this that other things troubled me. But (Blessed be God) I was supported under all; and God was pleased to work so, by his Spirit in my heart that I did assure my Self (from the grounds of His Mercy and Goodness; His Truth and Promises; His Providences and Methods of his dealing with me hitherto; and the Examples of others his worthy Champions for his Truth and Ministers of his Word) that He would deliver me from these dejections, confirm me in an humbly joyfull and comfortable Condition all my Life, and give me my desires long to praise him in the Land of the Living, and to spend my Self in his work to his own Glory and the Salvation of Souls. Desireing (in the mean time) patiently to tarry the Lord's leisure Psalm 27.16.

And now I began to discover that it was the Devil's Work to deject me and so hinder me by his Delusions and Temptations, and to discourage me in my way to such an end: because my troubles were about my much desired and longed for Calling, the Work of the Ministry; which aims most at the overthrow of Satan's Kingdome; and I had read that those in the greatest and highest Callings must look for the greatest Temptations; and that therfore it might be expected that Satan would strive to take me off or hinder me from such a Buisness. But I prayed earnestly to God that he who had Elected me from all Eternity /fo. 17r/ and seperated me from my mothers womb to win and pull Souls out of Satan's Kingdome, and Bondage to the glorious liberty of the Son of God; would pull me out first and give me liberty from his Temptations and injections, and arm me with the whole Armour of God against all his fiery darts, that I might follow my buisness cheerfully and with a Free Spirit. And I beged in David's words (Psalm 51. 12, 13.) Restore unto me the joy of thy Salvation and uphold me with Thy free Spirit, Then shall I teach transgressors thy ways, and Sinners shall be converted unto Thee.

It was one great relief to me in my troubles to consider how vain and idle my matter of troubles seemed to me to be when it was over, and another came in its Stead, and yet while the former was upon me it seemed the greatest of all. Two or three such experiences made me strive with my Self, to bear my Self down with the persuasion notwithstanding the reluctancy of an akeing mind) that the present trouble was as idle as the former if I could but see it, as I believed (from experience) in a short time I should, and indeed did.

But my greatest relief of all was when I poured out my Soul in tears, and Earnest Prayers to God to fill me with sound and lasting Comfort; and when I could the most freely, largely flowingly and affectionately open my mind to God in fit privacys & retirements I had always the most ease. And O that I could often remember it (so as still to practise it while I live) what delightfull Soul refreshing Converse and Communion, by Soliloquy and Meditation I had with my God in my daily Morning and Evening Walks in the Fields when I was at Cambridg, for these 3 Summers together (viz. 1667.–68.–69.) and what Effects they had upon my Soul!

/fo. 17v/ As to my Studys all this while I must Confess my Academicall Books of Philosophy and humane Learning were for the most part laid aside, save onely what bare necessity urged me now and then to take in hand which as it was forcedly and Unwillingly done, so (being never well instructed in a right Method of Studys) by drawing up a Method of my own head,* and appointing to severall

*Marginal note: possibly it may be ill done of Schoolmasters to cause youth to read Books by the halfs; when (at Schools) they cause boys to learn only 20 or 30 leaves of Virgil; and 6 or 10 leaves of Homer; and one Evangelist it may be of the New Testament and then put them into other Books.

hours and parts of the day severall books and Studys of a different kind; thinking to grasp all at once, and carry on altogether I carryed on none well: For one thing drive out another; and if at any time I was a little pleased with one, the time presently (according to my Method called me off unwilling to another which also (by that time I was well entred) I must leave again for a third so that I became really engaged in nothing; and did all as a Task; and my melancholly temper discomposeing me I profited little or nothing in that kind of Study.

But the truth is the Books which I most willingly took in hand, and the Studys which I most freely attended to were English Practicall Divinity such as suited my Condition and Designs; and such as tended to ease my troubled mind, as well as please it. Clark's Martyrologys and Lives exceedingly pleased and delighted me (which my chamber=fellow (borrowing it out of the Colledg Library) brought to my notice and I first borrowed thence and after bought)[50] The examples there mightily excited, and encouraged me, for here I met with persons in my own condition, and with the onely suitable company the University did afford me. I got some of Mr Baxters works which very much affected me[51]

So that (to return to my troubles) being further by the Examples and Directions in such Books as these; I suffered not God's providences to me (which I had experienced), onely to fluctuate in my weary mind But I took pen in hand, and committed them to paper to be ready for use. And I digested my Soul conflicts, and Soliloquys in the Written Meditations and Addresses following

/fo. 18r/ [52]And now O my Soul consider and ruminate a little with thy Self on these things Thou seest how graciously thy God has dealt with thee from the womb hitherto Thou seest unto what he hast called thee thou hast seen how many prayers of thine He had lovingly received and as graciously Answered how he has manifested himself unto thee a God Pardoning iniquity &c. how many Dangers he has delivered thee from from how many troubles and how great Afflictions. Thou hast seen how wonderfully He has kept thee at School and Places of Learning what little hopes thoughts or expectations thou hadst of ever attaining to the least of what he has now brought thee to; And how He has blest thy Father, with a Sufficiency of Means for thy education at all times. Thou hast seen what an overruning all wise disposing hand of Providence has gone along with thee in all thy ways what desires God has put into their

[50] Samuel Clarke, *A Generall Martyrologie ... Whereunto are added, The lives of sundry modern divines* (London, 1651, and later editions).

[51] Richard Baxter (1615–1691). *ODNB.*

[52] The following extract, ending at the end of fo. 19v, is written in a much smaller hand.

heart and that from a child and continued them what a complacency in their intended buisness he began long ago to work in their heart and continued it still. And now thou canst not be ignorant of the end he made thee for viz. His Glory nor of the application Office and Function wherein to answer it and endeavour your edification and Salvation of Souls.

Lo therefore how graciously he has disposed of these in order thereunto in fitting thee for and placing thee in the University where now thou art and kept thee here so well for so competent a time as now thou seest not that but thou must leave it. And now so far as thou knowest thine owne heart thou knowest whether thy desires tend and where they terminate namely the Subversion of Satans Kingdom in the hearts of God's chosen, and that not for any by respects but the Glory of God and thou knowest that he that which will live Godly in Christ Jesus must suffer Affliction and he who aims at the Ruin of Satans Kingdome must look for such opposition as no less than an infinite and omnipotent power can enable him to overcome

And now thou seest the Original of these troubles and to what they tend on one side namely (as they are provided by Satan) to disturb and discourage thee and if possible to impede and hinder thee in thy course. But consider O my Soul Satan acts but under Sufference There is an infinite power above him even of that God whose mercys thou hast experienced whom thou servest whose work it is thou desirest to be imployed in and for whose Glory thou ackest who has assured thee by his word that he sent his Son to beat down Satan and to destroy his works. Genesis 3.15. And should not those promises be of greater force to quicken and envigorate thy Spirit than Satans threats to discourage and deject thee Thou canst not be ignorant that that puts the bitter into all thy troubles is the fear lest thou should be so much the less serviceable by this or that &c. for thy Master's work Or else which is greater shouldst thou not live to do it at all And this is only Satan's work to daunt thee because that Calling most opposest him if it did not thou mightst be sure he would not trouble thee Thou hast read of those that have been thus discouraged and heard of others that have had the same fears with thy Self who have been faithful labourers in God's Vineyard Why art thou troubled because God hath taken away some excellent Schollers in your youth for causes and ends best known to himself What madest thou be troubled for fear thou shouldst be melancholy Hast thou not thought that few are distracted merely by the Study of God's Word or Divinity except by being over curious in prying into the Secrets of God or Nature; by worldly discontent or the like Why art thou troubled at any of those things Consider O my Soul the foregoing passages of thy youth their meaning and tendency Endeavour to live by Faith in the Promises and Providences of thy

God Why art thou cast down O my Soul &c. —— Psalm 42. ult. Hadst thou fainted O my Soul unless thou hadst believed to see the Goodness of the Lord in the Land of the Living? Thou shalt see it O tarry thou the Lords leisure Wait &c. Psalm 27. ult.

And now O my Soul (with Holy Job) Look beyond all these troubles to him to that orders them and learn to get good by all this by endeavouring to get thy Self into such a State as thy Afflictions are sent to bring thee into. Thou art not ignorant how fain David would have been delivered from all his Afflictions and wondered God punisht the righteous so, and yet he saw more afterwards and confessed it was good for him that he had been afflicted And Paul would as fain have been presently delivered from his thorn in the flesh too but God Answered him My Grace is sufficient for thee. And what dost thou think God sends these afflictions for but to work in thee either obedience to his commands as in David or Humility as in Paul: And I am sure if God did not thus humble thee thou wouldst be too proud and self concieted and have too many worldly ends in thy actions, and abundance of other evils which thou hast sometimes thought of would follow. Dr Harris would often say that he had /fo. 18v/ been quite spolied had he not thus been taken down for (said he) Young Ministers know not what ground they tread on till God lay them flat.[53]

Other reasons and ends of God's dealing with thee on this manner may be such as these.

1. Hereby the Lord would bring thee home unto himself and make thee really holy, to despise the World and set thyself to the work he has called thee to. 2. Hereby he would teach thee how to Comfort others dejected in Spirit. 3. To strengthen thy Faith in his Providence from the Experience of his mercys when thou seest the event fall out according to thy desires and Prayers. 4. That thou mayst live a life of Praises and Thanksgivings unto him when thou shalt see and observe his Providential Dispensations towards thee for Good. 5. To teach thee that whosoever will live godly in Christ Jesus shall suffer Affliction especially those whom God hath designed particularly for his own work His dearest Servants in the Ministry have been the weakest frailest men and most troubled and Tempted in their youth and entrance upon so great a Work. 6. Remember that thou in thy youth didst think what an easie life thou shouldst live if thou were a Minister and didst think to do any thing rather than Work for thy living and ease and pleasure were mostly thy ends and therefore since he hath determined thee to serve Him in that work 'tis a great deal of Affliction trouble and temptation that must bring thee home to

[53]Robert Harris (1580/1–1658). See, W[illiam]. D[urham]., *The Life and Death of that Judicious Divine, and Accomplish'd Preacher, Robert Harris* (London, 1660).

Himself and make thee act sincerely and really for his Glory as thy chiefest end. 7. To teach thee Humility that thou mayst not preach out of vainglory for praise or popular applause but only (as is said) for his glory in the Edification and Salvation of his people. 8. To teach thee experience in the points thou shalt handle and that which thou preachest unto others thou thy Self mayst not become a cast away.

And now O my Soul Remember O Remember how thou standest engaged as ever thou dost expect the favour and Goodness of God towards thee to act worthily in his behalf. Thou hast seen what God has done for thee and what he has called thee to O Remember and bethink thy Self what remains to be done on thy part. And first as thou art a Christian endeavour to be truly and really Holy Get an Interest in Jesus Christ and get footing in the provinces Get Humility and get Patience and Charity &c. let thy thoughts be upon thy work upon God and Heaven and thy future state. Let thy talk be gracious thy actions seemly thy whole carriage and deportment winning. And then as a Minister Follow closely thy Study and study such things as are of consequence the Scriptures and Soul concernments. Get all abilities endowments and qualifications for thy work that are acquirable and Pray to God for them who will not deny thee what's necessary for what he calls thee to. Pray and preach sincerely for God's Glory in thy Salvation of Souls Preach not wordy but worthy Sermons with demonstration of thy Spirit and with power. Go amongst thy people with the fulness of the Blessing of the Gospel of Peace. Comfort such as want Comfort and are in a fit Capacity of recieving it. Terifie the implacably wicked and obdurate Sinners. Catechise and instruct the weaker Sort. Reprove Sin in whomsoever thou findest it and endeavour the Salvation of all thou Comest in Company with Live more to God than thou hast done close with Him and adhere to him more. This if thou endeavourest to do God will bless thee and Comfort thee Confounding Satan before thee and subdueing him under thee He will make thee an Instrument of his Glory in thy Generation answer thy Prayers and Expectations to the Satisfaction of thy Soul and the Praise of the Glory of his Grace.

/fo. 19r/ But O infinitely gracious and merciful Lord God without whose help I can do nothing I turn to thee, I come to Thee Thou art He that tookest me out of the womb Thou didst make me hope when I was upon my (nurses) Breasts. I was cast upon thee from the womb Thou art my God from my Mother's Belly O be not farr from me when trouble is near for there is none to help. Thou hast seperated me from my Mother's womb by working in me a complacency in and desires after the Ministerial function. And what am I Lord or what is my Father's house that thou hast chosen me from amongst all my Neighbours Sons round about me and taken me from bodily labour and toyle and Sweat to so holy and honourable a Calling a Favour like to what thou shewed to the best of Kings (Psalm 78. 70, 71.) Even so Father it seems good unto Thee to chuse the foolish things of the world to confound the wise &c. 2 Corinthians 2. 27–29. And now Lord since thou hast inwardly called me by thy grace to so weighty an employment and of such grand concernment (for who is sufficient for these things?) Help me (blessed God) that I conferr not with flesh and blood that none of these sordid terrestrial objects which please worldlings may ever captivate my mind so as to draw it from Thee my God or discompose me for thy work. Thou hast let me see a little of Thee, and a little of thy wayes and a little of that which must be mine endeavour to bring others to O help me to pass the Form and shew forth the power of Godlyness and Religion in my life and Conversation Enliven and actuate these desires thou hast given me by thy Holy Spirit and help me to put these purposes into practise. And Holy Father let thy Servant find favour in thy Sight I beseech thee As ever thou hast promised to hear the petitions of those that call upon thee in thy Son's name And as ever any thing hath or may be got by prayer and as thou hast heretofore answered me O receive the humble petition my Soul desires to tender unto Thee. I have been afflicted and troubled O do thou Work in me those gracious ends which thou hast sent Afflictions and trouble for and then deliver me from them and teach me by thy Holy Spirit such a heavenly Art that I may overcome the strength of my Fancy and Imagination (which Satan works upon and by) by thy Word and Promise And when thou hast granted me a better measure of Health and Peace (which I beg of thee thou wouldst at length perform) O let me remember my troubles and what thoughts I had in them, as, that if I were but delivered from them what manner of person I would be and graciously make this as great a motive to the practise of my duty as thou didst the other a Spurr to resolve on it. And graciously effect that when I came to preach thy word and perform the Duties of my Calling all these delusions of Satan and endeavours of his by my melancholick constitution to trouble me may vanish that so I may have no Distractions in my work Impute not these mistaking disordered thoughts to me which Satan has injected and I have not consented to and all my own miscarriages forgive Help me to observe the Order and tendency of thy Providences towards and dealings with me. And Help me to live by Faith on thy Promises Help me to set a due Value and Estimation upon thy glory so as that in all mine actions I may act wholly for the same Help me to perform and promote Religious Exercises in the Families wherein thou shalt place me till thou givest me one of mine own. And now (Blessed God) since all thy Providences towards me tend to this one end to make me a Minister of thy Gospel O do thou make me a true Christian my Self and a faithful Sheperd of thy flock. Lord! it is the earnest desire of my Soul that thou wouldst make me truly Religious and truly serious as the message I am to deliver requires Make me a chosen Instrument of thy Glory in my Generation and Calling Thou mightest have had thousands better than I to have sent and hast only thy discriminating Goodness makes me to be what I am and what I am to be And Oh that thou wouldst make me like if but one of the least of those able faithful /fo. 19v/ painful preachers of thy word which are or have been Ministers indeed by thy own special Call and Appointment. Help me to act for right ends that as the end of my learning my Studies and other actions of my life hitherto has been the Ministry so the end of my undertaking that holy function may be not any second Self sinister Base or By respect but only thy Glory in the Salvation of Souls. Hear me Holy Father I humbly beg of thee and beseech thee for thy Son my Saviour Jesus Christs Sake. Give me a Delight in the Study of thy holy Word Power into my heart the gift of holy and fervent prayer Make me a Powerfull and Effectual Preacher of thy Word Give me all such abilitys and prerequisites both supernatural and natural, as may furnish me for thy Service and render me a Workman that needs not to be ashamed a Pastor after thine own heart A Scribe taught to the Kingdom of Heaven One that may have the tongue of the learned able to speak a Word in due season. Give me sufficiency of Learning and vigorous parts or faculties a quick apprehension a sound judgment and a retentive memory Grant me thy Gifts of Wisdom to find out discretion to dispose of Memory to recount and Utterance to deliver upright writings acceptable words even words of the truth to teach thy people knowledge Give me Experience in Every Considerable point that I may feel what I speak and then speak what I feel that I may first work necessary points upon mine own heart before I preach them to others

And for all the mercys which thou O Lord hast bestowed upon me from time to time I desire to Bless and Praise thy Holy name! for my Preservation from the womb and all thy Particular Providences towards me for Good: for my Creation Redemption and all the Blessings of this life: for my health; humbly beseeching Thee to add more perfect Strength thereto and to deliver me from all Infirmities Diseases and Distempers whatsoever my body may be subject to and the Impediments they may occasion that I may walk before Thee long in the Land of the Living to the greater setting forth of thy Glory And free me from all Melancholy dumpish humours that I may enjoy my Self in peace, and follow my buisness cheerfully. And now Blessed Lord, in order to the perfecting and putting in Practise all my foregoing Resolutions I here beg and implore thy gracious Assistance: that thou wouldst please, for thy Name Mercy Promise Truth and Sons sake to hear me, and answer these Petitions thy poor Servant has put up to Thee. And help me to believe and Trust in Thee for performance of all things agreeable to thy Will And Pardon me if I have asked anything amiss. I beg all and whatever else thou knowest needful for me who knowest better what to give me than I know what to ask for my Self I humbly beg in the (again mentioned) prevailing Name and for the Sake of Jesus Christ my Saviour To whom with Thee and the Holy Ghost I desire to ascribe all Honour Glory and Praise, and into whose hands I desire to commend my Self Spirit Soul and Body knowing that that cannot perish but prosper which is committed unto Thee. Amen.

Afterward I further added as follows.

Let the Doctrine thou shalst enable me to preach to others be wrought on my heart that's dead to Duty and cannot be such as methinks I fain would be But how durst I say I would be better when I do not do all I can in order thereto? For Jesus Sake hear me. Graciously accept of that Prayer which from the Consideration of thy mercifull Providence towards me I have here before tendered to the Throne of Grace and let it be a continually begging prayer to procure me thy unworthy Servant sound and lasting peace and Comfort in time of need. Mercifully deliver me from that spirituall Pressure under which I labour. Free me from the Temptations of Satan and the pravity and redundancy of that Humour by which he works And implant thy Holy Spirit and his heavenly Motions in my heart Give me true Humility and Cheerfulness and alacrity of Spirit Seriousness in Religion and a delight therein Laboriousness in my Calling as a christian and a Student And furnish me with Abilityes sufficient to the due discharge of that holy Function of the Ministry to which Thou hast designed me. Give me an affable demeanure in gesture and discourse at all times a solid serious spiritually breathing and tender disposition. Clear my call to the Ministry by providing me a fit place for my preparation. Give me the Spirit of mental Ejaculatory Prayer at all times especially when I am at a loss in any respect The Spirit of Thankfulness when I think of any mercy or favour of Thine the true and right way of regulating and governing my thoughts and rightly bias and habituate my mind and Soul in these my younger years that I may grow up more and more to be a serious and Confirmed Christian &c.

Confirm in me O Lord that thou hast wrought, and perfect the work that thou hast begun in me to Thy Glory. Amen

/fo. 20r/ [54]But now (by this time, and things being thus with me,) I begun to be very weary of the University. Melancholy I was, suitable Society I had none, the one or two (not very profitable companions)

[54]The text reverts to its original size from here.

that I did a little Associate with were in the Country as I wished to be and my Chamberfellow the chief of them (though he had a good place in the Colledg for his maintainance (and but of my own year) and I no preferment.) left the University also this Autumn. and tho their Examples afforded no plea for me, yet the want of their Society did. And as for others, their Society was generally worse than none, and it was one of the greatest mercys of my Life, that I was by any (tho sharp means) delivered from the Snares therof

That very little which I saw of it, (which could not be had but in Taverns) was a great deal too much: I was ever the object of their Scorn and derision: If I did but read a Greek chapter at Prayer times, or repeat my Sermon notes on a Lord's Day at night, in our Tutor's Chamber, when he required it; my very tone was enough for them to laugh at and jeer me for afterwards. For a Scholler to intend the Ministry or order his Studys more directly that way was matter of Obloquy and Scorn enough to them. Comedies and Playbooks were in greater Reputation, and a greater Credit to Schollers, than Divinity Books: And I must have suited them; and have drunk and been drunk with them, or have no company of their's. This seems hard for me to say; yet they that observe with what Ministers the Countrys are stored, will not I suppose be hard to believe it. Now if Society make an University, then was Cambridg no University to me; as things were.

/fo. 20v/ Howsoever I was like to get nothing there that would answere my charge of Living there: which could not be little; for I was in the dearest Colledg in Town and had not the least place of advantage in it, and as little hopes of any. My Tutor had done reading to me; and I had more opportunity for Studys that better pleased me, in the Country than there. Indeed my Friends in the Country did not like this, or approve my discontinuance; but in the Colledg I had my Tutor's approbation, and little by any (that I knew of) said against it. My Melancholy temper, and Inclination taught me to improve the foregoing Reasons to move my Father in the following Letter (now wrote to him) where I thus express my Self.

[55]Honoured and Dear Father.

I recieved yours &c.—— I have been very Melancholly ever since I came hitherto, and am sensible of the hurt it does me. I cannot fancy to tarry at Cambridg: A little thing troubles me and discomposes me for Study, so that (besides other divertisements) I cannot set my Self to my buisness with that Serenity and tranquility of mind I would contrary to my thoughts and expectations before I came. Doubtless

[55]The letter is written in the smaller hand.

these are all particular and speciall Providences of God for my good: The Lord open mine eys to see and follow them. My Tutor hath done reading unto us, and little we hear from him beside a Bill of expences at Quarter day. I do little here that I did not (or could not) do when I was in the country. Father, I am not at mine own disposall: The eternal God that made the world, and us mortalls for his Glory, who hath called me to serve him in the work of the Ministry, in order thereunto doth thus providentially dispose of mee. Surely he sees it best for me to be in the country where I may have better opportunity, more liberty and freedome to set my Self to that which must be the buisness of my Life. I confess a great deal of humane learning is required to the due discharge of that holy function; and 'tis daily matter of my prayers to God, that he would give me Sufficiency thereof to the right understanding of his Holy Word, to Answer opposers, and consider gainsayers in a word, to render me a Workman that needs not to be ashamed, a Scribe taught to the Kingdome of Heaven; one that may have the tongue of the learned able to speak a word in due Season; &c. If Cambridg could now afford me /fo. 21r/ any more in order therunto. I believe the Lord would provide for my continuance here; but since it is thus I desire to comply with his Will: knowing that all things work together for good to them that Love God. And O that I could adhere to him, close with him, obey him, and make it my delight and chiefest happiness to act for his Glory, with such Self denying Resignation as I could wish: And then —— you may see the consequences Psalm 37.5 and Proverbs 16.3. compared with Philippians 4. 6,7. —— Father I intend (by the will of God) at Michaelmas or thereabouts to leave the Colledg, resign up my Chamber and take the income and bring all away with me into the country, without any further trouble. I may make a Journey afterwards to take my degree; which is the advice of some, but I see the practise of more; and those not without preferment in the Colledg, if there were no more but that. And that little money I had in the Country, I have (with the Advice of my tutor) laid out for the best Books, and most Materiall for my purpose, I could think of, that I may have wherewith to employ one when I come down. Father I do not fear preferment in the Country when I shall be fit for it, onely it is matter of my prayers that I may (not out of any base or by respects, for any second, self, or sinister End, (such as to get a Living is), but) onely for the Glory of God in the Salvation of Souls, undertake the work of the Ministry: neither would I desire to run before I have a fair Call, to a fit place, in a fit time.—— The manner of my being at Cambridg these two last years may inform you (as it does me) that it is not out of any childish desire of Home I thus write unto you, but only the Providence of God.— I have no mor at present—— With my humble Duty to you remembered, and my prayers for you, &c.—— I rest (commending you to God)

Trinity Colledg
in Cambridg.
July. 3^{d}.
Anno. 1669.

Your Dutyfull
and obedient Son
John Rastrick

And in another Letter of August, 18. following I wrote,—— I am yet Melancholy which is one chief cause why I affect rather, to come into the Country and that so soon; but that's not all, I cannot see the great good I do here but learn Circumstances and see Fashions. &c.——

Your &c.——[56]

My father hearkned to these things, and (after he had communicated it to our Friends (Ministers) in the Country) willingly sent for me down the Michaelmas following; viz. Anno 1669. intending no more for the University till I should go take my Batchellour's Degree at the usuall Season.

/fo. 21v/ Being at Heckington my native Home, my Father put me upon praying in our Family every night, (a very unusual thing in that ignorant Town) and we endeavoured to perform that Duty in better Order than used to be formerly in our House. But that which I have chiefly to praise God for in this circumstance of my education; My Father earnestly pressed me to Pray by the Spirit, (For that was his expression for Concieved Extempore Prayer) and not by Forms: very much ado I had to be got to this in the presence of others; (tho alone I used no other) but my Father would have no nay, nor be content untill, sometimes by persuasions (urging the examples of others) and sometimes by chiding he had brought me to it: But this by use made concieved prayer so familiar with me and begat so much readyness and boldness, that it was a very great help to me when I entred upon the Ministry

October 10 following my return into the Country (being Lords Day) I fell sick of a flitting Tertian.[57] My first fit took me in Burton Church where I was (Mr Whiston Minister of Heckington being abroad) hearing Mr Goodknap preach on Jeremiah 17.7. of Trust in God. which I bore in mind throughout my Sickness; (which somewhat strangely held me every other week, and every other day in that week; untill the third ill week: in which (upon takeing a suitable

[56] Smaller hand ends here.

[57] *flitting tertian*: a tertian ague or fever occurring at irregular intervals.

cathartick[58]) I recovered.) and (being in a Melancholly habit of Body as I needed it, so) His text and Subject that day did much refresh and Comfort me. For it seasonably gave my Soul matter to work upon by Faith; and grounds to oppose that foolish and wicked conceit which now possessed my Fancy and disturbed me, (viz. that my distemper, (because I fell sick on one of the criticall or unlucky days) would hold me longer than ordinary, (I feared all /fo. 22r/ the winter at least) or have ill effects. But God restoring me so soon and safely did by this gracious Providence convince me of the vanity of such fancys and taught me better dependance upon Himself. And upon this occasion let me offer this advice and warning. Let no true child of God listen to the Devil, or be disturbed with such Astrologicall or other Vulgar Whymsys (see Jeremiah 10. 2,3–) For the devil may (if he get this hold of you, and find it troubles you) impose upon you in a 1000 instances and never let you be quiet. I remember the first day I learnt to write as I was going to School my paper blew away into the ditch: Some would have thought this a bad Sign; and yet (I praised God) I learned to write better than most of my Teachers. God be praised for his care, and Providence to his children.

November, 12. Anno 1669 on a Friday at night, there happened (at Heckington) a sudden Fire not far from my Father's house. Alarmed with a Confused noyse in the Streets my Father and I ran out, and soon saw what it was: the Smoke and Sparkes met us in our Gate=house, and presently Fire fell like Snow upon our thatched houses, and amongst the fresh Straw our yard was spread with from the Barns. Amazed at this I ran in, and (all my care being of my Books) I got a Sack and quickly filled it with as many of the best of them as I could, but could not readily get them carryed out; one came in to help me, but they were too many for him, and he went away and left them; and abler men were more concerned to quench the Fire, than about my Books: so that I was fain to leave them in the Floor, and run out and pray to God for Deliverance, which (as the case (which I saw so desperate) required) I very earnestly did. There was a large Stack of Barly in our next /fo. 22v/ neighbour's yard, upon which the wind drove the Flame which if it had taken, all our End of the Town must (in the ey of reason) have inevitably been consumed; and so near the fire it was, that (they wetting cloths <to>[59] cover[60] it with,) particularly a Shirt of mine which some had taken from a near ledg for that use, was (though kept with wetting) scorched yellow that it could be no more worn; (this mine eys saw;) and yet the Stack under them, and so

[58] *cathartic*: a medicine that has the power of purging or evacuating; a purgative. *OED*.
[59] Replacing *they*, above the line.
[60] *ed* cancelled.

all our houses was by God's wonderfull Providence preserved. Those at other times senseless neighbours could see the hand of God in this Deliverance, and cry out what a God have We! What a God have We! which pleased me to hear; for indeed it was remarkable. Thanks be to God for this unspeakeable Mercy.

January following one of my Mother's Sisters came and sojourned a few Weeks at our house One who being Melancholy was at that time very seriously inclined, she had lived with Mr Brocklesby (and brought me first acquainted with him) had a good understanding in spirituall things, delighted to hear me read good Books, and did freely and with good affection discourse with me about the things I read; with whom I had more discourse of that nature than ever before I had had with any. For I never had had the knowledg of, or familiar acquaintance with any one serious understanding Christian in my life (the Ministers of my acquaintance onely excepted with whom I was more as a Stranger or distant learner than familiar friend with whom I might be bold and free) So that her company was unexpectedly very grateful and refreshing to me, who never knew what the pleasure and advantage of suitable Christian Society and Converse was, untill the experience of this Tast. /fo. 23r/ I was troubled when she went away but held no Correspondence with her by any letters saving this one wrote the Summer following which (because it speaks much of my temper at that time) I here adjoyn.

[61]Dear Aunt

—— I may sit many months here at home, and not have one with whom I can familiarly converse, yet I desire to bless God for the privileges he has given me. I am ready to wonder sometimes (methinks) when I read of Mr Baxter's aquaintance with 100s if not 1000s (says he) of holy heavenly Christians and of his spiritual intimate familiarity with very many in all whom he had discoursed the image of God in such innocency, charity, justice, holyness, contempt of the world, mortification, Selfdenyall, humility, patience and heavenly mindedness in such measure as that he has had great cause to Love and honour them as the Saints of God: and the most of his converse in the world from the 22nd year of his age was with such (*[62] These are his own words) In what a Goshen[63] then did he live! For my part I did not know where to find one such Christian as this. If I came

*Marginal note: * Reason of Christian Religion page 299.

[61] The letter is written in the smaller hand.

[62] Richard Baxter, *The Reasons of the Christian Religion* (London, 1667), p. 299.

[63] *Goshen*: figuratively, a place of plenty or of light. *OED*.

to Newton and find one, and go to Metheringham and find another, likest unto these, thats much, yet I see them but seldom neither. Bless God (Aunt) for the love to and delight in Godlyness which he has wrought in you, and that you savour (as Mistress Brocklesby says[64]) of the best things; 'tis from the Especiall love of God towards you and 'tis an Estat of discriminating distinguishing grace and goodness. O see that you make it your buisness to endeavour after Conformation and Growth; and remember that upon this moment of time depends eternity and that the well or ill spending of this depends everlasting joy or Torment and that no man can make Heaven and Happiness too sure, let him do what he can. If you have any money in the world to spare buy some good books (tho they be dear) and read them hard fully over. Methinks Baxter's practicall pieces are the best that ever I read, because he speaks in good earnest, and near to the matter than most do (except such as Bolton Dod Whately Sibbs and especially Dr Preston, which are those he commended to his parish of Kidderminster.[65]) As he says,*[66] you may read an able Divine when you cannot hear one. And labour however to comprehend and bring within your capacity the Reasons of the Principles of Religion, and the coherence and dependence of one truth on and with another throughout. The Benefit of Books extends to futurity after this Life, they direct you to the never fading treasur, and teach you how to buy the pearls of great price which you cannot say of anything in the world beside. Have a care of the predominant disturber of your peace within you (viz.) Melancholy or fear when 'tis the passionate result therof. It [*sic*] it be possible keep a medium betwixt too much mirth and too much madness (as we say) you'l excuse the term. Melancholy is an humour that fills Satan's turn accordingly, and there's no one into which he will so powerfully insinuate himself as into that. Take Dr Harris's advice (to his children) in these words; Thats an (*) humour (says he) that admits of any Temptation, and is capable of any impression and distemper; shun as death this humour, which will work you to all unthankfullness

*Marginal note: * Preface to Saints Rest. Direct. 1st.
*Marginal note: * At the end of Dr Harris's Life.

[64]Presumably Richard Brocklesby's sister, since there is no record of his marriage or children in his will.

[65]For the Church of England clergymen Robert Bolton (1572–1631), John Dod (1550–1645), William Whately (1583–1639), Richard Sibbes (1577?–1635), and John Preston (1587–1628), see *ODNB*.

[66]Richard Baxter, *The Saints Everlasting Rest* (London, 1649, and many later editions). The reference does not enable precision as to which edition Rastrick used, but see p. 178, n. 371 below.

against God, unlovingness to man, and unnaturalness to your Selves.[67] And as for Fear, take something against them both together, and that in 3 words (which was one parcell of good counsell Mr Ball (he that made your Catechism) commonly (*) bestowed in all cases, viz.) Inform Judgment. Set Faith on Work Be of good courage.[68] I extend this to all trouble, fear and Sorrow except godly Sorrow; know but what that is and you may know how to regulate such thoughts and turn the Stream &c. — but . . .

Aunt, —— don't speak so much of my praise or comendations to any body (I add this because you went too far in mine own hearing, and I did not tell you of it.) If ther be any thing that's ought in me, 'tis none of mine own you know, therfore help me to praise God, and pray for me, and respect me so far as to take my counsell and I have my ends.—— I remain (with my prayers for you)

Heckington Your's (at your desire)
May 28.–70. in all Christian Service
John Rastrick.[69]

/fo. 23v/ This year (1670) I engaged in the close and serious Study of Mr Baxter (which of all my Study was the most considerable part) and therefore (my own mother haveing at her Death left me a little Stock of money which I set apart to buy Books) I now particularly bought all his best practicall pieces as I could light of them Which I mention the rather because God's Providence had now put them into my hands contrary to my Intention and design if not Resolution For being in a Booksellers Shop in Cambridg with my Chamberfellow there lay one of Mr Baxter's books in binding which me lightly and transiently looking at (for I cannot remember which it was) says my Chamberfellow 'twill be time enough to buy such books as those when we have taken our Degrees. But I thought with my Self (and I think said to him) I wod never buy such Books as those of a man's never educated in the University what could be got by them? &c. with such like under valuing thoughts. (for something I had heard of him and his Books; his Call and that of Crucyfying the world,[70] I remember we had in the house where I boarded at Sleeford, which

*Marginal note: * In his Life.

[67] W[illiam]. D[urham]., *Life and Death of . . . Robert Harris*, p. 111.

[68] John Ball (1585–1640), Church of England clergyman and religious writer. *ODNB*. Ball's biography was included in Samuel Clarke, *The Lives of Thirty-two English Divines* (London, 1677), pp. 147–155, with Ball's favourite saying on p. 152. John Ball, *A Short Catechisme* (London, 1615, and many later editions) was a bestselling work of its kind.

[69] Smaller hand ends here.

[70] Richard Baxter, *A Call to the Unconverted* (London, 1658, and many later editions); idem, *The Crucifying of the World by the Cross of Christ* (London, 1658).

those in the house much valued, but I little minded.) But soon after (he did not stay till he'd taken his degree) my Chamberfellow (aforesaid) buying his Reasons of the Christian Religion,[71] hugely commended it to me for the Learning of it, and philosophy in it &c. and told me he proceeded in the method of Des Cartes[72] (which our Tutor then read to us) from things more known to things less known in nature, beginning at Cogito, ergo sum. This I listened to; and (he lending me his to look over, to see how I liked it,) I soon after bought it; where I found, (not so much learning onely, but) so much Godlyness and Divinity in so serious and heavenly a Style, and a Spirit that so much suited me, that I was exceedingly taken with it, and could not stop here but thirsted after more of the same Author. I saw I had found a Treasure which God (blessed be his name) inclined my Soul to value. I bought soon after His /fo. 24r/ Call; and his Reformed Pastor;[73] and the more I read the more I liked.—— And then God wrought in me a Love to that heavenly man, and his Books which (as I said) I this year (haveing Freedom time and leisure) began to study more constantly and seriously than before. And afterwards I heard learned and episcopall men commend him; which much rejoyced me. And going to Cambridg this Summer for a day onely and being with my Tutor; I remember that he commended him and understanding that I had read his Cure of Church Divisions,[74] says he to me of it Does he not beat on both Sides bravely? and did much commend it, being then newly come out. After this I proceeded to his polemicall books also: by all which I profited incomparably more than by any Sort of books that ever I read.

For my Society in the Country this year I had all the preceding Winter Mr Whiston's[75] company as formerly but this Spring (1670) he left Heckington and removed to Moulton near Spalding in South Holland: which was a great trouble to many of our Town: but me it put to my tears to part with him. In his room there came an ignorant, idle, and malignant Minister to Heckington with whom I could have no Society;[76] who coming into our parlour saw a Book or two of Mr Baxter's on the Table, and talked on it afterwards, and accused me for reading (as he termed them) unlicensed or unlawfull books. At one time especially he uttered his distast against me in some company who thereupon sent for my Father who could better answere him. His

[71] Baxter, *Reasons of the Christian Religion.*

[72] René Descartes (1596–1650).

[73] Richard Baxter, *Gildas Salvianus; = the reformed pastor* (London, 1656).

[74] Richard Baxter, *The Cure of Church-Divisions* (London, 1670).

[75] Edward Whiston.

[76] Anthony Beridge, MA, vicar of Heckington (1670–1686) (patron: Lady Francesca Cobham); rector of Evedon, Lincs. (1687–1702). CCEd; Venn, I, 139.

accusation was that I should never be able to preach unless out of Authors: &c. Why says my Father do you never make use of Authors for your Preaching? He answered him, he had formerly used the help of Authors but had now laid them aside as to that Service: But Sir (replyed my Father) had it not been for Dr Boyse we had had no Sermon last Sunday /fo. 24v/ (for it was his constant manner at that time to take his Sermons out of Boys's Postills;[77] and (I haveing the book), my Father used (when I had delivered it to him) to read his Sermons on Lords Days after dinner word for word as he delivered them.) upon this he rode up and left the place and company (as he well might) with Shame and Confusion. My Father having given him not only that generall but a particular instance which he appositely set whom to himself. For the Subject he had been preaching on was on Luke 11. 14. (In Boys page 261) on the dumb devil; where he reminded him of this passage (page 263) That man is possessed of a dumb Spirit who suffers in his company profane Swaggerers to blaspheme the name of God without any controlment. Why then (added he) do you suffer such, without reprooving them; while you vent your Spleen against an innocent that never meddles with you! or to that purpose.—— but he had enough. And let this be enough to be said of him, and his unprofitable Society.

Mr Whiston being gone, I sometimes not only heard but conversed with Mr Goodknap of Burton (aforenamed) a very precious holy man whom I highly honoured and esteemed; and from whom I recieved much good.

But the most Benefit of all I (at this time) recieved from Mr Brocklesby aforesaid to whom I used to make a journey now and then to see <him>; and that on Saturdays that I might hear him the day following, and so be sure of something considerable for my labour. whose Sermons, Converse at Meals, and example did (indeed do) me the most Good; For much further Society and intimate Converse with him, I could not have; it being his Constant manner, a little after meals to get him into his Study, and leave me a book or two to keep me company the while: So that excepting at meal times, and in the Pulpit, and Prayer time in the Family, I saw him not. But /fo. 25r/ a wonderfull serious and heavenly man I discerned him to be, and no less learned: So that all the persecutions I had read of in the lives of others, I thought I saw summed up in in him. Whose fuller character and example and my observations of him I entred into my Papers as dillegently as his Sermon notes: especially when my visits could be but seldome. And the Truth is God's gracious Providence made use of these two things Mr Baxter's Books and Mr Brocklesby's Example, as

[77] John Boys, *The Workes of John Boys Doctor of Divinitie and Deane of Canterburie* (London, 1622).

the great means to instruct and mould, confirm, resolve and settle me in these my juvenile preparatory years: Thrice blessed be his name.

About Michaelmas this year (1670) the Lord restoring my Father out of a sharp Sickness: I entred a thankful memoriall of it in these words

[78]And now I am to remember a gracious act of mercy which the Lord has shewn me and my Father in hearing my prayers and raising him from so grievous a Sickness, from so near the grave as it has pleased god to bring him. He fell sick on such a day as Astrologers call unlucky, with such another diabolicall Atheisticall sign occurring as caused my mother (after the custome of the world) confidently to think and averr that my Father would dy (or however her Mother who was then very weak at Willowby) giving instances of what she had known at other times. This caused me (foolish Soul) to despond fearfully, but made me more earnest with my god in prayer for his recovery: and a strong hope (methought) I had that the Lord would restore him to the confirmation of me his poor Servant against all such aetheisticall, diabolicall, anti=providential principles, and to convince me of the evil and folly of such highly provokeing, and sinfull Observations: which by the admirable mercy and help of our God was graciously effected. To the glory and praise of his holy name let it be remembered, and the conviction of the Atheisticall world.

Thus, with a like recovery of my own the year before mentioned were two such remarkable Providences as took me off from the tormenting conciets of the nature abovesaid, whereby I had been deluded. In opposition to which (the notion and Life of Faith becomeing now more pleasant and facile to me) I entred a remark in the words following. or little varying.[79]

[80]I have observed how earnestly God all along pressed the Israelites to a faithfull and steadfast dependance upon himself and his word and promise; and how He has prospred them when they did so. I have /fo. 25v/ considered (tho it be hard, yet) how excellent and comfortable a thing it is to be serious in this, to be a thorow Bible christian: For a man to live by Faith in all the promises in all exigences;[81] yea to pick sure and steadfast comfort out of a promise made and performed to another person in particular; (as that of Hebrews 13. 5. for instance) I confess such a person is singular; but remember they are the excellent ones and most favoured of God, and prosper best by it. as Caleb and

[78]This paragraph, ending *Atheisticall world*, is written in the smaller hand.

[79]*or little varying* in smaller hand.

[80]These two paragraphs, ending *Deuteronomy 18.-10*, are written in the smaller hand.

[81]*exigence*: a pressing state of circumstances, or one demanding immediate action or remedy; an emergency; a difficulty. *OED*.

Joshua did.— A holy serious spirituall man will bear himself up above the instigation of Flesh, Sense, and carnall Reason: it is in a great measure free from fear; and can conclude and reckon upon Safety in times of imminent danger; and all by vertue of a promise; which God will make good unto him in kind; or else in value by giveing him patience, and comfort in a willing resignation and Submission of himself to Him and His Will. Read the Psalms of David, exceeding comfortable upon these accounts. Leigh on the promises.[82] Rogers of Dedham. Doctrine Faith cap. 11.[83]

'Tis therefore the veryest folly, and madness in the world for a man of reason to conclude of good and evill luk; upon beginning things &c. on such as they call good and evill lucky and unlucky days, or from Good and Bad Signs (of which no reason can be given) Judic: Astrolog: Divinat: &c.—— This is horid paganism and strikes point blank at the very Face of Divine Providence. See Leviticus 19.-26. Deuteronomy 18.-10.

And now (haveing entred & transcribed the above Remark.) I shall here Record it, to the Praise of God; and the Comfort of my Soul, and the Confirmation of my Faith: that my God gave me this year (1670) a compleat Deliverance from all my two or three former years Melancholy and trouble of mind, in Answere to my many earnest and importunate Prayers. To whom be Praise and unfeigned Thanks for it. Amen.

In January this same year (1670)[84] I took my Degree of Batchelour of Arts at Cambridge where I stayed but about a Month. And I remember I was not a little glad that I passed without takeing the Oath that is usually imposed upon the Schollers at that time, which happened by the oversight of him that gave it amongst such a Company.

Haveing[85] thus passed over my Preparatory years that I may not forget the Frame and Temper of my Spirit, which it was wrought to in the three or four last of them (during my Sickness and Melancholly), I think it fit to give some further account of that than I have yet done, before I proceed any further.

/fo. 26r/ My Sins and daily frailties and infirmities were a very great Burthen to my Soul not onely those of Commission but those of Omission also. I was too much addicted to Sloth and lying in bed in the morning and had much rather have made it out at night but that the affairs of a Husbandman's Family would not bear it: So that the

[82] Edward Leigh, *A Treatise of the Divine Promises* (London, 1633).

[83] John Rogers, *The Doctrine of Faith* (3rd edn, London, 1629). Rastrick's reference must be to the third, or later, edition, because the first two editions only contain ten sections.

[84] 1670/1.

[85] *Haveing* is written in a slightly larger hand, to separate the following section.

loss of my morning hours was not the least of my Sins. This temper I did not conquer; But afterwards when I had a room to myself I chose the night for my more serious fixed Studys which I was not onely naturally inclined to but found it by experience to be the most silent and truest time my head was then the clearest not so thick and cloudy as just after Sleep it was and I could always sit up untill 3 or 4 of the clock in the morning before I began to be sleepy though actually I did not usually sit up so long as sometimes I did. But chiefly I found that I was free from diversions as then and free from the fears of being called off for I was always of such a temper that I could do nothing but trifle, or seldome set to any thing when I knew I was to be soon called away nor could I well study in a strange place. So that I could never husband the Shreds of time as many can. But when I could not study at night, that I should yet loose my morning hours was a great trouble to me.

I was too much to blame in my behaviour towards my Father and angered him too often either by not going to prayers so soon at night as he would have had me; or too grudgingly performing any such little matters as did now and then intervene which he set me about And it troubled me exceedingly that I should so often offend after the same manner notwithstanding my frequent Resolutions to the Contrary. So that (in a particular Instance of this nature as I find it in the Papers of my Diary for that time) it cast me into the <lamentations and> Self=accusations following:

/fo. 26v/ [86]Good Lord! I had thought verily yesternight that I should never have sinned in this kind by disobedience any more! but I'l never trust my heart more. O that I could ly in tears, for the Sins that I am likely to commit! O damnable Hypocrite! O the loathsome pride of my Heart! O the profound difficulty of Holyness! What shall I do now?! Must I confess my Sins? I have sinned against God, my Father abhorredly abominably!—— Must I judg my Self? I have deserved Hell a 1000 times were Hell a 1000 times worse than it is, by reason of the heinous terrible agravations of my Sins. Methinks I hear, [87]You can spend time enough in bed but cannot afford your Father an inch! how long and how often has he waited on you, and how much has he Done for you? but you will not wait on him to th'dorr! &c. —— Well but what am I better for this? Must I ly in tears for my Sin? Alas I cannot! must I amend? Wo and alas this I cannot! I thought I could, but I cannot, or will not or something I am sure I do not. Thou Omnipotent God for thy Son my Saviour's Sake, upon thy Truth and Promise Help: or I am utterly lost undone! Thou hast promised to

[86]This paragraph, ending *Sinner*, is written in the smaller hand.

[87]This passage (*You can spend time ... th'dorr! &c.*) has been written in a distinct hand, perhaps to show that it was to be set in italics.

sanctify me, and it is Thy will that I should not Sin Why then is not Thy Will done? Thou who canst make me Holy as well as bid me be such: why then am I yet a Sinner?*

This was for thinking much to carry my Father his Dinner into the Field; (haveing somewhat offended him over night:) I did it but with so much reluctancy and ill will, as threw me into the preceeding lamentations when I got alone

I was moreover sadly disturbed and haunted with impure carnall inclinations and cumbred[88] with too strong a desire of the Flesh; which (with other things concurring did precipitate me too soon and hastily into Marriage as afterwards appears.

These infirmitys (and such as these too many) lay very heavy upon my Spirit: and I prayed: [89]Lord when shall I have a habit of the contrary vertues Vigilancy Studiousness Lab. Dilligence, Industry, Temperance, Humility, Seriousness, &c.—— and a delight in all? O the Beauty and Lovelyness of Grace and Holyness!—— O that I could love Vertue and Holyness for Vertue and Holyness Sake &c.——

And for Sins of Omission. If I happened into Company with Health drinkers (as once particularly at a wedding) and did not Reprove them; or did not reprove such as I heard take the Name of God in vain; or denyed a half penny to any poor sick Creature that begged it for Christ Jesus' Sake; or did any night neglect my then begun Duty of /fo. 27r/ Self=examination (as I too often did) or neglected to Visit any poor sick Neighbour, (to which I was too backward) and the like, O what a case was I in. I could have no rest or quiet in my Spirit for a good while after. If I met any poor blind lame person whom I took to be very needful and if I gave them nothing though they did not ask me it troubled me extremely. As once I met a poor blind boy led by another as I was riding betwixt Wragby and Bardney in the parts of Lindsey and because I gave him nothing (though they did not ask) I was so troubled and my mind did so ake that I could have no Comfort in my Journey for some hours after Thought I, how can I look to prosper? How if God should strike me with Blindness? and the like. Thus was my Soul afflicted under the Sense of Sin.

As to Dutys and the Temper of my Soul in them I shall onely Instance in the Sacrament of the Lord's Supper which now I had severall times recieved I looked upon it as so tremendous an Ordinance that the Aw and fear I had about it did very much interrupt

*Marginal note: The Lord pardon the Irreverance of my ignorant youth. I will not lay my Sin upon God.

[88] *cumber(ed)*: troubled (of mind), distressed. *OED.*

[89] This passage (*Lord when shall I . . . Holyness Sake &c.*) is written in the smaller hand.

and hinder that Joy and Comfort I should have had in it; and that benefit and advantage I should have had by it. I remember when it was administered to the Schollers in our Colledg Chappell at Cambridg I refused to go because it was said that every one was to be punished 12 pence* that did not recieve it: I was jealous lest my decietful heart should aim more at the saving of the money than the spirituall Ends: but I repented it afterwards when I understood that there was no such punishment exacted: and moreover that my Tutor preached at that time, whom therefore by missing that opportunity I never heard at all. I was afraid of Un=[90] /fo. 27v/ Unworthy receiving of it. And therefore when I did recieve I bestowed some Considerable time the day before in setting about the most serious Examination of my Self that I could both of my Sins and graces For my Sins I sometimes proceeded by the Rule of the Commandments as expounded and collected by the Author of whole Duty M.[91] and Assembly's Catechism; and wrote them down in order: but afterwards most commonly by a bare looking into my own Heart and temper and Practise. And I studyed to raise and Compose my Soul in the most serious and sincere Address to God; which (to make them the more solemn; and that I might proceed Understandingly I digested them into short Devotions while I wrote them down in my Papers some of Which I shall here transcribe.

[92]At Christmas. Anno 1670.

And now O holy and Blessed Lord that I am to recieve this Blessed Sacrament which Thou hast ordained for the comfort of Thy Servants as a Repast in their Journey and to seal unto them the Benefitt of the Death and Passion of Thy dear Son and as a Remembrance thereof unto them &c.—— O how must I prepare my Self for the worthy reception thereof, and a Comfortable Communicating therein. Where I have Examined my Self my Sins are spread before Thee. And where I have not O the abundance of Sins conteined in that very neglect! O the Pride, the Sloth, the Idleness, the Luxury, Intemperance and Uncleanness, the Disobedience Heard heartedness the Carelessness that I am guilty of! And O the Enhancing Aggrevations of all these! O the Horridness of the Guilt! O miserable wretch that I am! Am I in a State of Grace and have I Faith? I dare not presume! What must I

*Marginal note: By this it may be judged how improper it is to force men to Sacraments by external penaltys.

[90]This is not a catchword. It seems that Rastrick turned the page and decided to start at the beginning of the word.

[91]The authorship of the bestselling *The Whole Duty of Man* (London, 1658, and many later editions) remained a mystery throughout the period. It was probably written by Richard Allestree (1621/2–1681). *ODNB*.

[92]These devotions are written in the smaller hand.

do? Have I true and unfeigned Humiliation and Repentence for these Sins I dare not say so! O what must I do. Which way must I look? Whither must I go but unto Thee my Gracious Lord. O Thou who dost so lovingly and favourably condescend to admit thy Unworthy Servant to a Renewal of my Covenant with Thee, and Thou who hast made this Sacrament to be a Seal of Confirmation and growth in grace to Thy Servants; Behold the Servant of the Lord be it unto me according to Thy Word. I plainly see the Cursedness of my Estate by nature the need of a Saviour the necessity of this Sacrament and the Benefit thereof. And O that I had more longing desires of a more neer Communion with Thee my Lord therein. O my Unworthyness of so rich a mercy! O that I could be humbled for it! Lord Jesus accept of your will, and desires of my Heart after Thee, and if they be but sincere, Blessed be Thy name. O make this Sacrament Effectuall to my Soul to my Confirmation and Establishment in every good and perfect thought, word and work, to my growth and /fo. 28r/ encrease in grace to my proficiency and progress in serious Holyness. that Jesus Christ the Benefits and Meritts of his death and passion may be mine, that Thy Holy Spirit may be mine, to work in me every Grace and Gospell Duty; as Self-denyall, Mortification &c. O pardon these Sins of Pride Sloth &c. and work in me a habit of the contrary graces and Virtues as Humility Vigilance, Studiousness, Diligence in my Calling Temperance, &c. and a delight therein as verily and certeinly as I am partaker of the outward Signs of Bread and Wine. And because this is a special time of asking I humbly beg that thou wouldst give me all things necessary, as to my generall and speciall Calling as a Christian and as a {Student Minister}[93] O Qualify and dispose me for that great work. give me all manner of gracious Endowments, and Abilitys for that function, spirituall, naturall and acquired Cheer my Call; Bless and prosper me in all my proceedings in order thereto in Jesus Christ my Saviour, to the Glory of Thy Holy name, the Salvation of Thy chosen and the Comfort of me Thy poor Unworthy Servant.—— O let me walk before Thee in the Strength of this spirituall Food unto all well=pleasing. And Thou who hast said that he who eateth Thy Flesh and drinketh Thy Blood hath Eternal Life, direct thy Servant to and in all your means in order thereto. O that my ways are so directed that I might keep thy Statutes[94]

Another (which though wrote afterwards yet for the Affinity of the Matter, that they may be together) I here also add.

[93] Rastrick uses these curly brackets. *Student* is written above *Minister*, which has not been cancelled. The intention might have been to provide alternatives for a printed edition.

[94] End of passage in smaller hand.

[95]Examining my Self before the Reception of your Sacrament I find my Self guilty of Sloth, Idleness, neglect of heavenly and edifying discourse, A common careless stupid dead, secure senseless frame and temper of heart, a depraved disposition, propense to sin and backward to Duty. And (as a Minister) a want of Love to Souls and serious endeavours of doing them all the good I am able! Alas! for these things!—— Lord who knoweth how oft he offendeth O cleanse Thou me from my secret faults. And being to partake of such heavenly Ministrys O seal unto me an Interest in my Saviour to your casting down and demolishing the strong holds of Sin and Satan in my heart.—— How long will Thou behold Thy poor Creature in this misery and not pity me. How easily can Omnipotency help me and save me from Sin, and make me Holy and Heavenly and as I should be. Lord, it is a new (i.e.) a Holy and Heavenly heart that I beg for. Seal unto me your grant of this in your Sacrament. Methinks I long for this Heavenly Frame and temper with Sighs and groans. The Truth is it is long of my Self that I am so sloathfull and dead hearted; but methinks I can truly say I long after better, and should account it above all the world. O wouldst Thou but change the Temper of my Body that I might be freed from Sloath, and these headstrong inclinations thereto, and become vigilant. And wouldst Thou but renew and change the Frame and temper of my Heart, and Mind, that I might be saved from this Common deadness, and have a heavenly Inclination and freedom unto and fitness for Duty, I were a happy man!—— /fo. 28v/ Which request in the name of Jesus Christ that I make unto Thee with all the earnestness and might that I am able to put up a petition with. In the mean time I beseech Thee O my dearest Lord accept of thy poorest Servants Divines to wait upon Thee in this Their Ordinance, and meet me there and make it effectual to the Confirmation of my Soul in Christ and in Grace and for my growth and Proficency in Holyness. I desire earnestly to Devote my Self to thee and to close with the terms of the Gospell: O let the Match be made, and set now Thy Seal to it, and let not all the Malice of Diabolicall Opposition dissolve the Union. O give me a Portion of Thy speciall Grace, a speciall measure of thy holy Spirit, and a Heart suited to sacred and Heavenly Work, and seal unto me the grant of this in this Sacrament unto which Thou dost so lovingly and graciously invite me. O! it is in earnest and longing expectations of these that I desire to draw near thereto. O satisfy this poor hungry Soul with those good things that it so longingly breaths after: O let me see the effects of Thy power and Thy dear Love in this. Alas! What can I do of my Self, if Thou dost not uphold my goings in Thy paths, and help me to run the ways of

[95]This passage is written in the smaller hand.

Thy Commandment with an enlarged heart. But save me and help me O my dear Redeemer Remember me and my God for Good[96]

And again at another time.

[97]Still the same Sins!—— Lord! that I may be made whole, and cleansed and purifyed, and saved from mine Ungodlyness and Backwardness to my Duty. O seal the grant of Pardon and Further Strength in this Sacrament I am now through Thy Favour and Grace to Recieve. To thee I come, I seek, I cry, I call, I beg for the Divine Supplys of Thy Grace in order to the Heavenly Life. O let this Feast be a reviveing Cordiall to my Soul. Thou hast bidden me seek Thy For[98] and my Heart and Soul Answer: Thy Fear Lord do I desire to seek, Thy lovely, Thy Glorious shineing Countenance to my Soul do I implore. The Light of Thy Countenance: Thy Favour, Thy Grace, the pleasures that are at Thy right hand for ever, Thy Benignity and Loving kindness deny not this poor loveing, longing, panting breathing Soul gasping after Thee at Thy Feet. Hide not Thy face from me but hide it from my Sins for Thy name's Sake; And take me into Covenant and Union with Thee; and let me never violate that Allegiance that I have vowed to Thee. Renouncing the World, the Flesh, and the Devil, and all the powers and the works of Darkness; I here resolvedly chuse and take Thee for my God, my Saviour, and my Sanctifyer; and do here consent to take upon me the Yoke and Subject my Self to the Soveraignty of Christ O let this Match be stricken, renewed, ratifyed sealed, and Confirmed to the Everlasting Comfort and Salvation of my Soul. O crown my Resolutions with Thy Fiat, of the Celebration and Solemnization of this Contract at this heavenly Banquet: and then Blessed be Thy name. Amen.[99]

/fo. 29r/ I had withall this time a very awakned, and abideing Sense of the affairs of Religion and another Life upon my Soul; and a very high Concern for its good Estate with repect thereto; and of my Eternal Welfare. These thoughts ran much in my mind, which I shall best recall to my memory and Understanding by describing them in the same words in which I then expressed them. They were these

[100]I have Wondered at my Self (upon consideration of the severe punishment of the damned in Hell as it is described by the Author of Practice of Piety,[101] Mr Baxter, Mr Dent &c.[102] And after reading their Exhortations to Repentance and Conversion from such grounds

96 End of passage in smaller hand.
97 This passage is written in the smaller hand.
98 *For* (perhaps *Form*) is concealed in the tight binding.
99 End of passage in smaller hand.
100 This passage is written in the smaller hand.
101 Lewis Bayly, *The Practise of Pietie* (2nd edn, London, 1612, and many later editions).
102 Arthur Dent (1552/3–1603), Church of England clergyman and religious writer. *ODNB*.

and motives. And considering what Ordinances (as preaching &c.) were instituted for: What mean such tolling of Bells (thought I) and Congregating Assemblys every such set day if there be no reall cause and ground for this?) I say, I have wondered why I was no more affected and could be no more serious in such cases! Why, (thought I) do I not make my whole life a continued act and trade of Prayer and Praise and the Worship of God? Can I make God and eternall happiness too sure? What if I should finally miss of Heaven? What then!? Would it not repent me that I did not all I could in order to Eternall Happiness and continually bend my knees in prayer for grace to do more? Why do I not (I say) pray more and more fervently? Why is not my Talk gracious? Why am I no more serious? Why am I not afraid of Sin &c.— Why do not I set my Self to these things? and why not presently? What if I sould dy before? &c. in the case I am in! This is an Easy way, and broad enough if I go to Heaven, as I am: but I am told the contrary.— Now these thoughts have sometimes wrought me to more Earnest Prayers to God than ordinary (which shows what they would do if there were followed home and close) but have been so strangely gone, or snatched away that they have not produced in me those further effects which any man of Reason would think they should.[103]

Upon this I reflected on the common State and Condition of the generality of people in the world. Their lethargick stupid case was to me very sad: and when I wrote down those thoughts, I ran out so largely in the discovery of their common temper, (as to the concerns of Religion and their Souls:) the Reasons of it; and in such serious considerations to awaken them out of it, that I afterwards fitted it (with some small alteration) to that Text 2 Thessalonians 5.6. [104]Let us not sleep as do others, but let us watch and be sober: and preached it, as much to the Profit of the Hearers as any other Sermon. /fo. 29v/ For indeed, that men should profess to believe such great things as Heaven and Hell, and yet live so inconsiderately, stupidly, carelessly and negligently as they do, was to me, the most astonishing thing in the whole world! I thought often and much of their State; I could scarce see or hold with a neighbour, or other person but this was in my mind; What State is thy Poor Soul in? and most things I thought on, was in a serious manner, and with a religious respect and consideration. But as to my discourse I was always of so reserved a temper, that I communicated little: and it was always one of the greatest troubles of my whole life that I could speak so little to others of these things

[103]End of passage in smaller hand.

[104]*Let us not sleep as do others, but let us watch and be sober* has been written in a distinct hand, perhaps to show that it was to be set in italics.

though with an attractive receptive person that savoured of the best things I could be more free but to the common Sort of people I was strangely straitned in my Spirit unto an almost constant Silence unless it was by reading to them some serious book in course. I remember one Lord's Day the reading to my Self of Mr Baxter's Meditations at the end of his Saints Rest[105] so raised me that when I came out of the Parlour I catechised, and discoursed with my father's Family so seriously as that (by the mention he made of it to some next day at Sleford) I percieved my Father took great notice of it. (He sometimes would tell me I saved his Soul) But this was not ordinary, I too soon cooled again and remained so too long.

Another of my experiences these years was this: to use the words in which I then wrote it.

[106]I found that there can be no true peace to a Soul alienated and set at a distance from God Isaiah 48.22 and 57.21. O what damps and fears and terrour has my Soul been in; and with what horrour have I been stricken when (after deliberate commission of some known Sin or Omission of some known Duty, against the checks of Conscience: &c.) I have been sensible of the want of his presence: nothing that I did (methought) could prosper till I was reconciled to God again. I found that /fo. 30r/ the trouble and terrour of Conscience for a Sin committed, is incomparably greater than the pleasure of it! O that I and every one could deeply consider of this before we venture upon it, or please ourselves with the thoughts of it.

I found moreover that the surest and soundest Comfort ariseth from living by Faith in the Promises; (as I hinted before) and that the Consideration of the ways and methods of Providence is a wonderfull Comfort in all Afflictions.[107]

Another thing to be remembred concerning my troubles and Afflictions was

[108]I sadly experienced Satan's horrible Injection of monstrous hideous blasphemous thoughts and imaginations into my mind: as to wish, conceit, and conclude such and such a thing, and that of a sudden and such things as one would think it impossible for a man's brain to imagine: vastly aliene from and not all agreeing with the present Subject of his thoughts. and that so strongly as a man may be easily decieved not in the least to suspect Satan. They were cast into my mind mostly by way of a horrid Supposition, which my Soul infinitely loathed and detested, and therefore it was cast into a fearfull

[105] Baxter, *The Saints Everlasting Rest.*

[106] This passage is written in the smaller hand.

[107] End of passage in smaller hand.

[108] This passage is written in the smaller hand.

terrour and amazement and startled at the rising of them. My Remedy was (when I perceived them coming; and Satan as it were levelling his Dart) to have recourse to God in Jesus Christ by earnest prayer, and call aloud to him in my heart and beat him back with the Sword of the Spirit.[109]

This I wrote, but I remember more hereof than what I then set down. Sometimes a petition in mind would be violently (to my great horrour) turned into a Curse And it was not onely words but most horrid Visionary Fancys in mine Imagination. I was fain to resolve at last to be troubled at them as little as ever I could; for the more I was troubled, the more I was haunted with them. I cryed out in my mind many times in an hour, The Lord rebuke thee Satan. with other suitable Scriptures with which I repelled him (And this I have ever used to do since with the greatest earnestness, when Satan at any time assaults my Soul in any other kind and not in that blasphemous way) When I found a Cursed thought comeing, I learned the Skill to prevent Satan and turn it into a Prayer. But the best way was, (as it is with a Scold) to disregard him. /fo. 30v/ I am willing to be the more punctuall in this, because (as I find it much considered by the best Divines (Bolton Afflicted Conscience p. 532 to the end.[110] Perkins Cas. Conso. 2[d] Vol lib. 1. cap. 10. p. 39.[111] &c. Dan Dyke.[112])[113] Whom upon this experience I could the better understand and Recieve profit by; so) I since find this has not been my case alone (as I then was ready to conclude) but the case of very many (if not the greatest part) of the most serious and awakned Christians at one time or other most frequently at their first Conversion Many of whom I have known and Conversed with; and by my own experience I have been capacitated (as to Understand their Condition, so) to advise and help them about it; and formertimes (I bless God) with good Success.

And[114] now I proceed to the more publick part of my Life. The first place of my Employment in (or rather in Order to) the Ministry was at Fosdike on the Washes in Holland in Lincolnshire, <in> a Low and levell Country where I had often resolved secretly in my mind

[109] End of passage in smaller hand.

[110] Robert Bolton, *Instructions for a Right Comforting Afflicted Consciences* (London, 1631).

[111] Rastrick cites William Perkins, *The Whole Treatise of the Cases of Conscience* as it was reprinted in *The Workes of that Famous and Worthy Minister of Christ . . . M. William Perkins. The second volume* (London, 1631).

[112] Daniel Dyke (d. 1614), Church of England clergyman. *ODNB*.

[113] This bracket is placed at the right margin. The likelihood is that Rastrick intended to find a more specific reference for Dyke, or to add more references to his list of divines on this subject at a later date.

[114] *And* is written in a slightly larger hand, to separate the following section.

not to live howsoever; of all Countrys I loved not to think of Holland. But God often draws us, and provides for us where we lest imagine; and contrary to our own Designs; and so it was with me. Though I liked not the Country yet the place afforded me such a privacy and pleasant walks upon the Seabank where the Ships came up; (which I was very near;) as was not ungratefull to me. Here I was Curate under Mr Basil Berridg Rector of Algarkirk and Fosdike[115] and one of the Clarks of the Convocation for the Diocese of Lincoln. a person he was High in name, in place and Body and in Estate; but so High in Spirit and Temper also, that I could never suit with him, as will soon appear. Thither I went at the beginning of May, Anno 1671. He first procured /fo. 31r/ me a License to read prayers and Homilys and serve his cure which I took from the Ecclesiasticall Court met at Boston this Easter after Visitation, and this was all I did or could do for four weeks till the Season for entring into Orders should come. That Season approaching; I prayed earnestly to God for His Blessing and Assistance, and for his Holy Spirit to furnish me with Abilitys for his work and for the Discharge of my Duty. That he would make me a faithfull Labourer in his Vineyard and not let Satan hinder me: And that he would help me to Run the ways of his Commandments, and Teach the ways of his Commandments with an enlarged heart.

June 18. Anno 1671. I was Ordained Deacon at Peterborough by Bishop Heinshaw.[116] By the way I could not but observe the Profaneness of most of the Schollers when ordained; who rode out to see a fine house in the Country the same day and had talked at Dinner of doing some Extravagancy (which what it was I have forgot) but that the Landlord of the Inn restrained them (which I very well remember) from the Arguments of their having received Holy Orders and the Sacrament. As I was troubled with their Company so they were not (some of them) spareing of their reflection upon me for my so much Purity because I would not ride out with them. But glad I was when I returned home to my Undisturbed Retirement with liberty for more work; For though I was not licensed to preach (which that Bishop could not do in another Diocese) yet I now begun my catechisticall exercises; and delivered my Preparartory Introduction grounded on Hebrews 5.12. in the Desk or reading Pue. which served me severall Lord's days. August 17. the same year I took my generall License to Preach in the Diocese of Lincoln, of Bishop Fuller, being at Sir Edmund /fo. 31v/ Turner's at Stoke where he was entertained when

[115]Basil Beridge, MA (d. 1678) became rector of Algarkirk, Lincs. in 1638. His patron was Roger Fielding. CCEd; Venn, I, p. 139.

[116]Joseph Henshaw (1603–1679), bishop of Peterborough. *ODNB*.

he came on his Triennial Visitation to Grantham.[117] Here it may not be unfit to mention that the Reverend Mr Leigh of Silk=Willowby (above mentioned) was very Instrumentall in procureing me, both my Curacy and my License to preach.[118] Returning home with this I preached during my abode at Fosdike once in the Morning on the Lord's Day and catechised in the afternoon: And no more would Mr Berridg have me do. The first text which I preached on was Psalm 51. 12, 13. [119]Restore to me the joy of thy Salvation and Estate lift me with thy free Spirit: Then shall I teach transgressours Thy ways, and Sinners shall be converted unto Thee. I thought when I begun to preach just as I afterwards found that Melancthon did; (viz.) that men could not withstand the power of the Gospell, and Evidences for Religion, and the serious practise of it: but upon experience I quickly found as he did (viz.) that Old Adam was too hard for young Melancthon. While I was here and preached so seldome I wrote my Sermons very largely.

To get to be Curate or Assistant to some grave Divine, where a young man may begin to preach in some small Church or Chappell is thought by the best Men to be the fittest course for one that intends the Ministry to take at the first, or begin with; upon many accounts: chiefly the advantage of growing up under his Counsells Examples and Instructions. But it was not so to me here upon this last account I was under one who told me (very discourageingly) I was young and raw and must not think to be able to compose any Sermons fit for the people my Self and therefore he commended Dietericus[120] to me and advised me to translate him and preach those Translations for my Sermons to the people: For says he there are no Latin Schollers at Fosdike. (i.e) /fo. 32r/ to discover me.) But I must confess I did not take his advice yet this was the least that I disliked; His temper as to church affairs was worse. It happended on a time I was with him that we fell into discourse about the Nonconformists, and he affirmed that they were a Company of Unlearned Men; none of them had any learning; the chiefest of them (says he) is Baxter, whose Books are but Translations of other men's works they are but Bishop Davenport's works translated.[121] I asked him if he had any of them, he told me yes,

[117]William Fuller (1608/9–1675), bishop of Lincoln. *ODNB*. Sir Edmund Turner (1619–1707) of Stoke-Rochford, Lincs., Royalist and Surveyor-general of the Out Ports.

[118]John Leigh, MA (died in or before 1682), rector of Silk Willoughby (1661–1682). CCEd; Venn, III, p. 63.

[119]The biblical quotation has been written in a distinct hand, perhaps to show that it was to be set in italics.

[120]Conrad Dieterich (1575–1639), Lutheran theologian.

[121]Although this is an odd charge, the reference is presumably to John Davenant (bap. 1572–d. 1641), bishop of Salisbury, rather than John Davenport (bap. 1597–d. 1670), puritan

His Confession of Faith;[122] that being a Book which I had not seen, I desired to borrow it but he refused to lend it me, with this Answer No (says he) if you read nothing but what is good in the Knaves you will fall in Love with them. but instead therof he lent me a Virulent Pamphlet against Dr Owen, which he bad me take home with me.[123] This gave me trouble and amazement enough but was no temptation to me to change my mind at all. And it was not long before I got the aforesaid Book of Mr Baxters into my own Possession. But by this time I saw that I was like to have no help from him at all, and Glad was I to keep (as much as I could) away from him. and Mr Brocklesby being fallen deeply Melancholy was this year abroad at the waters for his health. So that I was left to my own Private Studys (which I had pleasant opportunitys for) and the Divine Direction which was best of all.

The people of this place were generally a Careless and ignorant Sort: but there were one or two Arminianized persons who held the universall point (one of whom (whose name was Ball) had been a preacher amongst those people) who were /fo. 32v/ more intelligent. These were the most Constant Comers to the Church tho they differed from me in those things My neighbour Ball (now mentioned) once when I was at his house) excepting against a Passage in one of my Sermons about the Death of Christ; did a little surprise me; but it did me good and put me upon a more concerned and therefore more advantagious Study of the Point to my better profit, and further Proficiency in the knowledge of those things than otherwise I should have arrived at.

But here I had no suitable Society. Mr Berridg, with whom I was most concerned, (who lived 2 mile off, in a house of his wife's (who came out of the Family of the famous Ferrar's of Little Gidding in Huntingdonshire[124]) and in Sutterton Parish was a high, Austere and Lordly man, would commonly let me sit bare before him as long as I pleased, and when I went to see him would sometimes roughly ask me what I came for and the like; So that unless I could have humoured him, and have been of his Foot-mark here was fitter to be gotten or hoped for.

minister in America. The reference is probably to Davenant's *Ad fraternam communionem inter evangelicas ecclesias restaurandam adhortatio* (Cambridge, 1640).

[122]Richard Baxter, *Rich: Baxter's Confesssion [sic] of his Faith* (London, 1655).

[123]Probably, George Vernon, *A Letter to a Friend Concerning Some of Dr. Owens Principles and Practices* (London, 1670).

[124]In fact, Beridge's wife was not a Ferrar but rather a Brooke; it was her sister Anne who married the younger John Ferrar in 1657. I owe this information to Joyce Ransome.

My Circumstances in the place wher I boarded were as hard. My Landlord could discourse of nothing but the Ores and Bores:[125] If I read any remarkable Historicall passage to him at any time he would say that was like the Story who should tell loudest Ly. He was backward enough to make good his word and bargain with me. I percieved he grudged my abode there; for he gave me to understand that he was weary of me when I put it to him. I could have no other place convenient in the Town For here I had a Chamber to my Self which I was much pleased in: but in winter (haveing no fire) to sit 3, or 4 hours after they were all in bed; and going cold to bed; and to rise in the morning with feet as cold as when /fo. 33r/ I lay dere[126] (sometimes,) did not do well. but that I could then have the most easily born for the advantage of such private and undisturbed Studys that it gave me.

My Stipend here was upon Agreement to be Twenty pound a year. But a Tax comeing out that year of the twentyeth part of men's Estates; Mr Berridg took off twenty shillings for that: and when I <expostulated>[127] with him; and asked him if he determined the like proportion of his Servant's wages (which he did not) yet it moved him nothing at all. He also stopped ten Shillings more for my preaching 2 or 3 Lord's days in another Parish; tho I omitted not to preach once at Fosdike nevertheless: onely for ommitting prayers there. And yet this was a man that had two if not 3 hundred pounds a year and much money (besides his two Parsonages) as the most common report was

My Affairs standing thus, I resolved to leave Fosdik at the years end howsoever and therefore accordingly, about the beginning of February (1671)[128] I gave Mr Berridg Warning to provide himself another Curate against May day And, (knowing then of no better place) I intended to return to my Father's at Heckington.

But without any Contrivance, yea and beyond all expectation of mine own God's Gracious Providence gave me the prospect of and Title unto another place of Employment before very many weeks were past. For Mr Scargell the Minister of Wiberton near Boston being Dead[129] and the people in that Vacancy being put to look out amongst their Neighbours for Supplys: amongst others I was spoke to to come and help them myself; (being 5 miles off thence.) /fo. 33v/ I

[125] It seems likely that this was a local phrase, used to describe the tides on the estuaries. *Bores* are tidal waves of extraordinary height, caused by the meeting of two tides, or by the rushing of the tide up a narrowing estuary. *Ores* are edges or banks, shores or coasts. *OED*.

[126] *dere*: hurt, injured. *OED*.

[127] Replacing, *ap. . .gazed*, above the line.

[128] 1671/2.

[129] John Scargill, MA (died in or before 1672), rector of Wyberton, Lincs. CCEd.

believe this came by the means of Mr Nicholas Graves of that Town (Brother to the Minister of Frampton of that name who lived also in his own at Wiberton[130]) a very sober man and (for a private person) very Understanding and well read: who had heard me preach Old Mistress Pulvertoft's Funerall Sermon at Fosdike sometime before. The day appointed for me to preach there was on Sunday the last day of March: accordingly I went thither that Lord's day morning to preach; and met with Mr Maleverer the Lord Castleton's Chaplain,[131] just come down to take possession of the Living, which was in the said Lord's Gift (and is the same that Bishop Sanderson once had when he preached his famous Visitation Sermon at Boston[132]) He agreed that (being come) I should preach in the morning; he being to preach himself in the afternoon: I did so, and went home to Fosdike as soon as I had done. But Mr Maleverer designing not to stay and live amongst them; but onely after his Induction to put in a Curate and be gone That town did unamimously desire that I might be his Curate. And therefore a Messenger came to me the next morning (which was April 1. Anno 1672) with a letter from the Church=warden wrote by Mr Maleverer. Order, and the consent of the Parish; Expressing the Satisfaction they had recieved and desireing me to give them a meeting at Wiberton that same day to treat with Mr Maleverer about this affair. Upon this I went and met their New Minister and severall of the chief of the Parish at the Parsonage house. He offered me 30li a year But I, (that could have been Glad to have got out of /fo. 34r/ Holland which I saw I was now like to continue longer in; and considering that my work was to be doubled; (for I was now by the Town's desire to preach twice every Lord's day) and that the Care of the Parish (he being to be continually absent and at very great Distance (I think beyond Sea) was to be left to me) stood a little upon 40li per annum. But he not willing to be brought any higher or to give more, The Neighbours (unwilling I percieved that we should part) urged me to accept it upon these terms; this being added by Mr Maleverer that though he should come himself I should continue there upon the same terms untill I could be better provided; which I liked well. Mr Anthony Graves (the sober Minister of Frampton before mentioned) set in, and answered my Argument from the double work, by the Provision of the Stock

[130] Anthony Graves, MA (d. 1701) is not otherwise listed as the incumbent of Frampton. He was appointed vicar of North Rauceby, Lincs. in 1673 and was rector of Little Casteton, Rutland (1674–1701). CCEd; Venn, II, p. 249.

[131] Thomas Maulyverer, MA, instituted rector of Wyberton, 1672 (patron: George Saunderson, 5th Viscount Castleton (1631–1714)). CCEd.

[132] Robert Sanderson (1587–1663), later bishop of Lincoln, became rector of Wyberton in 1618. For the sermon, see Robert Sanderson, *Two Sermons: preached at two several visitations, at Boston, in the diocesse and county of Lincolne* (London, 1622).

of Sermons that I must have laid in while I was at Fosdike; and he pleasantly told me that old nets would catch new Fish. And indeed (considering that God's Providence sent this in such a nick of time when I least thought of it, and had no whether else to go) this Offer was not in my Circumstances to be refused: and therefore upon their desires (which swayed much with me) I accepted of it. Which when I had done, it was desired by them all that I should preach there once a day untill May day that I could remove, which I did; (excepting one day (April 21.) when (lying at Madam Walcot's[133]) I preached at Lincoln to two of the greatest Auditorys I had ever appeared in before: being invited also to preach the same day at Surflet before My Lady Cobham and Sir H. /fo. 34v/ Heron, had I not been other ways engaged.)[134] And for this preaching at Wiberton once a day this month it was that Mr Berridg stopped ten Shillings as is before related.

But here being no convenient place for boarding where I could have a room to my Self and I being wearyed with Boarding (as was said) at Fosdike and loath to venture into the same Circumstances again; and my Inclinations standing to another kind of Life I removed at May Day to the parsonage house at Wiberton: where, (Contenting my Self for a few weeks with what a poor Woman who lived in an End of it could provide me) I marryed (on the 25 of June following) Jane the youngest daughter of Mr Henry Wilson Batchelour of Divinity and Rector of Foldingworth and Benningworth in the parts of Lindsey and one of the prebends of the church of Lincoln.[135] And in that parsonage house we lived while I stayed here.

[136]May 25. Anno Domini 1673 I was Ordained Priest at Lincoln by Bishop Fuller: Before which I had kept a Day of Fasting and Prayer in preparation for the same. The Subject matter of my Prayers and Petitions were to this Effect. viz. That God would Bless me and enable me to discharge my Duty, in this Weighty Function and give me such a Measure of his Holy Spirit as might Capacitate and Qualify me for the same. That he would give me a free and clear Call, and a Divine Mission and such sincere and upright Intentions in this

[133]Probably Mary, wife of William Walcot of Walcot (d. 1689). See, *Lincolnshire Pedigrees*, p. 1033.

[134]Frances, daughter of Sir William Bamfield, was the second wife of John Brooke, Lord Cobham (d. 1660). She was buried at Surfleet, Lincs. in 1676. See G. E. Cokayne, *The Complete Peerage*, 14 vols (London, 1910–1959; Stroud, 1998), III, pp. 338–339. Sir Henry Heron of Cressy Hall in Surfleet died in 1695, aged seventy-six.

[135]Jane Wilson (d. 1684), daughter of Henry Wilson BD (d. 1665), rector of Faldingworth, Lincs. (1630–1665); rector of Benniworth, Lincs.; prebendary of Lincoln Cathedral (1641–1665). CCEd; Venn, IV, p. 428.

[136]From this point the manuscript is clearer. This appears to be because of a change of pen, or re-cutting the old, resulting in a finer point.

great Undertaking that his Glory in the Conversion Edification and Salvation of Souls might be my only ultimate end. That God would furnish me with all Abilitys for this Heavenly <spiritual> Calling <natural and acquired> and give me a quick Apprehension and a clear Understanding an Enlarged Invention a sound Judgment and a Retentive Memory; a gracious Elocution ready Utterance and moving Gesture: A Head full of Matter a Heart full of Affection and both full of his holy Spirit: a Composed Mind and a sanctifyed Heart. That he would make me Vigilant and Diligent /fo. 35r/ in my Studies and direct me to a right Method therein and such a Complacential Delight therein and in Prayer Preaching and heavenly Converse as might counter ballance or weigh down all carnal pleasures and that he would Bless my Studies with such a Proficiency and Improvement in Knowledg and to such a Stock of Learning and acquired Endowments as was requisite to make me an Accomplished Minister and a Powerful Preacher of his holy Word a Scribe taught to the Kingdom of Heaven and one that might have the Tongue of the Learned able to speak a Word in due Season. And that He would give me such a tender Love and Compassion to poor Souls as might prompt me to Endeavour their Conversion all the ways I were able. That he would give me another Heart suitable to this Work and Charge and that I might feel new and heavenly Motions carrying me out to the same: that he would heal my great Imperfections and Answer me according to my great necessities and save me from my common careless loose and dead Frame of Spirit; that I might have such a Sense of the Work that should be upon my hands as might with the Concurrence of his Holy Spirit animate and raise my Endeavours: and that he would help me to act as His and not as my Own in the Whole Course of my Life. That He would Providentially dispose of me freely clearly and fully to some place where I might do the most good though there were the less Means or Maintenance even as might be most agreeable to his Blessed Will and might lend most to his own Glory; that he would help me to study Work more than Wages: and make me a faithfull and successfull Labourer in his Vineyard: and that by my pains in his Harvest a great Increase might be brought into his Barn. And that I might lay out my Self in his cause and service for the Honour of his name and become an Usefull Instrument of his Glory in his Church.

At Wiberton where I was yet Curate I lived in very great Straits, and laboured under very great discouragements. For from May day 1672 (when I entred,) to the 4th of January following (and I know not how long after) I had not recieved above 5li for Preaching in that place. And, (to look two or three Months back,) the Lord Castleton's[137] Steward left in trust with Wiberton parsonage, &c. tampered to get

[137] Sir George Saunderson (1631–1714), 5th Viscount Castleton.

me out; and the detening so long my due pay seemed to be one of their Methods to effect it; though I never recieved the full of what was due to me in that place to this day, but was very hardly and unjustly dealt with. Another Minister was appointed for the place and came to it (before I went away) under the Notion of a Curate; but it was to the Parsonage it Self, which he procured to be resigned to him and settled on him by such means (as was /fo. 35v/ reported) as are but too much used, and likely to be so till Christ shall come to cast the Buyers and Sellers out of his Temple.

But God's Providence is mine Inheritance: Just at this very juncture of time the Vicaridg of Kirkton fell void by the death of Mr Cheney late Minister there who was buryed the 26th of March 1673.[138] I helping to carry him to the church, The Town being destitute, they got me to preach there the next Lord's day being Easter Sunday in the forenoon, and after that for several Lords days continuedly once a day, rarely looking out for any body else. And soon after two of the Inhabitants of Kirkton came to my house at Wiberton (in the name of others) to invite me to give the chief of the Inhabitants of the Town a Meeting on an appointed day at the house of one Christopher Wallis not without some Generall Intimation of the Design of it. So I went, and found a considerable number of the principal of them met together: where they gave me their Call <to be their Minister> and Unanimously agreed to make a Purse and at their own charge to send me to London with one Mr Seagrave[139] with a Petition to the Company of Mercers (who are the Patrons of that Living) to present me thereto: So we went with their Petition signed with 77 hands and made our Address to the Clerk of the Company Mr Godfrey;[140] And Mr Seagrave spared for no Cost or Dilligence to procure friends amongst them. So a Court of Assistants was soon called and on Lords day June 22 I was ordered to preach at Saint Micha<e>ls Cornhill before the Company, which I did on that text. Ephesians 5.15. we dined at Mr Norton's a Member of the Company[141] who desired a Copy of my Sermon and some time

[138] Thomas Cheyney (d. 1673), vicar of Kirton in Holland, Lincs. (1659–1673). CCEd.

[139] Perhaps the same Seagrave who married the sister of Rastrick's mother-in-law (Wilson). See p. 184 below.

[140] Michael Godfrey (1624–1689) was the sixth of the eleven sons of Thomas Godfrey (1585–1664) and thus brother of Sir Edmund Berry Godfrey (1621–1678). He was a leader of the City Whigs, probably sympathetic to nonconformity, but attended an Anglican church. See J. R. Woodhead, *The Rulers of London, 1660–89: a biographical record of the aldermen and common councilmen of the City of London* (London, 1965), p. 77; Ian G. Doolittle, *The Mercers' Company, 1579–1959* (London, 1994), p. 84.

[141] Henry Norton, as a member of the Mercers' Company, served as surveyor-accountant of St Paul's School. See R.B. Gardiner (ed.), *The Admission Registers of St Paul's School from 1748 to 1876* (London, 1884), p. 394.

after had it The next day I recieved the Companys Presentation to the Vicaridg of Kirkton at their Generall Court.[142]

Here (to divert a little) I had the Opportunity and advantage to hear Mr Baxter preach which I did June 13 and 20 his Friday Lecture. at his Meeting house near Fetter Lane. and on the Lords Day June 15. in the Morning not being then employed my Self Tho I was troubled to think how /fo. 36r/ I must give an account of the same to Mr Jarwood Minister at Kentish town a Relation or Acquaintance of Mr Seagraves, with whom we were that day to dine; and he had advised us to hear Dr Tillotson, or Dr Stillingfleet, and told us where they preached:[143] But when upon his inquiry I was forced to tell him who we had heard, said he, That's well!— and he fell into such a Commendation of Mr Baxter as mightily pleased me: He said he saw abundance, and was able to rule the Church by himself &c.

But to return. When I came down into the Country I went straightaway to Lincoln to the Bishop for Institution. But when I delivered my Presentation to his Chaplain (whose name was Hammond[144]) he read it with a sort of scornful Smile, and said, he was sure my Lord would not accept it, because it was in English; reflecting upon the Company of Mercers as fanatically constituted and inclined, and as if they took Latin for the Langauge of the Beast &c. So he carryed it up to the Bishop and presently the Bishop comes down and told me he could not grant me Institution upon that Presentation for the reason his chaplain had mentioned, and bad me write for a Latin one; but told me however that if the Living should laps to him he would confer it upon me, I should not loose it. So I lost my Journey at that time,[145] and came home re infecta:[146] and wrote to the Company an Account of all this. But before a Latin Presentation could be procured the Living lapsed, and I went again to Lincoln to urge the Bishop's Promise, which he remembred, and fulfilled: and September 25. 1673 The Bishop did Collate me into the Vicaridg of Kirkton aforesaid:

[142]Mercers' Company, London, Acts of Court, 23 June 1673: 'Mr John Rastrick being an humble Suitor for the same [the parish of Kirton], who by the appoyntment of the Court of Assistants preached yesterday at St Michaels Church in Cornhill and having received a Certificate from the Towne of Kirton testifying his exemplary life and conversation and the good they have received by his painefull preaching together with their earnest desire to have him settled amongst them The Court thereupon approving of him, Made choyce of him to be Vicar of the said parish, and presently, in the Court Sealed his presentation.'

[143]John Tillotson (1630–1694), archbishop of Canterbury; Edward Stillingfleet (1635–1699), bishop of Worcester and theologian. *ODNB*.

[144]John Hammond DD (d. 1723), chaplain to William Fuller, bishop of Lincoln; canon of Lincoln cathedral (1671–1723); archdeacon of Huntingdon (1673–1701); rector of Chalfont St Giles, Bucks. (1701–1723). Foster.

[145]*at that time,* inserted in the margin.

[146]*re infecta*: with the matter unfinished.

(which some told me brought the Bishop more money than if he had granted me Institution upon my presentation.) But during this Stop I preached at Kirkton nevertheless all this Summer every Lords Day; and oft on the week day did other buisness there. Till on September 29 I took possession of the Church, and removed thither with my Family the next day.

Kirkton is a considerable large Country Town scituate in that low and level /fo. 36v/ part of Lincolnshire called Holland about 3 mile southward of Boston and is the same that Camden mentions as denominated from its fine Church which is indeed the stateliest Structure that ever I saw in any Country Town. Blome gives the best account both of the Church and the Town.[147] There are two main Endslips or Villages that belong to it (that have no chappells) the one to the South East called Skeldike, the other to the North West called Kirktonholm (which are both in the Maps) the whole Parish being about five miles long besides many other Rows and Clusters of houses within that compass going by other names. So there was a large and encouraging Auditory; and (when I went first) several sober people, the remains of those Religious times when Mr Cotton and Dr Tuckney were Ministers at Boston;[148] the fame of whose Piety Dr Tuckney tells them (in his Preface to Mr Cotton's Notes on Ecclesiastes[149]) outtopped their Steeple: Kirkton also having had many able Ministers in it. But the number and distance of the Inhabitants gave me a very sensible concern, and I was very uneasie under the Burthen that lay upon my Shoulders; I knew not what to do for so many Souls that were also most of them so remote from my dwelling; nor how to discharge my Duty in a place that (as my Worthy Reverend Friend Mr Brocklesby told me) was as large as the Diocese in the primitive Church (at least many of them) were. Yet, When in a Sickness I had once I expressed to that friend how much I was concerned about the Charge of Souls in that place and parish he said to me, You serve a Good Master: which one word did very much Comfort and support me, and I often thought of it since. My maintenance here being but small not above

[147]Richard Blome, *Britannia* (London, 1673), a volume that Rastrick cites when describing Kirton in *An Account of the Nonconformity of John Rastrick M.A.*, p. 3. This is an edition of William Camden's *Britannia*, first published in Latin in 1586.

[148]John Cotton (1585–1652) was vicar of St Botolph's, Boston from 1612 until he resigned his living and sailed for New England in 1633. Anthony Tuckney (1599–1670) succeeded Cotton and went on to gain national significance in the 1640s as a prominent member of the Westminster Assembly of Divines. He resigned Boston in favour of Obadiah Howe in 1660. *ODNB.*

[149]John Cotton, *A Briefe Exposition with Practicall Observations upon the Whole Book of Ecclesiastes. By that late pious and worthy divine, Mr. John Cotton . . . Published, by Anthony Tuckney, D.D.* (London, 1654).

40li or 50li per annum at the most, I could not procure any Assistance: What I endeavoured (young weak and raw as I was) by the Grace of God that was with me was as follows.

1. I preached constantly twice a day on the Sabbaths besides all anniversary and occasional Funeral Sermons. And I did it after as awakening rowsing and pressing a manner as I could till my Sins and afflictions daunted and dejected me that /fo. 37r/ I could not afterwards get up the Confidence and boldness to speak with that kind of seriousness and zeal that I had formerly done: Though I always managed my work with a down right plainness and studyed to be faithfull.

2. I catechised publickly the youth of the Parish when the days were long, and while they would be got to come, in the Church before the Evening Sermon, and that very largely; it may be I held them somewhat too long: But I had a mind to go through the chief Heads of Religion every time I catechised that such as came might have as full a view of it at once as I could help them to. and this I did not in the manner of continued Speech after the manner of Expositions and Sermons but in an interrogatory way. and having seen Mr Herbert Palmers Catechism[150] I took his Method (which Mr Doolittle and others have since followed[151]) and so contrived my Questions that the less ripe especially might have little more to Answer than Yes or No; and than I further explained or pressed it as I saw cause. Its true I used the Church Catechism,[152] and must do so in the place and capacity I was in in the church: But that (the Creed especially) gave me occasion to speak to all the necessary Principles of the Christian Religion, the Scheme of which (by Gods Blessing on the many Catechisms, Methods of Divinity, and Practical Books which I had read) I had pretty well digested: And the Questions in it about the Baptismal Covenant (particularly the renouncing the World the Flesh and the Devil &c.) I very much both approved and improved: and that so necessary, so usefull and concerning a thing should be omitted in the Assemblies Catechism[153] (where so many abstruser things and criticisms are taken in,) I confess I always even to this day greatly lamented. though in other particulars and respects the Church Catechism might and ought to be amended; and is not comparable to that of the Assemblies. This catechising of mine much

[150] Herbert Palmer, *An Endeavour of Making the Principles of Christian Religion . . . Plain and Easie* (Cambridge, 1640, and many later editions).

[151] Thomas Doolittle (1630/1633?–1707), clergyman and ejected minister. Rastrick is presumably referring to *A Treatise Concerning the Lords Supper* (London, 1667, and many later editions).

[152] The catechism in *The Book of Common Prayer*.

[153] Again, Rastrick does not specify the larger or shorter catechism.

took with the People and was much remembered and talked on by all Sorts, even many years after I left the place: But what Success it had, or what considerable good it did I did not see or observe. One thing I will mention, my asking the youth what the Soul was put all the Town into Self inquiring reflections, and there was a great talk and noyse upon that Subject, and many strange ignorant /fo. 37v/ and odd opinions about the Soul came upon that occasion to be uttered: So I gave them a fuller account thereof in a Sermon or two which I preached to them from Genesis 2.7. (after abridged in my first Doctr on Matthew 16.26) upon which the people were quiet and well satisfyed; and those Sermons seemed to have a more visible effect than most that I ever preached in my life.

3. I gave a dozen of Bread every Lords day for some years to as many of the Poor (who commonly were the most ignorant) as would come to the Church; that so I might do good to their Bodys and Souls at once.

4. I bought one half Score of Mr Baxter's Calls to the Unconverted at one time, and another half Score at another time, and gave them amongst such of the Poor as I thought most needed them and could read them.

5. In Visiting the Sick I was always (the Lord knows) too backward; being of a too Melancholized reserved temper, and loath to be disturbed from my Study; especially when I had far to go, and I could not do it under half a days time. Yet I seldom failed when I was sent for yea and most curiously I went whether I was sent for or no when I understood (by the Bills they sent to be prayed for) that they were sick: for I could not be easie till I had been with them. In this work I found some would talk all, that I could scarce get in a word; some would say nothing at all, that I could not understand their Case, and how to apply my Self thereto; which made it hard for me that needed so much attraction and pumping before I could be any whit enlarged in spirituall discourse. Most (I found) were stupid and insensible of their Souls case and concerns; and some would tell me, They knew not how to live better than they had done if they were to live again, that needed I thought to reform their Course.

6. But that great Work to which I was the most averse of all was that of Private Personal Instruction from house to house. In the latter end of the year 1675 I made an Attempt in that kind, as near as I could according to Mr Baxter's Directions at the latter end of his Reformed Pastor.[154] As I remember I chose Friday in the Afternoon weekly, and took /fo. 38r/ three or four Familys (or as many as I could) in a Day. Some refused to admit me, and those that I got some

[154] Baxter, *Gildas Salvianus*.

Neighbour or other to send for to their houses, not letting them know that I was there, and so I got an Opportunity to speak to them. But little good could I percieve done by this: some I thought were rather worse. Only I got the knowledg of and acquaintance with one honest pious poor Fisherman whom I knew not of before to have been so good, and he heartily recieved, heard, and welcomed me. But this work went so hardly on that (with[155] grief I relate it,) I did not hold out in it. It was only that part of the Town called Skeldike (which lies next the Sea, where I begun) that I got through, when I purposed and hoped to have gone through the Town from Sea to Fen. The cause I must needs say was in my Self. a sinfull Bashfulness and Melancholy Reservedness; before mentioned;) straitned and sparing in Discourse of spiritual things, especially to such as I thought were Strangers to them, that yet most needed it: So that every thing of that kind came guglingly[156] from me like liquor out of a narrow mouthed Bottle. One time I had a fair oppertunity in Skeldike, viz. a Churching, or some such like Occasion where several of the Neighbours were met together yet then though my heart mused within me I did not speak with my tongue. And I have often in Company sat thinking what to say till I said Nothing. Such was this slow Temper of mine that I never was good at a Repartee, nor a sudden Unstudyed Answer. I could do nothing till I was well entred. And therefore when I was to preach at any time in a strange place I had rather read prayers my Self than that another should do it because this opned my mouth and begat in me that parrhesia[157] that I wanted, and look of the Amusement of the Congregation that commonly look most at Strangers. So when I had any such instructing work to do, as Visiting the Sick, and this last mentioned, I had rather if it lay within my reach to perform it on a Lords Day in the Evening when I was warm and enlarged with preaching, than in the Week day when my Spirit was cooled. So with an aking heart and Unwilling mind did I oft go about this work untill the stated performance of it was left off. which I beseech the Lord of Mercy to forgive.

But I bless God I was yet so faithfull to their Souls and to my trust that commonly when I had heard any of my parish /fo. 38v/ my Neighbours and acquaintance especially had done anything amiss I spoke to them after the best manner that I could and reproved and admonished them. Though often (from my fore mentioned temper, or rather distemper) my private discourses were either not taken notice

[155] The letters of *to* have been changed to *with*, followed by *my* cancelled.

[156] *guggle*: to make a sound like that made by liquid pouring from a small-necked bottle. *OED*.

[157] *parrhesia*: frankness or freedom of speech. *OED*.

of at all, or else they were taken ill; yet I did it as well as I could. And when I did not speak I wrote letters. And had I wrote more it might have been better could I have been sure of a fair and candid acceptance and interpretation: But if to Enemies, there would be need of caution. My writing of this kind has been exposed and laughed at amongst the drunken crew. Otherwise I could have chosen that way for therein I could have freely fluently and as methodically as I could with all cogency and argumentation speak to the case of a particular person, as to severall I did. Most of my Converse was now confined to my Neighbours and acquaintance the yeomanry and farmers of that Town with whom I commonly used to be very plain even to their displeasure; when I saw cause to be so. Much ado I oft had to get them out of the Alehouse and sometimes they would cheat me: viz. pay their Shot, go out, and take their leaves of one another, and as soon as my back was turned they would <go> in again.

But yet my sinfull Straitness as to good and pious Discourse and my neglect of Personal Instruction in a more general and solemn manner as before begun was a great trouble and Grief to me. Glad could I have been of a smaller Parish or Lecturer's Place or the like; though mine was a very desirable Auditory to preach to, if that had been all that was to be done. It made me much of the mind that where it could possibly be there should be more than one Minister in a place, every one not being fit for every thing or gifted for every purpose. Romans 12.6. 1 Corinthians 12.4.–6. So Moses and Aaron, and Aaron was the Mouth. Exodus 4. 14–16. So Paul and Barnabas; and Paul was the chief speaker. Acts 14.12. So Christ sent the Twelve two by two Mark 6.7. that they might with more ease and Success carry on their Ministry and mutually strengthen encourage and Comfort one another. Accordingly I commonly found myself much more enlarged in and unto this duty when I had my dear friend Mr Scoffin[158] with me, at times when the youth came to my house to be instructed, as on Lords Day Evenings they sometimes did. He was a /fo. 39r/ man exceedingly fit for this work being very communicative and delighting in Religious discourse and though but a Teacher of Children he had a heart set upon doing good to Souls in this kind which afterwards (God's Providence concurring) brought him into the Ministry to the great comfort of many, and he served the church and Souls with much Acceptance and Success. When he and I have been together and when Melancholy did not too much depress or straiten my Spirit, I could

[158]William Scoffin (1654/5–1732) became curate of Brothertoft, Lincs. in 1681 but quit in 1686, sixteen months before Rastrick. He became the Presbyterian minister of a church at Sleaford. *ODNB*; and Edmund Calamy, *The Nonconformist's Memorial*, ed. Samuel Palmer, 3 vols (2nd edn, London, 1802), II, p. 165.

be much more enlarged my Self when he had begun and entred me, than I could be at other times, in publick excepted. So I, that could have given any Competent Salary to an Assistant that were fit for this work, if out of my small Living it could have been afforded, did think that I might possibly be able to procure him and that I could not be better fitted. So I discoursed him about it; and would have given him his Board and such further Salary as I was able; and he was to do the Private Work of my Parish, in catechising, visiting and instructing <the people> from house to house. [159]on Condition he might be accepted of the people in that Relation, and for that end. Accordingly therefore when he had done at Mr Shaw's at Wiberton[160] where he had been Teacher to his only Daughter he removed to my house; And I gave the people publick notice in the Church that if any of them had a mind to recieve Instruction for the Souls Good of themselves and their Families, upon Information given or word sent me I would help them to such Private Means as I was able. And I had the better pretence for this because people (Servants &c.) would often say they had rather been Catechised in private than before all the Church: But the Town slighted him, and not one gave me notice of their desire of any such thing. So that buisness fell; and Mr Scoffin was in a little time after better recieved in a more publick Capacity and Station. And I thought my Self more clear after their refusall of this endeavour.

Teaching Work was not all neither that I thought I had to do in the due Discharge of my Ministerial Function. I could not excuse my Self without being sometimes concerned in Acts of Discipline and Goverment and that more particularly as follows.

1. I thought the Church's Way of admitting or entring persons into a State of Adult Church Membership and taking their Baptism upon themselves which is done in con= /fo. 39v/ firmation was not practicable at least regularly; Since a Bishop came so seldome into the Country and when he did come did it in such Confusion and Disorder Confirming so few and those commonly the worst: and that therefore the charge seemed hard upon the Suretys to bring all the Baptized to the Bishop to be Confirmed. I therefore made much use of that Question in the Church Catechism, Dost thou think that thou art bound to believe and do as thy God? and God ? promised for thee? I asked the riper and more intelligent youth that question in a more solemn Manner and told them what it Answered to, and worded it more * directly and positively: And I told the Church that the Suretys

*Marginal note: * explicitly, or emphatically.

[159] *accordingly* cancelled, after *house.*

[160] Probably John Shaw of Wyberton (d. 1686). For the family, see *Lincolnshire Pedigrees*, pp. 868–889.

that thought they could not have <the children of> their charge to the Bishop, should bring them to the Catechism which was Materially the same with Confirmation: And so should the parents in the first place do.

2. I was not satisfied to Baptize all the Children in the Parish promiscuously be the parents <be> what they would. But because it was seldom but the one or other of the Parents Father or Mother was at least Civilized I actually refused to Baptize none but the Bastards, where the case of the Parents* was more plain: and yet not all these neither. My <so> use therefore was this: When <any> such came to me to have their children Baptized I used to reprove them for their Sin to bring them if I could to Repentance; and I told them, if at the time of Baptizing their child they would publickly in the church declare (that) their Repentance, and renew their Baptismal Covenant in terms, and promise Ammendment for the future, I would Baptize the child, otherwise I would not. So some of them were willing to this, and did answer publickly the Questions which I put to them to the forementioned purpose, and their children I Baptized: others would not submit to this, and theirs I refused. It's true I had no power in the Church's Constitution to do this [161] till they had been presented, and so should do Penance: but its likely that they did not know but I had: They having had also one good use there (though contrary to the canons before by time, viz. for the Father to appear with his Child at the Font as well as the Suretys.*[162] So though the Ecclesiastical Court might have looked upon my forementioned practise as an Usurpation of their Authority yet there was no notice taken of it: Though for not Baptizing the children of the impenitent parents I was afterwards presented and troubled; as may be further related in due place. as I was also much blamed for it by the people (and one Non. Con. Minister*[163]) as too rigorous and cruell to make the Children suffer for the Parents faults.

/fo. 40r/ 3. In the matter of the Sacrament of the Lords Supper I was no less concerned than in the former I could not admit all: and in so great a Parish it may well be thought there would be many loose and scandalous persons and that some of them (altogether unfit

*Marginal note: * unfitness by their scandalous Sin to give their children a Title to Baptism was more plain (as it follows.)

*Marginal note: See the 20th Article against Mr Cartwright in Fullers Church History of Britain Book 9. page 200.

*Marginal note: Mr Pues of Suffolk.

[161] Two words cancelled and rendered illegible.

[162] Thomas Fuller, *The Church-History of Britain* (London, 1655).

[163] John Pew, MA of Giselham, Suffolk. *Calamy Revised*, p. 388.

for this Ordinance) would pass to it. I thought I was obliged as the Minister of Christ (and not of the State or the Bishops only) to repell such. I thought that a living after (or according to) the World the Flesh and the Devil renounced in Baptism was to forfeit the Rights Relations and Priviledges that came thereby; and that therefore a Suspension from them ought in that case to be made. This found me some Work. Some that offered themselves would take my advice, when I thought them unfit and dissuaded them from it, and would keep away, and not make much Stirr: But there was (one especially, and he the chief Gentleman in the Parish) that would not be thus ruled. His name was Mr William Hunt. In the year 1678 a little before Easter I sent him a Message by his Brother in Law to forbear comeing to the Sacrament the approaching Season for reasons I then gave him: but he would not take it; but on Saturday Easter Eve he sent for me to the King's Head about it I wrote to him telling him that if he would [164] declare his Repentance for his former ill life and Promise Amendment I would admit him; but this not satisfying I went to him; when I came there he demanded whether I would give him the Sacrament or no? and <having taken>[165] me into the Dining room he clapped the door behind him and said in a dreadfull rage We'll die together in this room but I'll know &c. upon which a neighbour in the house rushed into the room to prevent Mischief, and I urged him to repent and promise to amend: But he refused and said, Must I make a God of you? So I positively denyed him as one utterly unfit in such a Temper for such an Ordinance. But this did not serve; for the next day Easter day he appeared in his place in the Chancell amongst the communicants notwithstanding what I had said to him, expecting it, as I suppose, from me: But when in the Distribution of the Bread and Wine I had missed him, or passed him over, he then in a passion spoke, and asked me the reason of it? which /fo. 40v/ may easily be imagined was no small disturbance to us in so sacred and solemn a Duty. I said nothing to him but only stept to the Table and read that Paragraph of the Rubrick before the Communion Office that forbids the Admission of such to the Lords Table as he was known to be; and so went on to my remaining Work.

This done, I advised with my best Friends the Ministers of mine acquaintance what I should further do. i.e. whether I should give the Bishop notice of it as the Rubrick directs: but they disswaded me from this and told me that would create a certain and troublesome Suit; whereas if he should not present me himself, as it was likely he would not, the thing would die and peace be upheld. So I took

[164] *promise* cancelled.

[165] Replacing *leading*, above the line.

their Advice and informed not against him; and he at that time was silent and gave me no further disturbance by any publick Law procedure.

But the Noyse that this made both in Town and Country was very great. All (except two or three) blamed me for what I had done; and no body would stand by me in it. The Congregation was so far from being offended at such men's communion, or pleased at my endeavour to preserve it pure that they were greatly offended at me for They cryed what had I to do to meddle in that kind? Let every man examine himself and the like. So, some time after this a meeting was appointed by their means to make peace (as it was accounted) between Mr Hunt and I. But the Ignorance and Strangeness in things of this nature among the common people that appeared at that meeting I confess I can neither well express nor forget My buisness was to work Mr Hunt to Repentance or to profess and promise it; upon which I should not refuse him. This he would not be brought to, or not to do it so seriously as to make it credible. I cannot remember that my Neighbours pressed him at all to it: most of their work was with me according to their forementioned Sense they had of my Carriage in it. So however in the close a peace it must be, and I must recieve Mr Hunt again; which I did the next Sacrament, and for two or three years after, without any more disturbance all that time: though he was no better a man than he was before, but rather grew worse and worse

/fo. 41r/ After this <and after all this tryall> I saw cause and thought it my Duty to deny Mr Hunt the Sacrament again a * second, (if n<o>t a third time) but he came and talked there, (after my refusall of him) as he had done before. and afterward did not let it pass as he had done before, but informed against me in the Ecclesiasticall Court at Lincoln, and Procured a Citation, which the Apparatour served on me; and also at the same time, and for the same thing he brought his action against me at Common Law; and sent for a Writ for me; which yet I think was not served. For now my Neighbours procured another Meeting to be <now> at Boston before Mr Morland the Minister there, who needs must have the hearing of this Case, and be intreated

*Marginal note: * at Christmas An. D. 1681
A line below, another marginal note: And my giving the Sacrament at the same time to Mr Richardson a worthy Non. Con. Minister sitting did very much provoke him as appeared by his talk![166]

[166] John Richardson, BA (d. 1687), incumbent of Bottle-Bridge, Hunts. (*c.* 1650); then rector of St Michael's, Stamford; ejected 1662. Richardson later lived at Kirton in Holland and was buried there. See Edmund Calamy (ed.), *An Abridgment of Mr. Baxter's History of his Life and Times. With an account of many others of those worthy ministers who were ejected, after the Restauration of King Charles the Second* (London, 1702), pp. 451–455.

to reconcile us.[167] He came, but said nothing that I can remember to any purpose, and after a while went his way and left us to our Selves. The Management of this debate was much after the old rate, and the Issue much the same; a peace it must be again:* the Town I think was to allow Mr Hunt all the charge he had been at, and he was to stop all proceedings. And so he comes to the Sacrament again, without Repentance in him, or Remedy for me in Cases of this Nature. But none other in Kirkton gave me so much trouble upon this account. Onely Mr Scudamore the Teacher of the Free (Grammar) School in that Town,[168] being by me kept back from the Lords Table (April 16. 1682. Easter.) upon reasons that I thought required and would justified [*sic*] it wrote me three very scurrilous Answers to the Letter I wrote to him that insisted but on his Repentance, or declaration thereof to me only; (as before to Mr Hunt.) But he troubled me not with his presence at the time, or any after prosecution.

4. Another thing that troubled me was the Publishing the Excommunications and Absolutions of the Ecclesiastical Court (especially after I had for some years been Minister there) For those commonly crossed my Judgment. With what temper or dislike I published the excommunication of some Anabaptists in the Town I have almost forgot. But some time after when they were prosecuted by our Officers (Mr Hunt one, and the main) upon the Act of twelve pence a Sunday, and (refusing to /fo. 41v/ pay) had their Goods taken by distress I paid the money for them my Self and redeemed the Goods and sent them then home. I know they had their faults, and that of Unchurching all but themselves not the least but they were pious and honest* Christians; and I (at least afterwards) thought that they should not be excommunicated for their Opinion about Infant Baptism.* So I saw cause to beg pardon of God for my concurring therein.

But afterwards we had some <other> persons in the Town that were presented (for not coming to Church I suppose) and it came to an Excommunication. That I had no Scruple to publish because I knew they deserved it, being loose livers, and next to Heathens without all Religion. But some of the Chief of the Town urged them to get their excommunications taken off at a Visitation approaching; Penitent or Impenitent, that they seemed not much to regard But

*Marginal note: though I bore him no ill will in all I did

*Marginal note: * holding all the essentials of Christianity.

*Marginal note: * And though they came not to the Church they failed not to Worship God in their own Assemblies.

[167] Henry Morland, BD (died in or before 1702), vicar of Boston. CCEd.

[168] Clement Scudamore (d. 1684), schoolmaster of Kirton in Holland Grammar School. CCEd.

I knowing the persons Impenitence and Unconcernedness about it themselves, was not forward to perswade them to get off. However, before Chancellour Howell they came to that End; and, (which I grieved to see, and think off) an Oath is put upon them to Obey their Ordinary, which they must take, and did, before they were Absolved. But then this Absolution was to be published by me, though I knew that they were unfit for it. But (whether on purpose, or upon some necessary occasion I have almost forgot) I went from home that Lords Day it was to be done, and a Neighbour Minister did it in my place.

By this time I begun to be sensible of the Snare and Burthen of Conformity: and saw that there was no abiding in that Publick Capacity and Station with the Discharge of my Duty and Trust, and with Safety to the Truth, and the Peace of my own Mind. This, (as it put me upon many successless Attempts of a Removall to some lesser Parish or Lecturers place, untill my Scruples of the Terms of Conformity rose so high as to check such endeavours; and brought me then to many Semiresolutions of giving up all and quitting my Living; So it) disposed me to go out when the Door afterwards came to be open. But by what Steps my Non-Conformity came on I come now more particularly to relate.

/fo. 42r/

Of my Nonconformity.

I had not much Doubt or Scruple in my mind about the Terms or Matter of Conformity when I first entred upon it. Though I had known other Times and some other men and seen the Bartholomew Change, yet I did not take very much Notice of it being but 12 years old, nor did I understand the reasons of the Difference nor the true Scale of the case when I was more Capable of Considering it. Though I remembred the Difference of Practise, and how men talked when I was a child against the Common Prayer, and for Praying and by the Spirit, &c. and though I thought and hoped that Suplice and Ceremonies would be laid aside before I should come to be a Minister; and could have wished that I might have been excused some Conditions of Entrance <when I did come to it> as Subscription &c. which therefore I have thought since could not be done Ex Animo in the High Church Sense, probably intended: yet, That which mainly satisfyed me was (next to my Education in the University) the example of so many learned Pious Able and Worthy Conformists that I knew or was acquainted with in the country round about me, as, Mr <Robert> Sharp and Mr <Edward> Whiston Ministers <vicars> successively of Heckington my native Town. Mr Roe Rector[169] of Howell. Mr <John> Walker

[169] *Rector* inserted in the margin.

(my Master) at Great Hale.* Mr <Jeremy> Goodknap <Vicar> of Burton. Mr <Richard> Brocklesby <Rector> of Kirkby-Bane, and after of Folkingham. Mr Justice <Rector> of Lesingham. Mr Leigh <Rector> of Silk-Willowby. Mr Lucas Rector of[170] Newton. Mr Randolph <Vicar> of Dunnington. Mr Graves Vicar[171] of Frampton. Mr <Samuel> Whiting <Vicar> of Sutterton. Dr <Obadiah> How,* <Vicar> and and Mr Naylor <Lecturer> both of Boston. Besides Mr Catlyn <Vicar> of Horbling, and the two Mr Males at and near Folkingham &c. whom I less knew but had heard of.[172] Men so eminent, that (as I have heard) it was Observed by the Londoners, there was not such a Knot of Ministers of their character to be found in the like Compass of Ground throughout all England, as in this Part of Lincolnshire south of Witham. Now I should have thought it inexcusable and shameless Pride in me to pretend to be Wiser and Better than such Ministers as these: Nor could I take a way which I could not Defend, or refuse what I could not Disprove; whatever little Misgivings I might have in my mind about it.

But when I was in the Ministry and settled at Kirkton where Buryals of the dead were more common, I was in the (1st) place soon awakened to consider those charitable passages (as they are called) in that Office which suppose a strict Discipline in the Church and the persons buryed

*Marginal note: Vicar of great Hale

*Marginal note:

Mr <Jeremy> Vasin <Rector> of Skirbeck.
Mr Male Rector of Folkingham.
Mr Male Rector of Ormesby
Mr <William> Laughton Rector of Somerby
Mr Cooper Rector of Pickworth
Mr Cheyney Vicar of Kirkton.
Mr Johnson Vicar of Spalding.

[170] *Rector of* inserted in the margin. The capital *R* of *Rector* has been adapted from *of*.

[171] *Vicar* inserted in the margin.

[172] Several of these men have been mentioned already. The others are: Jonathan Catlin, MA (d. 1708), vicar of Horbling, Lincs. (1661–1708): Venn, I, p. 308. William Cooper, MA (died in or before 1676), rector of Pickworth, Lincs.: CCEd. Martin Johnson, BD (d. 1678), vicar of Spalding; Master of Spalding School: Venn, II, p. 479. William Laughton, MA, rector of Somerby, Lincs.: CCEd. Humphrey Lucas, MA (d. 1682), rector of Newton, Folkingham, Lincs. (1662–1682): CCEd; Venn, III, p. 113. Loth Male, MA (died in or before 1662), rector of Folkingham (1625–1662): CCEd; Venn, III, p. 168. Samuel Male, MA, rector of Bigby, Lincs. and instituted rector of Aunsby, Lincs in 1668: *Calamy Revised*, p. 334; CCEd. John Naylor, MA, lecturer of Boston: CCEd. Robert Randolph, MA (d. 1671), vicar of Barnetby le Wold, Lincs. and later vicar of Donington, Lincs.: CCEd; Foster, III, p. 1233. Thomas Roe [Rowe], BD (died in or before 1668), vicar of Granchester, Cambs. (1623–1634); rector of Howell, Lincs. (1634–1668): CCEd. Jeremy Vasyn, MA (d. 1679), usher of Boston School (1628–1633); rector of Skirbeck, Lincs. (until 1679): CCEd; Venn, IV, p. 294. Samuel Whiting, MA (died in or before 1692), vicar of Sutterton, Lincs.: CCEd; Venn, IV, p. 395.

thereby to be of the number of the Faithfull. These passages I had but little encouragement to use often: and therefore I commonly altered some of them, and left out other some: For I durst not wish my Soul in the case or State of the most I buryed, /fo. 42v/ nor contradict my preaching by pronouncing them all saved, or but probably so. Though at the Buryall of such as I had hopes of I altered not a word. I could not percieve that this was taken notice of at first: nor was I ever presented or prosecuted for making this Alteration. Though at length I was bitterly exclaimed against for so doing.

Some little alteration I also made in some other of the Offices: as in Marriage, putting the word Honour for Worship; the latter sounding harshly;* but the former warranted by 1 Peter 2.17 Honour all men. and 3.7. give honour to the wife.

2. As <to> the Common Prayer used in the Ordinary Worship of every Lords Day, I thought it sound for the Matter, but not well ordered for the Form. And therefore I always omitted the Concluding Prayer of St Chrysostom with the Benediction following it, when the second Service was to be read: For I thought it odd to make an end, and seem to dismiss the people with a Blessing, and then presently to begin again! And I commonly left out the Lords Prayer, at least once, being that it was so often read: Which, one Attorney Johnson observing when I supplyed the Ministers place at Spalding, he rose up out of his Seat (as I was told) and said, What Devil have we got here.[173] But one thing I will Observe, that I must blame my Self for viz. that through the very much Use of the same Words, I could not fix my Mind or thoughts to go along with them: So that, though I read them as deliberately and seriously as I could, so as that some were almost brought to be in love with them thereby, yet I could seldome think of what I said: which made me disrelish that kind of Service that did not suit my temper; Though I believed it might be fittest for some.

If now it be asked how all this could suit the Engagements I had laid my Self under to a strict Conformity? I only say that as to the Point of Cannonical Obedience I did at first think, as I was taught, that I was the Judg of the licita and honesta:[174] But as to the Ex animo Subscription, especially the Assent and Consent Declaration, I must confess I did begin to chew upon that, upon the mentioned occasions.

*Marginal note: * & disliked by many

[173]Probably Maurice Johnson (1661–1747), who was admitted to Clement's Inn in 1684 and Inner Temple in 1700. Johnson was a barrister in Spalding and the father of Maurice Johnson (1688–1755), barrister of Inner Temple and founder of the Spalding Gentleman's Society in 1710. *ODNB*.

[174]*the licita and honesta*: the oath of canonical obedience to the bishop was not absolute but 'in omnibus licitis et honestis mandatis' (in all lawful and honest commands).

3. About Michaelmas 1678 the Popish Plot broke out I was just recovered out of an Autumnal Fever when the Rumor surprised me having heard before some general flying accounts of the Papists Attempts, and as if they would not slay the Kings Death, and as if things tended to a speedy Revolution which made me more inquisitive about it. And from thenceforth the talk of News when /fo. 43r/ friends met together kept out Discourse of almost everything else. Many were under sad Apprehensions: though the best and wisest had the best Courage My Melancholy made me suspect and fear the worst; and I was very much concerned how to escape the Ruine that I (and wiser men than I) thought impending. And now was there such a Fermentation and Division in the Land as I had never known in my time Whig and Tory came to be the distinguishing names I was reckoned amongst the Whigs. King Charles dissolving Several Parliaments Ordered a Declaration of his Reasons for so doing to be read in all churches. For this the Nation Addressed him with their Thanks &c. Our Holland Address had a petition in it to have the Laws put in Execution against Dissenters. Many of my ductile unthinking people signed it; even the chief of my Parish. I was exceedingly grieved at this, and reproved them publickly for it: (in my Sermon on Isaiah 55. ult.) I told them, For men to Address Authority for the Putting Laws in Execution for the Banishment Murder and Ruine of so many 1000 persons in the Land so much better than the Drunken profligate [175] Addressers, is a wickedness not to be paralleled with any Ordinary Crime! How heinous a thing to call that a Bulwark of the Church &c. For this was one of the Expressions in the Address.) This the Lord gave me Boldness to speak, and when I had said it, he yet preserved me.——Thus Providence let me see whether High Conformity tended; and drew me to love and chuse the better Side. But after this <also> so many Cramping State Papers were Ordered to be read in the Church that we must seem to comply with, that I was more inclined to be out of my Publick Station upon that account. And this was another Step.

4. In the year 1679 Mr Baxters Non=Conformists Plea for Peace[176] came out with some other of his Books of Church Controversies soon after,[177] which as soon as I heard of I procured and read.[178] And Anno Domini 1681 came out his Treatise of Episcopacy[179] which I also read. These Books gave me a fuller Account and a clearer Notion of the

[175] Illegible word cancelled.

[176] Richard Baxter, *The Nonconformists Plea for Peace* (London, 1679).

[177] *soon after* inserted in the margin.

[178] For Baxter's works in these years, see A.G. Matthews, *The Works of Richard Baxter: an annotated list* (Oxted, 1932).

[179] Richard Baxter, *A Treatise of Episcopacy* (London, 1681).

Case of Conformity and Non Conformity than ever I had before; and I did not think that the Case had been such as I hereby percieved it was. I was satisfied the meer Dissenters had a great deal of Reason on their side. I knew no true Answer given to the forementioned Books of Mr Baxter's: Maurice I read, but <that gave me no Satisfaction at all> it rather confirmed me in the Notion and Opinion that the former had given /fo. 43v/ me.[*][180] Its true, I was not at first fully and absolutely resolved in the Case, at least what one should do that had Conformed in ignorance; but from hence-forwards, I was much more in doubt about it than I had been before. And particularly, whereas I had but slight thoughts of his Opinion about Church Discipline, when (at the University I first read his Reformed Pastor,[181] I had other thoughts of the Necessity and Usefulness of it now; and saw that though we had reformed Religion; and <in part our> Worship;[182] the form of Church Government had never been reformed at all, though so needful to be done.

5. Another thing that Conduced to and furthered my going out was the many dissapointments I met with in my Endeavours of a Removall which I attempted for these following Reasons. (1.) The W<e>ight and Difficulty of my work made me long for a better Parish that might possibly have a more Governable People or for a Lecturers Place where Preaching might be all my Work, in which (if I was good for any thing) my chief Talent lay. (2.) The Air and Country was judged not to suit my health being low levell Fenny and near the Sea. Mr King the Non Conformist of Lesingham asked me when I lived at Wiberton why I chose to live in such a Country, bad (he said) for any Constitution, and therefore for mine: and he bore this so much in mind that I after recieved a Letter from him of September 12. 1673 with the Offer of Ashby from his Namesake Colonell King[183] but being then engaged with Kirkton, (which, upon the account given him of the place and people he advised me rather to chuse;) I thankfully declined the Colonell's offer, and came hither. But (though the Heavens were as fair and Beautiful there as elsewhere, and we had a more constant Sun, yet) I could never like the Country, and seldome escaped an Autumnal Fever. And in my long Illness and Stoppage in my head in the Spring

*Marginal note: * viz. that the ancient Bishops sat with their Presbyters in their governing Acts &c.

[180] Henry Maurice, *A Vindication of the Primitive Church, and Diocesan Episcopacy* (London, 1682).

[181] Baxter, *Gildas Salvianus*.

[182] *in part* cancelled.

[183] Colonel Edward King (d. 1680) of Ashby-de-la-Launde, Lincs. had been a key figure in Lincolnshire politics in the 1640s and had been appointed by the earl of Manchester as governor of Holland and Boston. See A.A. Garner, *Colonel Edward King* (Grimsby, 1970).

1675 my greatest Relief was Rideing abroad into the High Country where I usually was well but sensibly Ill again upon my Return into Holland: besides, my Melanchollу Temper for which nothing was worse. (3.) My Living was small and my charge Encreased; which some thought was the best and chiefest Reason of all. (Though I thought I could have been glad of a small Living in the High Country in a smaller Parish.) When therefore several Chief Members of the Company of Mercers London were down at Boston (May Day 1677) about the Concerns of the Parsonage of Kirkton which is in their disposal; Mr Godfrey (Brother to Sir Edmundbury who was murdered by the Papists.) and Mr Lapp[184] were at my Church at Kirkton on Lords day April. 29 and came to my house, and taking notice of my last mentioned circum= /fo. 44r/ stances they resolved and Promised to remove me when any Competent Preferment fell in their Disposal. Accordingly the next of theirs that became Vacant to my knowledg was the Lecture at Huntington (This was in August 1679) But this was so small except 20^{li} per annum were taken from the Poor's part that I was perswaded by some of them (when at London) to decline it. The next that fell in their <disposall>[185] was the Lecture at Grantham of the Lady Campden's Gift endowed with 80^{li} per anum (Fellow to another of hers at Wakefield in Yorkshire.)[186] This was a very desireable place; and so great were the endeavours used and partly made for another, that my Friends gave me little encouragement to hope for it. However, The town of Grantham was unanimously for me, and petitioned the Company of Mercers upon my account; and my Old Friends Mr Godfrey, Mr Oliver Wallis[187] &c. were my friends still, and laboured for me to the utmost. In the mean time I was as much in doubt about the conditions of entrance there, (viz the declaration of Assent and Consent &c.) as I was about proceeding in the Practise of Conformity, (and chiefly <in> Promiscuous Admission to Sacraments) where I was. In this Case, (before I designed for London) I betook my Self to

[184]Presumably the same Walter Lapp who in 1681–1682, as a member of the Mercers' Company, served as surveyor-accountant of St Paul's School. He was preceded by Oliver Wallis (see below, n. 187) and succeeded by Michael Godfrey. The surveyor-accountants of St Paul's School were drawn by Statute from the Mercers' Company. See Gardiner, *Admission Registers of St Paul's School*, p. 394.

[185]Replacing *Gift*, above the line.

[186]Lady Elizabeth Camden, the widow of Baptist Hicks, 1st Viscount Camden (d. 1629). By her will of 1642, Lady Camden bequeathed £3,100 to the Mercers' Company to maintain two livings in Yorkshire, Lincolnshire, or the Bishopric of Durham. The legacy was received in 1651 and livings bought at Wakefield and Grantham. See Gordon Huelin, *Think and Thank God: the Mercers' Company and its contribution to the Church and religious life since the Reformation* (Leeds, [1994]), p. 57; *ODNB*.

[187]Oliver Wallis (d. 1699) was surveyor-accountant of St Paul's School, 1680–1681. Gardiner, *Admission Registers of St Paul's School*, p. 394; Woodhead, *Rulers of London*, p. 170.

God for direction and Resolution, in the most serious Manner I could; and set two, or three days apart for Fasting and earnest Prayer about it; Begging of God if it might be Well and according to his Will, that he would further and prosper it; but if otherwise that he would signally cross it. And so I preparerd for my journey. But when I set out, I found my horse was so lame that I could scarce get a mile to an end. I went to the next Smith, who drew out a Nail which the blood followed; For the man had pricked him that shod him for this Journey: And where to procure another Horse in so short a time I did not know; nor did I seek to do it, but went to a Neighbour house to write to London, and send what was to be sent by Post, and so returned home: where it was wondered at that I should be so cheerfull under so great a disappointment. But I took it as God's decision of the Case in Answer to my prayer. The next News I heard was that I lost it but by two Votes; he that got it had 75, and I had 73. and that if I had been there I had certeinly carryed it. (This was February 13. Anno Domini 1681/2.)[188] So /fo. 44v/ great a respect had the Company to the Granthamers Petition; and so carefull were they not to impose Ministers upon the people that they were concerned to provide for, against their own Consent. Which must be said to their praise. But very angry were the people of Grantham at me for my neglect in this buisness: Though as to my Self I had the greater Peace and Satisfaction by having taken the Course that I had done: And the more when I understood that Lecturers (more than Ministers of Parishes) are bound by the Act of Uniformity to a Monthly Declaration of their Approbation of the Common Prayer &c. which hint was first given me by my worthy Reverend Friend Mr Joseph Farrow Curate at Boston and afterwards Chaplain to Sir William Ellys. which post he took because he could not Conform himself.[189]

Just whilest this Buisness at Grantham was in Agitation, Another thing fell out that Issued as strangely as it: I was desired to preach at Wigtoft (about two miles south West of Kirkton) one Lords Day in the afternoon in their want of a Minister. After Sermon some of the chief of the Inhabitants came to me to desire my Assistance and Advice to help them to a Good Minister. I recommended two

[188] John Arthur, curate of St Christopher-le-Stocks, London, won the election, beating Rastrick and a third candidate, John Oswald, curate of St Vedast, Foster Lane, London. Arthur and Oswald presented their petitions in person, while Rastrick's was read in his absence, 'his abilitys [being] well knowne to the Company'. The election was made first by show of hands and then by poll. See Mercers' Company, London, Acts of Court, 13 February 1681/2.

[189] Joseph Farrow, MA (d. 1692), licensed as curate of Boston (1680); chaplain to Sir William Ellis of Nocton, Lincs. (1683–1692). Venn, II, p. 124; CCEd. Sir William Ellis (1641×7–1732), was a Jacobite politician but also a committed Protestant. *ODNB*.

to them, to one of whom they applyed themselves, but he was too young for Orders. Soon after one or two of them came to my house at Kirkton, and (whereas I thought it was for further direction and Advice) it was to desire me to be their Minister my Self, telling me that the Town were unanimously for it, except one man that had a kinsman of his own in his ey. I positively denyed them: and well I might being then engaged in the buisness of Grantham. Nevertheless they would proceed and make means to the Bishop (the patron of it) to have me in, whether I would or no. So though the other Party designed a Journey to Bugden[190] for his Friend, yet they who went for me were before them, and got to Stilton and there Baited.[191] While they were refreshing themselves and their horses at Stilton, the other party went by and went through without Stop to Bugden. When my Friends came there, they percieved that if they had not made that short Stay at Stilton, they had done their buisness and prevailed for me. So narrowly was this missed! Its true, I knew nothing of all this till afterward, and should hardly have /fo. 45r/ gone; (though they offered to make a considerable Augmentation of the Living and to do for me what I should desire.) But, lest I should not be satisfied with the Issue of Grantham, This like Gideons Fleece[192] might seem a double Assurance and Signal of the mind of God about these matters.

And it was but about 9 or 10 months before all this (viz April 1681.) that the Inhabitants of Burton Pedwarin (Mr Goodknap their Minister my much valued Friend being dead) were earnestly desirous to have me to succeed him: But they could not obtein the Favour of the Patron, their Landlord, Sir Thomas Orby;[193] though sought with the Towns earnest Petition, and the Tears of him that went with me to London about it. I kept a Day or Two of Fasting and Prayer before this Journey upon this buisness also, that so, which way so ever it went I might be sure it was after God's mind; and that I might be the better satisfied, and I was so.

Upon all these Providences and Events (Though its possible God might have other reasons and ends in them than I knew of) yet I was more and more perswaded that the Cause of Conformity was not of God; And that it was his Gracious Design in these Crosses to prevent my Renewall of my Guilt.

[190] *Bugden*: Buckden, Huntingdonshire. Although he took some time to leave Oxford, Buckden Palace became the favoured residence of Bishop Barlow of Lincoln.

[191] *bait*: (of travellers) to stop at an inn, originally to feed the horses, but also to rest and refresh themselves. *OED*.

[192] For the story of Gideon's Fleece, see Judges 6:36–40.

[193] Sir Thomas Orby (d. 1692), gentleman usher to Henrietta Maria while in exile in Paris; created baronet by Charles II in exile in 1658.

And therefore when the November* following (viz 1682) Good Madam Savile[194] offered me the Presentation to her own Town Newton Living, a pleasant little place, a Competent Maintainance, and near my Learned and Dear Friend Mr Brocklesby yet I voluntarily and deliberately refused it, meerly because I could not be free to do that again which I had once done before, and now saw so much cause to question the Lawfulness of doing.

6. Another Prologue to my Non-Conformity was the Concern I had with the Courts Ecclesiastical; And the Debates I had with the Court or Church Officers and Governours as Chancellour Archdeacon and Bishop.[195] I found they were far from concurring with me in what I thought reasonable and just, or standing by me in the Discharge of my Duty; They being always more zealous for the Observation of their own Rites and for Obedience to their own Laws than God's: Conniving at the Breaches of the latter, but punishing beyond all Measure the breaches of the former though never so small. So far from Encouraging /fo. 45v/ any Moderation and Temper, (whatever they say to invite men into the church,) that it begat in me no good Opinion of the Constitution. To give some instances.

August 28. 1682 there being a Funeral Sermon to be preached, the Apparatour Egregiously disturbed us openly in the Church. For, while I was reading the Lesson for that Occasion, he came up to the Reading Seat, boisterously and insultingly with Whip in hand, and spoke to me, and asked "Why don't you wear the Surplice according to the Canonical Orders?" I said nothing to him; but went on, and he took a Seat in the Church with Mr Hunt who followed him, and <who> (with the Inn Keeper at the Kings Head, (as was supposed) prompted him. But in Prayer time before the Sermon he made such a noyse and Stirr to the Clark to bring the Surplice out, that when Prayer was done I spoke to the people to put that drunken fellow out of the Church: They attempted it, but he would not move; So he sat

*Marginal note, perhaps intended to be inserted as the subsequent paragraph: So February 25. 1683 I received a letter from a Principal Member of the Company of Mercers with the Offer of Reepham Living near Lincoln but refused it. And this I add that no man may say that I turned Non Conformist for Bread; or because I could get no preferment in the Church of England. Few Meetings would afford me the Maintainance which I had in my Living.

[194]Madam Savile (m. William Savile) was of the Lincolnshire cadet branch of the Savile family.

[195]William Howell (1631/2–1683), historian and civil lawyer; chancellor of Lincoln cathedral (1678–1683): *ODNB*. John Cawley, DD (d. 1709), son of William Cawley, regicide, archdeacon of Lincoln (1667–1709); deprived 1687 and restored: CCED. Thomas Barlow (1608/9–1691), bishop of Lincoln: *ODNB*.

him down and slept* out the Sermon: and I went on and buryed the Corps without the Surplice. This disorderly Action we signified to the Chancellour Dr Howell (one of the best and learnedest of them; who wrote the History of the World in 3 folios:[196] and whom I had several times seen with Mr Brocklesby.) and we moved that the Apparatour might be put out of his place: And at the Visitation following I spoke with him about it: But (after all) the Apparatour was continued in his place; and Chancellour Howell fell hard upon me and reproved me for not wearing the Surplice at Funerals, &c. (which its true I did not think decent in so publick a church yard, almost surrounded with the Crossing of two great Roads.) But I asked him if I should wear it when it rained? He said, No; but; (asked) "Did it Rain?" I answered, I was not bound to accuse my Self in answering that Question but I told him that there might be Causes* that would justify or Excuse the not wearing the Surplice at some times as much as a Shower of Rain at least: to which I remember no reply that he made.

But the Surplice was a small matter in Comparison with some Others. April 30 1684. Mr Hunt (aforesaid) appeared against me* at the Visitation at Boston publickly in the church before the Arch-Deacon (Cawley) Accusing me for not Baptizing /fo. 46r/ two or three Bastard Children; and for giving the Sacrament to Mr Richardson sitting. (a worthy Non Conformist Minister in my Parish who scrupled that Gesture <of kneeling>) and the like matters. So in the Afternoon I appeared before the Arch Deacon at his Inn: and found that I had been accused about my Method and Order of reading the Common Prayer; and when I gave him my reason (according to the purport of what is before=mentioned) he said, "That was a Presbyterian Principle. But when my refusing to Baptize the bastard children was discoursed on, I thought to have justifyed my Self by the [197] exception in the 68 Cannon, which I thought had extended to Christening, (as well as Burying;) and that no child of a person or persons excommunicated, or deserving

*Marginal note: * Save that once he awakned and said, He thought I would never have done Babling.

*Marginal note: Now if I could not be quiet in the Exercise of my Ministry without such rude and violent Assaults as these it was very hard.

*Marginal note: So did Sir John Oldfield of Spalding against Mr Talents Vicar of Moulton (Brother to the worthy Non Conformist Talents at Shrowsbury) for some such like matters.[198]

[196] William Howell, *An Institution of General History*, 4 pts in 3 vols (London, 1661–1685).

[197] Illegible word cancelled.

[198] Sir John Oldfield (d. *c.*1706). Francis Tallents (1619–1708), clergyman and ejected minister: *ODNB*. Philip Tallents, MA, minister of Lilford-cum-Wigsthorpe, Northants. (1654–1662); ejected and subsequently conformed as vicar of Moulton (1678–1705): CCEd; Venn, IV, p. 198.

to be so, (by impenitency after some previous and notorious crime committed,) ought to be Baptized: and that the fault was in the Court by neglecting to bring their Mothers to Pennance. But the Cannon was brought, and otherwise expounded by the Archdeacon, who affirmed, that I had no power thereby to refuse or delay to Christen any child whatsoever (or of what Parents so ever) brought to the Church to be christned. [199] And indeed it is plain (though I understood it not till <then>[200]) that the exception is to the person deceased only (as to Buryal) and not concerning the child brought to be Christned. But when I told him my own Opinion about it notwithstanding; and that it was reasonable and scriptural to proceed upon the grounds I went on; and urged the ill and abused Consequences of a General and Promiscuous Admission, He said, That was a presbyterian principle too. And that was all I got of Him: Save only some few hints as if it was intended to proceed against me for these things: But I heard no more from them at this time.

August 9. Anno Domini 1686. The ArchBishop's Visitation was held at Boston by the then Bishop of Peterborough (White) and Sir Thomas Exton.[201] The Country ringing of his Violent Carriage in the southern part of the Diocese, (Buckingham and Bedford Shires;) and I hearing what kind of men of the Clergy the Bishop fell upon with the greatest Fury, I went to the Visitation at Grantham (the next before ours) to observe his Proceedings that I might be the better prepared what to say and do in Answere thereto at Boston, and not be surprized. There I understood /fo. 46v/ that the Bishop intended to make a Tour by Kirkton to see its fair and Cathedral=like Church as other Bishops had done before him; and I must be there in my Gown to wait upon the Bishop; Who, now he stood affected to me, I partly guess by the discourse one told me was had of me at dinner at the Visitation at Grantham. So on Saturday August 7 in the afternoon the Bishop comes, lights out of his Coach and (I meeting him at the Church Stile he) passed by me without taking any notice of me by Word or Gesture, and into the Church he goes and I after him: But when he came into the Chancel he found that that made him open his Mouth; for things were not ordered there according to the High Church Mode as it may be expected. The Company of Mercers haveing been altered, (as the rest of the Corporations in England were) some of their new members sent down orders to have the Communion Table set Altar Wise and

[199] Illegible word cancelled in margin.

[200] *then* has been written above *now*, which has not been cancelled.

[201] Thomas White (1628–1698), bishop of Peterborough and nonjuror: *ODNB*. Sir Thomas Exton (bap. 1631–d. 1688), lawyer and politician: *ODNB*.

railed in:* But those who concerned themselves about it not knowing how to do it, (for I, glad of their mistake, willingly let them go on in their ignorance,) they had set the old long Table endways as it had stood before and Seats about it for the people, and one long Rail that just at the top of the Steps crossed the Chancell from Side to Side and Spikes upon the Rail. Here was work enough for the Bishop. He asked what did the Spikes do there? and ordered them to be taken out by Munday morning. Then he asked <me,> What were those Seats for? I told him for the People to sit on Why, (said he) Do you sit at the Sacrament? I answered Yes, when the Psalm was singing. Psalm! (said he) what have you to do with a Psalm at the Sacrament? So then I told him plainly, My Lord, at Communion times we have the Communion Table brought down into the Body of the Chancel and go not within that Rail at all. I? (said the Bishop,) By what Rule or Order do you do that? I told him By the Rubrick of the Common Prayer that Ordered that the Communion Table should stand in the Body of the Church or Chancell where Morning and Evening Prayer are wont to be said. To this Sir Thomas Exton replyed, That is, but, except it be otherwise appointed by the Ordinary. Said I, Sir Thomas There is no such Exception. So then they called to see the Surplice suspecting (as I con /fo. 47r/ cieved) whether we had one: I was glad of this for the Common Prayer Book lying in the same Chest I was resolved to let them see the Rubrick. So the chest being Opened I took up the Book (which lay upon the Surplice) and turned to the Rubrick and read it, [202] and said to them, You see I need not go into the Chancell at all but may bring the Table down into the church; for Morning and Evening Prayer are never said in the Chancell. To this Sir Thomas replyed That the second Service is to be read in the Chancell but I returned There is no second Service in the Evening Prayer but the Table is to stand where Morning and Evening are wont to be said: To this they replyed nothing. And as to Sir Thomas's fore=mentioned exception which I had let him see was not there to be found, The Bishops Chaplain said The Exception was in another place and he took the Book to turn to it; But after he had turned it over a pretty while and found nothing of it he silently laid it down, and they all turned their Backs and went out of the church immediately and said not one cross word more. But in the Street at Taking Coach

*Marginal note: But what Care was taken at the Reformation to turn the Altars into Tables, and for what Reasons; see Fox's Acts & Monuments Volume 2. page 699, 700.[203]

[202] Illegible word cancelled.

[203] John Foxe, *Acts and Monuments*, 3 vols (London, 1632). Rastrick's page references identify this as the 1632 edition.

the Bishops Carriage was to me very much altered; for, he drunk to me in a glass of Sack: (which our Church Wardens had provided for him.) and he took me by the hand and gave me many familiar Instructions about the Administration of the Sacrament which he would have me to celebrate more frequently &c. But (though I believe I might have come off after this as well as most, yet,) all this did not make me resolve to forbare or suspend what I had prepared to speak at the Visitation approaching, in Case the Bishop should proceed here as he had done at Grantham.

So the Munday following (August 9. 1686.) the Visitation came on And (after Sermon) when the Ministers were called over, the main Question which the Bishop put to Every Minister particularly was this, (as it had been before at Grantham) viz. Have you pre=examined and Catechized Your Church=Wardens upon all the Articles in the Book given them in charge as one Carefull to preserve them from the guilt of Perjury? This came to my Dear and pious Friend Mr Scoffin's turn (Curate of Brother Toft) before it came to mine: and when the Bishop spoke /fo. 47v/ to the Chappell Wardens about him Mr Scoffin turned him about and earnestly intreated them to say nothing for favour or affection but the Truth; To which the Bishop scornfully replyed, Oh! how careful you are to save them from perjury! But Sir Thomas Exton called for his License, and kept it; and so turned him out.[204] When I saw this I had much more Courage and Resolution to deliver my mind to the Bishop when it came to my turn, which I did in Answer to his aforesaid Questions as followeth.

[205]My Lord

"I have not examined the Church=wardens upon your Articles, and do think I cannot in Conscience safely do it. (Here the Bishop begun to say something and to interrupt me, but I begged leave to speak out what I had to say, and obteined it and went on.) "For so tremendous is the Oath they take (in my apprehension according to your Lordship's Interpretation of it and Examination upon it, (an Oath which I durst neither impose nor take for all the World) that I have no mind to have any hand in it. For, (1.) I think I should be accessory (by so doing) to that Guilt of Perjury which I foresee they will certeinly bring upon themselves and cannot be prevented by any such examination or Advice of mine. (2.) Whereas that Oath of theirs in the concurrent Opinion of all men that ever I conversed with used to be interpreted with Latitude, and supposed to be both imposed

[204]Rastrick's account casts new light on Scoffin's resignation. Cf. Edmund Calamy, *The Nonconformist's Memorial*, II, p. 165.

[205]Rastrick indicated that this was a passage of quotation by writing 'cc' all down the left margin, rather than by using a smaller hand.

and taken in a favourable Sense and Construction with allowances, This way of examination upon every punctilio'[206] puts upon it the most strict and rigid Sense that the Words are capable of bearing, and obtrudes it upon them accordingly which makes their perjury more direct and unavoidable: And for ought I know might be forceing them to present such things (or else be perjured) as by the Laws of the Land (Ecclesiastical) may not be presentable. (3.) Whereas in the common Course their ignorance might in some certein /fo. 48r/ (small) measure excuse them, and take off some of the guilt, This will make their Sin to be knowing wilfull and deliberate. (4.) I think they are sworn to present such things by the Articles as in Duty to Christ and fidelity to his Interest and Religion they ought not to present if they did know of them: and I think I cannot examine them upon the Articles in the manner your Lordship would have me, but I must be guilty not onely of approveing, or seeming to approve such Presentations and Proceedings, but even of promoting the Design. As for instance,* if neighbours meet together for Religious Exercises if it be but the Ignorant's going to a more Understanding Neighbour's house on a Lord's Day at night to hear the Ministers Sermons repeated, (When Judg Hales exhorted his children to go to the Minister's house to that end.[207]) if these be but called Conventicles; and the like. My Lord, I like the Informers Trade so ill that I tremble to think these poor men should be sworn to the Office; and I had rather a Millstone were hanged about my neck and I cast into the Sea than that I should have the least hand in such things, or part in such guilt.

When I had gone thus far Sir Thomas Exton urged upon me my Declaration of Assent and Consent to Conformity made at my Entrance upon my Living. To which (directing my Speech to the Bishop) I gave this following Answer

"My Lord. I have observed that the Highest of our Church of England men who Answer the Non Conformists do [208] understand and Expound the Terms of Conformity (Subscription and Declaration &c.) with a Latitude, and assert the necessity of a favourable Construction; and wonder the Dissenters should insist so much upon Trifles and punctilios, like men of very narrow and scrupulous Consciences:

*Marginal note: * So in the more moderate and sincerely pious Sort of Dissenters if they dare not come up to every point of Lay Conformity, Or the Ministers if they do not indulge them notwithstanding.

[206] *punctilio*: a small or trifling point; a nicety of behaviour, ceremony, or honour; a scruple. *OED*.

[207] Sir Mathew Hale (1609–1676), judge and writer. *ODNB*. *Several Tracts Written by Sr Matthew Hale* (London, 1684) includes his 'A letter from Sir Matthew Hale . . . to his children'.

[208] Illegible word cancelled.

And I have ever been told that the practise of the Church must /fo. 48v/ expound her meaning: Lex currit cum praxi, and Lex non curat minima, being Rules in Law:[209] But I have further to my no little Wonder observed that when such as your Lordship come to inquire into the Practise of some of us, you examine it by the letter of Conformity understood and expounded in the most strict and rigid Sense that can be: You urge upon us our Promises and Subscription and you aggrevate the least Omission to the Height: So that we are insnared in this case, first courted in by plausible Constructions and then racked and served* and squeezed at no rate. But now therefore (My Lord) If Conformity be to be understood strictly and rigidly without Latitude in the Sense in which I percieve your Lordship expounds it, I do here declare my unfeigned repentance of it, and beg forgiveness of God and man.[210]

When I had said this I stopped; and Sir Thomas Exton cryed, Admonish him, Admonish him. Said the Bishop Admonish him? He must be deprived, doth he not say, he repents? And I spoke further, My Lord if your Lordship thinks I do mischief in the Church I must Desist: said the Bishop, In the name of God desist then. I thought I must then have had my Living taken from me, and been turned out as my Dear Friend Mr Scoffin had been a little before me: And the Book of Cannons was sent for in order to make use of the Cannon against revolters against me. But Having delivered my Conscience in what I had already said, as soon as another Minister or Town was called I went out of the Church and left them.

That Evening the Bishop sent for our Church Wardens to Mr Morland's Vicar of Boston and examined them upon all their Articles from the beginning to the end and extracted from them these six Articles against me that I was presented and prosecuted upon viz

1. Our Minister doth not read the Litany on Wednesdays and Fridays

2. He doth not Constantly wear the Surplice in all his Administrations.

/fo. 49r/ 3. He doth not usually administer the Communion on Christmas Day unless it fall on a Sunday nor on Whitsunday

4. We believe our Minister doth not read over the Cannons and Articles of the Church twice per annum

*Marginal note, perhaps an alternative way of phrasing this: We are first stroaked and blinded till a Bishop get upon our backs and then whipped and spurred and ridden breathless.

[209] *Lex currit cum praxi*: the law follows common practice. *Lex non curat minima* (usually rendered *de minimis non curat lex*): the law does not concern itself with trifles.

[210] End of 'cc' in left margin, indicating end of passage of quotation.

5. There are two Children unbaptized in the Parish which the Minister refuseth to Baptize

6. He Converses with Mr Richardson an Excommunicate Person.

This done the Bishop had the Church=wardens tell me that he desired to speak with me at his Lodgings the next morning. Accordingly I went; and when the Bishop heard I was there, he sent for me up into his Bed=chamber from amongst all the rest of the Ministers who came to wait upon him, and with whom the Hall began to fill: And there was I with the Bishop all alone for I believe an Hour or more; and he was much more mild and familiar in his discourse than he had been the day before. His Design and Buisness seemed to be to talk over again the matters that had passed the day before and to give me his Instructions. So a great deal of Discourse he had with me about Conformity, the Common Prayer and Ceremonies and the like. He understood (he said) I was a man of tenderness enough; but as to Conformity defective in the External part But (he said) The least defection from the strictest Conformity let in Popery, which (he said) the Non Conformists industriously furthered. That all the Designs and Attempts for a Comprehension were all Popish Designs. He wondered at the Scruples of the Non=Conformists so Answered as they had been Magnified the Public Church Service and Liturgy. As to Closet Prayer (he said) it was but once mentioned in the New Testament. And for Publick Prayer Thomas Cartwright (he said) was the first that brought it up.[211] He said the Litany was the best Body of Petitions perhaps in the world. That the People might be brought to Devotion; which he pretended to assert from his own Experience; mentioning some Church into which he some time went where he saw the people all upon their knees like people going to die. This was the Gesture of kneeling in prayer. And for the /fo. 49v/ Surplice there was no excuse from it. And how might he wear his Rotchet? &c.[212] But he seemed to falter somewhat about the Case of the Unbaptized Bastard Children: and mentioned something of Calvin's Opinion about it; which how he represented I have forgot. I urged that the Bastards Mothers (though prosecuted) had not been brought to penance, and then one might as well Baptize the children of Heathens as theirs &c. So he said, He would take care of that, (viz. that they should do penance.) Then (said I) I shall take care of the other, viz that they be Baptized. (Though by the way I should much more respect their Repentance declared upon my Instance, than upon their Courts: the latter being more forced, the former more free.) But the Women were

[211] Thomas Cartwright (1534/5–1603), theologian and religious controversialist. Public prayer was an important issue in his dispute with John Whitgift. *ODNB*.

[212] *rochet*: a vestment of linen, like a surplice, worn by bishops. *OED*.

poor, and there was nothing to be got by them; so they were never Censured. And no repentance would they shew or publickly declare upon my motion, as others in the same case had done.

In all this discourse (though I said not much, yet) I told the Bishop plainly where I differed from his Lordships Judgment and that I did not think the Common Prayer adapted to all occurring Cases &c. And I retracted nothing of what I had said the Day before. I must confess that I could not but extreamly nauseate the forementioned Discourse of the Bishop. He bad me read Dodwells Letters of Advice about Studies Theological &c.[213] Saying, If faith may be given to any Man I would give it to him. I enquired for the Book but the Bookseller there had it not.

[214]So sometime after this I was cited into the Ecclesiastical Court at Lincoln 25 miles off from my Dwelling: but when I came There, there was no proceedings against me that day, but I was only to retein a Proctor against the next Court. That fell out to be the very day when King James's Declaration for Liberty of Conscience came first down into the Country; so I found when I came there now this second Journey that the Court was very much down in the mouth, and far from the heat and Violence in their proceedings that I expected. To that Article about Conversing with Mr Richardson as excommunicate the Judg said to some of the Court that I might do that for his Conversion. So my Answer to the 6 forementioned Articles being called for, and that it must be in writing, I retired and /fo. 50r/ drew it up in hast, and* delivered it in; and I never heard more from them since about those matters.

Such a Declaration as this from King James was never expected or foreseen as I remember of any that I conversed with: So it was a strange Surprize. But though the meaning and Design of it was pretty well understood; yet all good men rejoiced that by this means Truth and the sober Non Conformists had their Liberty, and that the sanguinary Laws were suspended or laid aside, and the hands of Persecutors tyed. My worthy Reverend Friend Mr Richardson was much taken with it: but just at this juncture, while he was designing a return to his Work, (within a week or a fortnight after he had read the Declaration at large,) by a very dark providence he fell sick and dyed to my no small trouble and loss.

*Marginal note: not haveing any Copy I cannot now account for that Answer.

[213]Henry Dodwell, *Two Letters of Advice: I. for the susception of Holy Orders. II. for studies theological* (Dublin, 1672; 2nd edn, London, 1680).

[214]From this point, Rastrick uses his smallest hand, perhaps as a result of using a finer pen.

Soon after this the Apparator comes about with a Gratulatory Address from the Bishop of Lincoln, for the Clergy to sign to be presented to King James to thank him for his Declaration for Liberty aforesaid. This he brings to me; But because I could not declare my Approbation of the Toleration of Idolatry I refused to sign it (as I never did for one Reason or another sign any of the <many> Addresses of those times.) Though I was not without frequent Thoughts of quitting my publick Station, and making use of the same Declaration as I not long after did.

For now, though I had no reason to expect much more trouble from the Ecclesiastical Courts yet my mind grew very uneasie in the Practise of many things in Conformity which I thought I could not well tell how to avoid. So I resolved to go out. But one time the latter end of this Summer 1687 while my thoughts were fluctuating and deliberating about it; and haveing a new Text to chuse, and not knowing where to fix, I was resolved to dip my finger into the Bible, and Try what I should first light upon, (whether any thing relating to my then Case and Doubt and Duty:) and it proved to be 1 Corinthians 7.18. Is any man called being circumcized? Let him not become uncircumcised: is any called in uncircumcision? Let him not be circumcised I was surprized at it, and I thought there could not be a fitter text in the Scriptures to my case; considering the near resemblance between Conformity and Non Conformity with us, and Circumcision and Uncircumcision in those times.* and I thought it might be read, Is any man Called (i.e. convinced converted or brought to the Knowledg of the Truth &c.) being a Conformist let him <not> become a Non Conformist (or relinquish his Publick Station &c.) Is any called being a Non Conformist let him not Conform. Though as to the first Branch I am satisfied that it was my Duty to r<e>fuse Conformity to such things as I was Convinced were sinfull: Yet it seemed to Justifie their Advice who thought it my Duty to keep in, and do what I could, and omit the rest, till I should (for such Omissions &c.) be cast out by others. This I must confess gave some check to me and demurr;[215] and was one thing that made that when I did go out it was not with the fullest Satisfaction that could be. But yet I thought it was not safe to be Governed and determined by such a Lottery or fortuitous dip (which I had read some able Divines (if I mistake not) declare against) but by Judgment and Conscience Enlightened and guided by the Word of God taken together in its true Coherence and Scope and applyed to

*Marginal note: * Saving this great difference that Circumcision had been of Gods Institution and so might be with more reluctancy parted with &c.

[215] *demur*: hesitation; pause; state of irresolution or doubt. *OED*.

the particulars of my practise. And in Conclusion (to be short) these following things pressed

fo. 50v/**1. I was sufficiently satisfied that what I did at my Entrance to Conformity and taking my Living was sinfully done, and what I thought it not lawfull to do again: and I was taught by the best Divines that *Repentance ought to be made as publick as the Sin; and that therefore it was incumbent upon me to make my Dissent as publick as I had made my Assent to be; and therefore in the same Congregation to declare the one where I had declared the other: But this I could not do without being out by the Law.

2. I was not easie in the Practise of what the Law asked a Conformist to. Though I read the Common Prayer and wore the Surplice as much as most, (the Cross in Baptism indeed I had begun to omit for some time) yet I knew that in the Administration of the Sacraments I ought to make great distinctions. I knew I ought to repel from the Lord's Supper such as yet turbulently pressed thither, as I shewed before. And for Baptism though I had not such frequent occasion with clear reason to reject infants brought thereto, it being seldom but one <or> other of the Parents was at least sober (commonly the woman) yet I knew there was too great Cause to refuse more of them than were offered by such lewd women as were obstinate and impertinent in their Sin. of which latter I have given an account before.

And I promised at my Ordination to exercise the Discipline of Christ as the Lord hath commanded; and though it be added also, <u>as this Realm hath recieved the same</u> yet I was satisfyed, and it was

*Note, running along the very top of the page: What the Reformers thought of sinful Oaths see Sleidan (English.) page 216 bottom, and page 341. line 28.[216]

*Marginal note: Said ArchBishop Cranmer in a Speech of his to the Lords about the necessity of Reformation If any common error had passed upon the World, when that came to be discovered every one was at liberty to shake it off even though they had sworn to maintain that error.

Burnets Abridgment Hist Ref. page 141. top.

A man is bound in Conscience to reverse and disclaim that which he was induced unlawfully to engage himself by Oath to perform.

Bp Hall prop. concerning Oaths and Covenants before his Episc. by div. Right. prop. G.[217]

*Marginal note: * Baxter Reformed Pastor preface page 3 line 21 Hildersham on Psalm 52 Lecture 34 page 171. Doctr.[218]

[216] Johannes Sleidan (1506–1556); John Sleidan, *The General History of the Reformation* (London, 1689).

[217] Gilbert Burnet, *The Abridgment of the History of the Reformation of the Church of England* (London, 1682); Joseph Hall, *Episcopacie by Divine Right* (London, 1640).

[218] Baxter, *Gildas Salvianus*, sig. A3r ('when the sin is publike, the Confession must be publike'); Arthur Hildersham, *CLII Lectures upon Psalme LI at Ashby-Delazouch in Leicestershire* (London, 1635).

plain from hence <1.> that Discipline (i. e. the exercise of it) did belong to my Office, and Order as Presbyter. And 2. <I knew> that where the Commands of Christ and the Practise of the Realm clashed I was bound to proceed according to the commands of God. And 3. nothing was plainer to me than, that if it was my Part and Duty to Baptize and give the Lord's Supper, it was my Part and Duty also to Judg to whom they did belong, and whom to give them to: and by consequence also to Exercise a Judgment of my own about the Suspending of these Rights, i.e. about Excommunication and Absolution. Or else I saw I was not Master of my own Acts in these things: And I thought if I must Answer for my own Acts I ought to be Master of them, and not another that is not to Answer for them for me. But it is well known I could have none of this Power of freedome in my Publick Station. Nor would my people own or stand by me in the forementioned Difficultest part of my Duty. Though I had been in some places where there were fewer and more complying people its probable I had not gone out, especially after I had told my mind plainly to the Bishop (if that would have satisfyed my Conscience as to <my Sin of> Subscription and Assent at Comeing in) if I could have gone on safely and Comfortably in my Work.

But as my Circumstances were, and mind framed (not now to mention the Bishop's charging me in the Name of God to desist from Publick Employment which might be the effect of his passion and bitterness. (and might not be thought to bind me by my Oath of Cannonical Obedience) Nor to mention my taking my Afflictions to be for my Conforming Sins; Or my discerning few Seals of my Ministry, which might be the effects of my own Melancholy) I resolved to withdraw. And therefore having in several serious shewn Reasons, why all ought not promiscuously to be admitted to Sacraments (either Baptism from 2 Corinthians 7.14. Or the Lords Supper from 2 Corinthians 5.7) I did in a discourse about Schism from Romans 16.17. abridg Mr Baxters Plea for Peace,[219] and state the case of Con= and Non Conformity. and retract my Cannonical Subscription Oath and Declaration formerly made, which threw me out November 27. 1687.*

See all my Sermons on these Texts Numb 47 & 27.

/fo. 51r/ This might seem to be a very rash and desperate Action! But it may be considered, that

*Marginal note: Since the writing hereof I find that November 27. was the very day that Mr Richard Capel quit his Pastoral Charge after the same manner i.e. voluntarily without being thrown out. Life page 263.[220]

[219] Baxter, *The Nonconformists Plea for Peace.*

[220] Richard Capel (1586–1656) resigned the rectory of Eastington, Gloucs. on 27 November 1634, being unwilling to read the reissued Book of Sports. See Samuel Clarke, *A Collection of the Lives of Ten Eminent Divines* (London, 1662), p. 263; *ODNB.*

1. It was no new or strange thing.* Many Divines of the Reformers were at first Papists. And many Non Conformists in Charles the 2^{nd}s time had been Conformists before the Warrs.

2. I know I retained not only the same charity but also the same Esteem and Veneration for the Learned sound and Pious Part of the Church of England that I had done before; and therefore I was no Schismatick where I was not uncharitable Accordingly the Christmas after <my going>[221] out, I recieved the Sacrament Publickly at Frampton, at the house of my good Friend Mr Ishmael Burroughs[222] (he allowing me my Gesture; for I did not kneel) hereby explaining what I had done, and declaring that it was not from schismatical Principles, nor <in or by>[223] an avowed and totall Separation that I had departed from the Church of England. Accordingly I after took all the Opportunitys to hear all the able Conformist Ministers that I could in all the places where I lived. Resolving, (as not to lay aside my Office of Preaching when God should call me to it, so) not to depart from the Publick Established Church further than needs must. So I was the same man still that I was when in my living; For then I heard all the Non Conformist Ministers that I could, as now I did <many of> the Conformists; having a high Value Honour and Reverence for all able and worthy men of either way: Though I exceedingly disgusted the Dissenters hereby, as I had done the Church before. So that I often thought and said (as the State of things was in England) that I was neither fit for Church nor Meeting. But who can help it?

3. I thought (for all the Cry against Schism) that what I did was Capable of a Good and Charitable Interpretation, Even amongst Conformists by such as were willing to make it. For in a time when the people every where might and would have private Teachers, it were better they had such as would teach them the Truth than those who would lead them into errour. And perhaps if more able Conformists had stept amongst Dissenters and endeavoured to preserve them from running mad, as but too many of them were too prone to do, it might have been the best Service that in such a time could have been done

*Marginal note: At least (said Bp Bedel) I shall have the better reason and suffer cause to resign to his Majesty the jurisdiction which I am not permitted to manage.
Letter to ArchBishop Usher in the Life of Bishop Bedel page 107.[224]

[221] Replacing *I went*, above the line.

[222] Ishmael Burroughs, BA (1657/58–1734), schoolmaster of Folkingham (1680); curate of Frampton, Lincs. It is not clear when Burroughs left his living, although he was certainly the Presbyterian minister of Wisbech, Cambs. by 1694. He moved to London in 1724 and died in 1734. CCEd; Venn, I, p. 263.

[223] Replacing *only of*, above the line.

[224] William Bedell (bap. 1572–d. 1642). *ODNB*; Gilbert Burnet, *The Life of William Bedell, D.D., Bishop of Kilmore in Ireland* (London, 1685).

the Church. Especially if the publick places they served in were very small.* Not but that I did and do really Dissent from the Church of England as above and in my last Sermon expressed; but yet the strictest conformists that /fo. 51v/ think me to err in this, may believe me to be serviceable in the forementioned respect if the reflection be upon my acting in a separate Capacity. And my conscience beareth me Witness that in my more Private Station in all the places where I have served I have not been spareing both in practise and Preaching to set my Self and express my Self against the Vices and Errours of Dissenters, though it has been so much to my hindrance and disadvantage in outward or worldly respects. And I hope there are not many that will think that a Dissent from the Church of England in the mentioned things is as dangerous an errour as those of too many Dissenters which undermine the Foundation of the Christian Religion.*

4. And as to the event, I add, that it has been a wonder to me that God (I speak it to his praise) should have given me so many years (now 15 years) Liberty of Preaching his Gospell in as great Congregations as that at Kirkton which I left; which is a thing I could not hope for at that time; For I went out before the Act of Tolleration past. But popery would have silenced more than my Self.

From November 27 1687 till the Beggining of February following I never preached in any place publick or private. But I sometimes went to my own Church at Kirkton: but most commonly to Boston, to hear Mr Pell a worthy Non Conformist Minister newly settled there;[225] which I did to my great advantage; having heard him often on his week day Lecture there (Thursday) while I was in publick employment; but now for the time more constantly; with whom, or from whose hands, I sometimes recieved the Sacrament of the Lords Supper. But I dwelt in the Vicaridg house at Kirkton still, untill the week before Lady Day following, when my worthy Successor Mr Reeve of Tattershall (whom the people chose, to whom I resigned, and whom the Company of

*Marginal note: and they but few people of their own to preach.

*Marginal note: I did not resolve to lay aside my work, For I was well assured it was my Duty to preach notwithstanding I could not do it in a publick capacity or Station. Mr Baxter's Apology for the Non Conformists Preaching I could not Answer And though Dr Stillingfleet say upon occasion of the confessed difference betwixt the case of Ministers and people how the former can preach lawfully to a people who commit a fault in hearing them I do not understand (in his Sermon of the Mischief of Separation) I think it is as plain on the contrary way How the people can commit a fault in hearing where it is the Minister's duty to preach I do not understand.[226]

[225] William Pell (bap. 1634–d. 1698), clergyman and ejected minister. *ODNB*.

[226] Richard Baxter, *An Apology for the Nonconformists Ministry* (London, 1681); Edward Stillingfleet, *The Mischief of Separation* (London, 1680).

Mercers, at the people's petition, presented) was ready to come into it, and where he lived but about half a year and dyed.[227] It was put in good repair by the Town for me; and so I left it with an Orchard of my own planting. Dr Tuckworthy's Father formerly vicar of Kirkton had (most probably) lived in it, where the Dr was born;[228] and the next Minister Mr Pues a few years:[229] but after he left it no Minister dwelt in it till I came thither: Mr Pues (for most of his time,) and his Successours having lived in their own, or some hired house nearer the church.

I was indeed once desired to preach a Funeral Sermon for a Neighbour after I was out; which I had prepared to do on Job 12. 14,15 because he had got his Death by riding in the Fen, and taking wet in the time of a very great Flood: But his Widdow thinking that I would not use the charitable passages in the Office of Buryall, expressing the hope of his Salvation, if I did use the main of the Office it Self, changed her mind and got another to do it.

/fo. 52r/

Of the Treatment my labours and Ministry met with in Publick my Troubles from Enemies and God's Deliverances.[230]

Different was the Acceptance my labours met with in publick according as Times, Men, and Things, The Subjects I Preached on, and my Management of them were. To give some instances.

In the beginning of June 1676 I took a Journey to Oxford in the Company of a Neighbour carrying with me (my Neighbor Town) Frampton's Petition to Bp Barlow* (then at the Colledg)[231] against their wicked drunken Minister; who being but a Curate, or haveing no other title but a Court License, they thought the Bishop if he pleased might easily remove. So I delivered the Petition to the Bishop in his Study, and dined with him upon his Invitation; but it came to nothing. But my fellow-travalier going to see a Relation of his one Mr Knibb Schoolmaster at Ayno occasioned our Stay there some

*Marginal note: Here I asked the Bishop's leave to Baptize children in private without bringing them to the church afterwards, and I obteined it.

[227] Daniel Reeve (died in or before 1689), vicar of Kirton in Holland. CCEd.

[228] Anthony Tuckney, DD (1599–1670), whose father (William) was vicar of Kirton in Holland. *ODNB.*

[229] John Pue, MA (d. 1652), vicar of Kirton in Holland (1611–1652). Venn, III, pp. 404–405.

[230] Title set apart and indented.

[231] Thomas Barlow gained the bishopric of Lincoln in 1675 but had still not visited either Lincoln or Buckden by July 1678, *ODNB.*

Nights, and one Lords Day. Mr Knib had a Cure, not farr off;[232] but he would neither invite me to help him, nor admit my going to hear him; but he wrote a letter and sent me to Banbury, to Mr White Minister there at that time, (and afterwards at Kidderminster.[233]) So he invited me to preach for him in the afternoon, which I did in a very good auditory. After Sermon came the Maior several of the Aldermen &c with the Maces, to Mr White's to give me a Treat and thanks for my Sermon. and we talked of Lincolnshire, and especially of Mr Brocklesby, whom most of them knew; (for he had boarded in that town some time before when he drunk Althorp Wells) and my acquaintance with him procured me here the more respect: And greater I had not met with than this Town expressed: and Mr Knib told me afterwards at Kirkton that he had many thanks from them at Banbury for sending me amongst them. Here it was pleasing to <me to> see the Church, Town, and Tomb of old Mr Whateley formerly the famous Minister of this place: as I was also to see and ride through the Country where such famous Worthies as Mr Dod Dr Harris &c. (Whose lives I had read) lived and laboured.[234] And so much for my undeserved entertainment at Banbury.

July 30 following (viz. 1676.) I preached at Boston (the next market town to my dwelling) on Ephesians 2.2. My Subject was, A Saint or a Devil. Which to make out, I brought in so many Storys of Spirits &c. and notions that Dr More's books lately read had filled my head with, as gave great Offence, and were received with laughter and Contempt; and laid the Foundation of that distast that increased against me in that Town to the very last.[235] Its true the point was plain and sharp and I thought would displease; but I rather studyed to profit than to please men. And quod cogitamus loquimur;[236] The Subject made great Impressions on mine own Spirit and I thought might do so on others. But I think since, all things proper for a Discourse or Tabletalk are not proper for a Sermon nor decently to be delivered in such an Auditory.

[232] Presumably the Mr Knibb who had a living at North Aston, Oxon., six miles from Aynho, Northants. CCEd.

[233] Richard White, BD, vicar of Banbury, Oxon.; instituted vicar of Kidderminster, Worcs. (1677). CCEd; Foster, IV, p. 1616.

[234] For the biography of John Dod, see Samuel Clarke, *A Generall Martyrologie* (London, 1651), pp. 404–416; for that of Robert Harris, see W[illiam]. D[urham]., *Life and Death of . . . Robert Harris*.

[235] Henry More (1614–1687), philosopher, poet, and theologian. *ODNB*.

[236] *Quod cogitamus loquimur* was probably lifted from the preface of Baxter, *Reasons of the Christian Religion*, dedicatory epistle, where Baxter translated it as 'That which is most and deepest in our thoughts, is aptest to break forth to others.'

/fo. 52v/ In the beginning of September 1677 my wife being extreamly Melancholy I carryed her to Cambridg in Sturbridg Fair[237] time to divert her. And Baiting at Huntingdon on Saturday our Landlord (Soaper) percieving me to be a Minister and knowing their Town to be unprovided for the next Day I was prevailed with to stay and spend the Sabbath amongst them. For this I was altogether unprovided having no Notes about me: expecting nothing but to be an Auditor at Cambridg where I knew I should not be invited to preach. So I was fain to go to work and recollect what I could of a Subject I had preached not long before and digest it in the best Order I could for the time. My Landlord telling Sir Lionel Walden[238] (whose turn it was, in the Vacancy the Town was then under to provide for that day) of a Stranger that he had procured, and of his Unpreparedness; said Sir Lionel, If he has no Notes I'll not go to Church. My Landlord told him yes, I believe he has for he called for pen, ink and paper into his Chamber &c. So I preached at All hallows in the morning after which Sir Lionel took me and my wife home to dinner. and in the afternoon I preached at St Mary's near the Bridg. After Sermon as I returned to my Inn, Sir Nicholas Pedley[239] took me in, and expressed his kindness and thanks in wine: and after I came to my Inn I found the Maior and many of the Aldermen come to Give me thanks and a Treat there; where I had not sat long but Sir Lionel Walden comes in amongst them and brings me Twenty Shillings for that Days Work. A remarkable Providence I took this to be and what I had reason to be thankfull to God for. I had not been used to such kindness and respect from persons of their rank.

October 17. the same year 1677. I preached the Visitation Sermon at Boston before Dr Howell Chancellour of the Court at Lincoln and Author of the History of the World in 3 folios[240] Which Sermon though serious Plain and Pungent yet was not ill accepted of the Clergy. Dr Howell's approving Glance at, and Reflection on it in his Speech to the Clergy might (it may be) prevent their unkinder Censures. And an undue representation of the Ancients preaching, (as if it were but once on the Lord's Day,) with a Gird or two at the Sectaries, might (with

[237] Stourbridge Fair, Cambridge lasted from the end of August until the end of September. Its charter of 1589 stated that it 'far surpassed the greatest and most celebrated fairs of all England'.

[238] Presumably Lionel Walden (1620–1698), MP for Huntington (1661), and for Huntingdonshire (1685); and not his son Lionel Walden (*c.*1653–1701), MP for Huntingdon (1679, 1681, 1685). See B.D. Henning, *The House of Commons 1660–1690*, 3 vols (London, 1983), III, pp. 649–651. Walden House still stands on George Street in Huntingdon.

[239] Sir Nicholas Pedley (d. 1685) of Huntingdon. Pedley's daughter, Elizabeth, married Edward Stillingfleet (1635–1699), bishop of Worcester. *ODNB*.

[240] Howell, *An Institution of General History*.

many) attone for what else might be more displeasing. The former of which I heard afterwards that the Clergy (such as preached but once a day) laid hold on, and Commended: And I do greatly repent that every [*sic*] I said it; and it always irketh me to think of it: and especially when I find it so different from that account Dr Cave hath given of the same matter. (Primitive Christianity Part 1 Cap. 9 page 278.279.[241]) Though I constantly preached twice each Lords day my Self.

/fo. 53r/ I was as yet well enough satisfied with the Worship and Constitution of the Church of England. My preaching was after a more rowsing awakening manner than I could afterwards reach; though weak and barren in other respects and far from Exactness. I have oft thought since that I had not a Fund or Stock proportionable to such an Expence of Affection and that a bare imitation of Mr Baxter and Mr Brocklesby in that particular might carry me higher than the inward Furniture of my mind and Heart would supply: and possibly it might be too affected and histrionical. I had power enough but charged with small or hail Shot. However it were, my Sermons were as yet (generally speaking) well enough recieved, though they did little good: and I had not that I knew of any Enemies in the church.

But after that I had refused to give the Sacrament of the Lord's Supper to some that I thought unfit: and upon the Fermentation that went through the Land after the Popish Plot broke out 1678 I had some malicious Enemies rose up both at home and abroad that expressed even a Mortal Emnity and Opposition to me; which my plain dealing brought upon me from such as could not bear it

One of my Parishoners and Friends at Kirkton Holm, was Tennant of certein Lands belonging to Magdalen Colledg in Oxford lying at Frampton near us, and the Steward and certein fellows of the Colledg use to come on a yearly progress into these parts, to keep a Court and recieve their Rents; and they lodged and [242] feasted at my Neighbours house; and he used to invite me to dine with them In the year 1679, it fell out that they lodged here on the Lords day October 12. and whereas it was expected that some of them at least would have come to church and made some Conscience of the Publick Worship and Service of God there was not one of them came, neither in the fore noon nor afternoon: and how they spent the day at their Lodging, people were free to talk, and draw infrences therefrom tending to bolster themselves up in their neglect of Religion, and Profanation of the Sabbath, and the like consequences easy to be conjectured. This so troubled me, that the next day instead of going to dine with them

[241] William Cave, *Primitive Christianity: or, the religion of the ancient Christians in the first ages of the Gospel* (London, 1673).

[242] Illegible word cancelled.

I wrote to the Burser with his mate and the rest of them a sharp letter wherein I plainly told them what mischief they might do in the places where they came (and particularly my own) by their examples; and how apt people were to indulge themselves in all looseness and irreligion upon their Observation of the same, especially in such as they &c. This Mr Henry Allein in his Answer stiled Billingsgate raillery — told me they saw under my own hand my impudent uncharitable and phanatical temper — asked me if I did it to try my faculty /fo. 53v/ against there was an Opportunity for Rebellion? adding, "indeed this charge ought to run higher – you deserve this and ten times worse." &c. Thus he. And yet my letter was not so sharp as my Visitation Sermon (though it might be too rough and blunt,) and I told them I meant it but as a serious Memento to them; and that I honoured their persons and Professions notwithstanding. But this was not all: The year after, as I was going to dine with them again, being invited by my neighbour and Friend that enterteined them (Mr Coleby) I met the Steward going to the Court, and saw he had a Countenance full of fury towards me. So when I was got thither; Mr Coleby (whose child I was also that day to Baptize) comes to desire me to withdraw to prevent mischief: for the Steward had declared if it had not been for my Cloth and Order he would have stabbed me; So I withdrew: and soon after the Angry Steward was taken away by Death, and never came into our neighbourhood more. And I remember not that ever I dined with these Oxonians more in any anniversary progress they after made as they constantly do into these parts.[243]

No less bitter were my Enemies at home. In the Winter of the year (1680) One of Stamford a Stranger to me lying in his Travails at the King's Head in Kirkton and hearing the Malicious Speeches of two of mine Enemies against me (of whom I suppose the Innkeeper himself might be one) left word at a Neighbour's to give me notice to have a Care of my Self, for he believed they meant <to do> me a mischief when they saw their Opportunity. It was for what I said in my Fast Sermon on December 22 (before) on Jeremiah 5.9.

And the year after (1681) I was informed that a Knot of mine Enemies being got together at the same Inn, drunk on their knees to my Confusion.

Anno 1682 being at Stamford on a Lord's Day I was called to preach at St George's Church the Minister being sick; which I did on Ephesians 6.12. In Sermon time some went out of the Church;

[243]The Steward of Magdalen College, Oxford from 1673 to 1680 was one Mr Keat(e); the three bursars in 1679 were Dr Edward Yerbury, Mr John Younger, and Mr Annesley. For further information on Yerbury and Younger, see J.R. Bloxam (ed.), *Magdalen College and James II, 1686–1688: a series of documents* (Oxford, 1886).

Others (Gown men) showed their dislike there by their carriage. Next morning all the Discourse at the Coffee-house was against me for my Sermon. Dr Cumberland (after Bishop of Peterborough)[244] defended me amongst all the Company; for which I went to give him thanks at his own house: haveing been acquainted with him some small time before.

One night at Stamford lodging at Mistress Reynolds Sister in law to Mr Richardson my dear and worthy friend. at Prayer time in the Evening there was a great Noyse and disturbance in the next house upon it and these words were heard – Have him before the Maior: Does he come to Conventicle here? And yet there was none but I, and the family I lodged in!

Anno 1683. my house was searched for Arms.

/fo. 54r/ In the Close of the year 1684 Mr Scudamere Teacher of the Free School in Kirkton dyed. In the Vacancy the Heir of Sir Thomas Middlecotes the Founder[245] who was now Mr Ryley of Welborne[246] was to Nominate or Present a Schoolmaster and there was (by the Act of Parliament that settled the School and the Orders of it) Feoffees in trust appointed to Examine and Approve him whom the Gentleman aforesaid should Present Of whom the Vicar of Kirkton for the time being was one. So I thought it my Duty to take the Key of the School, and the Copy of the Orders into my possession until the rest of the Feoffees should meet and order the Disposal of it, or should be called to Approve of a New Schoolmaster to whom it might be delivered. In a little time Mr Ryley aforesaid comes and brings a young man to put him into the School without Concerning or Consulting the Feoffees about it. So they sent for me to the Inn and demanded the Key of the School that they might give the young man possession I told them I could not do it in faithfulness to my trust without the Consent of the rest of the Feoffees or the Majority of them who ought to have been there to examine and approve the person But they would not stay to send for the Feoffees but grew hot and angry and so I left them and went to see a sick neighbour that dwelt hard by thither the Gentleman followed me and in great Passion again demanded the Key; (amongst other angry expressions I remember he said to me, I hate a Presbyterian at my heart.) But I was resolvd not to betray the people nor my Trust, and would not yield it. Whereupon they went (Mr Ryley and a Gentleman companion with him &c.) and they broke

[244]Richard Cumberland (1632–1718), bishop of Peterborough (1691–1718). *ODNB*.

[245]Sir Thomas Middlecott established the Free (Grammar) School at Kirton in Holland in 1624.

[246]Perhaps Robert Riley of Welbourn, Lincs. (d. 1703). For the Rileys of Welbourn, see *Lincolnshire Pedigrees*, p. 823.

open the Door of the Free School with force and Violence and so gave the young man possession. And afterward a writ was served upon me about it, to which I put in Appearance: but it was not prosecuted; For after I saw that neither the rest of the Feoffees, nor the Town would concern themselves in the Case, it let things go as they were; after some time I delivered the Key, and the Copy of the School Orders to the young man they had put in, and so the business fell And afterward it appeared the young man (Mr Gaze of Spalding[247]) came in by Corruption, having bought the School of Mr Ryley for a Summ of Money. But it grieved me to see the carelessness, indifferency and unconcernedness of men in a matter of such Moment as the education of youth is that none would appear against so bold a Violation of Law and Equity in this matter!

/fo. 54v/ April. 2.1685 the Apparator brought me the Clergy's Address to the new King James 2 which I refused to subscribe upon the account of that passage therein where the Subscribers call the Church=Government as then by Law Established the Desire and Comfort of their Souls: which I could not do; for it was the grief of mine.

I refused also to set my hand to the Order for chusing Dr Fuller of Lincoln our Convocation man when it was brought me by a Neighbour Minister.[248] After these things (chiefly my refusing the Address for which it was threatened that the King should particularly know it) I met with such measures as expressed my Enemies Resentments. For

July 11. Anno Domini 1685. Sir John Oldfield of Spalding Deputy Lieftenant sent some Officers and Soldiers to search my house for Arms (As it had been once before in 1683 about the time of the Plot the Lord Russell dyed unjustly for[249]) Who swore if the News of Monmouth's Rent had not come I must have gone prisoner to Hull with the Dissenters. And he had brought a Troop or part of a Troop of the Militia horse to Boston for that purpose.

On July 16. following the Quarter Sessions of the Peace was held at Kirkton. The Justices sent a Constable for me and put upon me the Oaths of Allegiance and Supreamacy which I readily took: and was after Glad of this that the world might see it was not out of Principles of Rebellion that I refused the Address: And that if there should come any further Test which I could not take I might refuse it without such

[247] Edward Gace, BA, appointed schoolmaster of Kirton in Holland, January 1685. CCEd; Venn, II, p. 187.

[248] Samuel Fuller (bap. 1635–d. 1700), chancellor of Lincoln cathedral (1670–1677); dean of Lincoln cathedral (1695–1700).

[249] William Russell (1639–1683) was executed in 1683 after the exposure of the Rye House Plot.

an Imputation: For if a Test for Loyalty and a Test for Religion should be tacked together I might not be suffered to take the one without the other and so the refusal of it might be taken in a wrong Sense which the seasonable and single taking of this I thought might rationally prevent. And as for King Kames he did not like the imposing and taking these two mentioned Oaths which swore the Nation against Popery: yea and on that Supposition against himself.

It was (as I was after informed) moved at this Sessions that I should be bound to the Good behaviour for seven years (which as the Gazett informed us had just at that time been part of Mr Baxters Sentence[250]) but this was stopt.

Mr Hunt having before given out that he hoped in a very short time to sheath his Sword in my hearts blood (his very words) /fo. 55r/ I now took the Opportunity Mr Hunt being also present to inform the Justices of this But they were so far from doing me Justice or so much as giving him a Reprimand for the same that they rather encouraged him; speaking of him before his face as a Person of undoubted Loyalty. &c.

This was at the Kings Head Inn or Tavern the keeper of which Mr Port a Norfolk man and one of my greatest Enemies was dead but a little before viz June 27. His Mortal Emnity to me for seven years past being commonly known. When he dyed many both in Town and Country took great Notice of it with Admiration at the Providence of God in it to me in particular it happening especially at such a Juncture of time! Mr Scudamore the Schoolmaster, and another bitter Enemy of Goodness being also dead but a few months before.

I was about this time informed that Dr Roads (a Justice of Peace for the Country,) and Mr Morland Minister of Boston, and Mr Jackson Lecturer of the same[251] met and advised and wrote a Letter to the Bishop of Lincoln Dr Barlow against me and a Neighbour Minister or two Mr Burroughs, and Mr Scoffin, my dearest Friends representing us as intollerable Fellows and the Disgrace of our Function and the like: And that Mr Jackson carryed it: but I heard nothing of it from the Bishop.

September 7. 1685. The Assizes being held at Lincoln; The Judg (as I was after informed) would have had the Chief Constable of our Wapontake[252] to have presented me for not reading the Common

[250] *London Gazette*, issue 2047 (29 June 1685), p. 2.

[251] Israel Jackson, MA, Lecturer of Boston (1685–1707). CCEd; Venn, II, p. 455.

[252] *wapentake*: a subdivision of certain English shires, corresponding to the 'hundred' of other counties. *OED*.

Prayer: chiding him for not Walking his Circuit to see how the Ministers did their Duties: adding, They say there's one Rastrick that reads not. &c. Charles Coppin a young Attorney at Boston would have had him present me But the Chief Constable Mr Allein though a high Tory denyed the Report about me and would not do so untrue and unjust a thing. This Judg had been at Kirkton with the Oxonians once or twice as Steward of Magdalen Colledg and there its likely heard enough against me from such as Mr Hunt &c. if he had not heard what had passed in 1679 before related.[253]

/fo. 55v/ Times and Things being thus black and Threatning; King Charles being dead, and James 2 (a Professed Papist) succeeding him in the Throne whence Popery was expected to overrun all, &c. It pleased God to draw forth my Spirit (with three or four more of my best Friends) in Earnest Prayer for the Church of Christ for the Nation and for our Selves with much unexpected enlargedness and fervency, and unto much Assurance of God's favour and protection. And we did the year 1685 keep many private days of Fasting and Prayer at each others houses; sometimes at my house (the Vicaridg) sometimes at Mr Rasor's (Mr Richardson's son in law[254]) and sometimes at Mr Scoffins in the Meers for the Churches Deliverance, and our own from the threatening Storms and Dangers: And much Comfortable Communion we had with God and, with one another on those days. Such as I then set down I shall summarily mention Ex. Gr.

March. 13. at Mr Richardson's Chamber. 1684.[255]
March. 23. (1684)[256] at Mr Scoffins.
April 2. (1685.) at my own house (when Apparatour came)
April 3. (1685.) at my house a little longer time.
April. 17. Good Friday. at Mr Rasor's.
May 4. at Mr Scoffin's.

June 2. at my own house. where we particularly remembred Mr Baxter of whom I had heard the day before that he had been tryed and found guilty upon two Inditements for his Paraphrase on the New Testament.

[253]Sir Richard Holloway (bap. 1629–d. 1699), judge. Holloway was Steward of Magdalen College, Oxford in 1681. He was close to Judge Jeffreys and was one of the judges before whom Algernon Sidney was tried. His links with Magdalen were evidently loose, since he appears to have advised James II to proceed in his (unsuccessful) attempt to install Anthony Farmer as the President of Magdalen in 1687. *ODNB*.

[254]Humphrey Rasor married Dorothy Richardson (b. 1655, daughter of John Richardson, rector of St Michael's, Stamford) on 16 October 1681 at her father's church.

[255]1684/5.

[256]1684/5.

June 19. Fast at my own house

November 6. I and my wife alone together upon the same publick account as before.

Soon after (that same Month) the Parliament which we thought would have ruined us, but how wonderfully God overruled it we all have seen.

July 29. (1686) Fast for the Church with three or four but where I have not noted.

The Effect of all this was surprizing, and what few at that time could have expected being Contrary to all mens imaginations. Though my Reverend and Worthy Friend Mr Richardson would after say upon King Charles's Death and James's Succession that he had no dreadfull apprehensions upon him from the change, which he (a very wise man) spoke upon Publick Considerations; Yet who could have expected the Non Conformists Liberty so soon and from such a King? 'Tis true we prayed that they might be restored to the Publick Churches, and more Publick Service there; but how much more for their Ease and Safety at present did God provide than if they had been put to Contend with a profane and malignant age by the Distinctions in their Minstry they would in all likelyhood have made! And the Revolution that soon after followed made by others, and brought about by the Non=resistance men themselves and followed with a Repeal of the sanguinary Laws, and Settlement of the Liberty by Act of Parliament, which all men wondered how it could have been effected: Yea and the Liberty we had hereby for Family Religion which the malignant populacy begun to insult (as may be seen in my own Case mentioned before) All these are such wondrous Mercys as call for the most gratefull Acknowledgments to a prayer=hearing God, and the best Improvement by a saved people.

/fo. 56r/

Of my Remove to Spalding;

King James 2[d] having published his Declaration for Liberty of Conscience April, 4. Anno Domini 1687. All places where there was any competent number of Dissenters from the Church of England or of persons who were not satisfyed with their publick Means and Ministers, and had a Sense of their spiritual Needs were for providing themselves Ministers and Forming themselves into distinct Societys that they might have more agreeable preaching; and might worship God in that manner that their Consciences told them was most agreeable to his Word. Amongst the rest some of the Inhabitants of Spalding in Lincolnshire sought out. But the Anabaptists were beforehand with those I call meer Dissenters, or Non=Conformists (to give them no other Denomination) and by the means and Agency of Thomas Grantham the Head of the Arminian Anabaptists in

Lincolnshire (if not in England)[257] they greatly encreased, and were like to carry all before them: So that the other Dissenters cryed out earnestly for help, or else they said they should <all> be gone over to the Anabaptists. So they first sent, and then came to me at Kirkton, with repeated Desires that I would come and dwell and preach amongst them in that Town. This I considered on, and Mr Pell advised me to it. On the 2[d] of February commonly called Candlemas day I first preached there at the House of a serious ancient Christian John Kirk; (who had been formerly Servant to Dr Chaderton Master of Emanuel College in Cambridg;) And so after, for 3 or 4 times on the week days; till at Lady Day 1688 I removed with my Family to Spalding. Which had it been sooner, it might have been better: for there were such already turned Anabaptists of better estates than <any of> the Dissenters that I was concerned with: one of whom often said, that if I had been there, and our Society been formed half a year sooner he should have joyned with us, and not with the Baptists. But he could never be recovered. Besides that there were others that left us and went over to them after I was settled in the place. And here I could not but Observe the strange Alteration of men and things: For these people who before when I was in Conformity would occasionally hear a Funeral Sermon from me, would now never do so much as that. So that now notwithstanding my hard Circumstances in the Church, and exceptionable Complyances with it, (affording them their Objections) were altered, yet I could do less with them than ever before.

As soon as I had removed to Spalding One of the Principal Members of that Congregation dyed: and the first Sermon that was preached in the place prepared and dressed up for our Meeting was his Funeral Sermon. He was a worthy pious and intelligent person and the loss of him was a great Grief and Affliction to me. The /fo. 56v/ Providence was dark and I knew not how to expound it. I was afraid God was displeased and it cast a great Damp upon my Spirits. and still more alarmed and amazed when God took that famous Old Christian John Kirk before mentioned from us almost a quarter of a year after. (or 4 months at most.) The best interpretation that I could put upon this was that it may be God might preserve those two alive to that time to do that work and settle the Meeting there and after this that they were reserved to do was done He then saw fit to remove them. For I believe had they been dead before, I had never gone to Spalding. But what a loss had I of their Assistance and Society which I both needed and greatly loved. Their loss renewed my Childish grief of parting with my Parents. Even as when my worthy Friend Mr Richardson came first

[257] Thomas Grantham (1633/4–1692), general Baptist minister. *ODNB*.

to Kirkton for a while, and went away again, I could not part with him but my heart was full.

Before the said John Kirk dyed, they desired to have the Lords Supper administered amongst them. I that had not been used to administer Sacraments otherwise than by a Form did not think my Self sufficiently able to do it now without one and therefore I desired and propounded it to them that I might do it by the Reformed Liturgy drawn up by Mr Baxter when he and others were commissioned by Charles the Second to treat about the alteration of the [258] Common Prayer.[259] About or a little before my giving up my Living at Kirkton I and some serious Christians had a Private Sacrament at Mr Scoffin's which was Celebrated by me, by, and according to the mentioned New Form; with which some judicious and devout Partakers were very much affected: And O how passionately did we all wish (though some of us were and had been long Dissenters) that that Reformed Liturgy had been settled by Law, when it was appointed to be drawn up to that end! But this would not down with our Dissenters at Spalding: though I told them of the excellency of that Form; and my own unfitness through Strangeness and want of Use &c. to perform it of my Self. No, they were resolved to trust God with my heart and Mouth. So I studyed to get the Matter of the Sacrament or the Doctrine of it into my Head, and Commit my Self to Divine Assistance for Words and Management. So I was forced to leave my Crutches in all Emergent Offices and Duties; which proved (God So ordering it) a very great Advantage to me in the after discharge of these parts of my Ministry.

My Work and Order of the Publick Worship of God at Spalding was as follows I always begun the Service Morning and Afternoon with a short Prayer for Assistance and Acceptance Then I read a Psalm or two according as they were in length and after that a Chapter in the Old Testament, and then another in the New which were read /fo. 57r/ in Order except Fasts &c occasioned the choice of some other One of the chapter I always expounded both noons beginning with [260] the Prophets and after the Historical Books of Old Testament[261] When this was done I set a Psalm; then prayed and preached: and in the Afternoon after Evening Sermon we closed the Service of the Day with a Psalm. Besides this when I went first I preached a Lecture on Week days (Wednesday) till the small attendance of people thereon occasioned the leaving it off: and at

[258] *Liturgy* cancelled.

[259] Richard Baxter, *A Petition for Peace: with the reformation of the liturgy* (London, 1661).

[260] Illegible word cancelled.

[261] *of Old Testament* inserted in the margin.

those Lectures I also expounded a Chapter in Course. We had the Sacrament of the Lord's Supper Monthly the first Lords day of every Month without much Interruption. (though some <intermission> by Divisions was occasioned.) And on the Friday before (after the Lecture was laid down) we constantly met and I expounded a Psalm in course and prayed; and this partly for the afflicted church; and partly in preparation for the Sacrament approaching. Besides what Fasts we had at other times for the Church and besides those appointed by Authority.

I stayed at Spalding till I had expounded (within a very little) the whole Bible. which was <in> 9 years. And it was chiefly part of the Psalms which I took in Course Monthly (as was said) that I stayed not to [262] finish. But I cannot easily express the great Benefit I recieved (whatever others did) by this Course of Exposition. It engaged me to read my Commentaries, and so brought me into better Acquaintance with the Scriptures. I drew up no Notes in writing in order to this work:* but having read the chapter with some Comment the Evening before and so got the Scope thereof into my mind, and Sense of hard places, I left the rest to divine Assistance at the time of Performance. And I have great reason to bless the Lord for inclining me to this Course.

I gave my people here this liberty and advantage (if it was one to them, as it was to me) viz that if any of them had a mind to have me preach upon any Particular text I ordered them to pin a Note upon the Cushion naming the Text (it needed not be known from whom) and I would preach upon it. And many of my Sermons at Spalding were on such texts so appointed. And it much took off that uneasy distraction of Mind about chusing a New Text when an old one was done which many Ministers experience: And was of use to the Souls of the people; every one knowing his own wants better than I could do my Self. &c.

I did also one while Catechise the willing youth (which were not many) their Parents and Masters being present, at my own house (when I had removed into the Town) on the Evenings of the Lords dayes; till I had gone over the Catechism Principles of the Christian Religion; which I expounded to the Auditors as familiarly as I could. And some wished it had been done in the Meeting more publickly. But the time there was employed as is above mentioned. And I had gone /fo. 57v/ over the whole Body of Divinity in my Publick Preaching, when I went first to this place; And that by handling five points of

*Marginal note: * Or but very seldom as when I was at Lynn.

[262] *expound* cancelled.

Doctrine, as so many Principles of Religion, which I raised from that one Text. John 3.16.*

In this place God exceedingly blessed me with more Soul refreshment and Ministerial Enlargement (especially as to Publick Duties,) and more cheerfulness than I had at Kirkton: So that I was convinced I had been more Melancholy there than I did at the time apprehend; in my temper and constitution especially though not so dolourously Melancholy as I had been at Cambridg as was before mentioned.

The Publick Minister of Spalding Mr Pendelton[263] being an excellent Scriptural Preacher I took all opportunities to go to hear him: as on the Mornings of Fast dayes (not Meeting our Selves till one of the clock.) at Christmas, and other occasions when we were not employed in our own Meeting; which was a great Comfort and Advantage to me. But this was not well digested by the people my hearers, many of whom refused to follow me. But I thought I was bound to leave the Church no further than I needs must. And I knew not why any should be against my profit. and it suited my Temper as before mentioned; And no bad effect that I discerned followed it, nor was our Congregation at all lessened by it.

Being one Lord's Day at Wisbich and knowing how Excellent and solid a Preacher their Minister Mr Coldwell[264] was, (having heard him one Holyday when I was there:) I resolved (tho against the earnest repeated desires of the Dissenters there to the Contrary) so to order

*Marginal note: When I was at Spalding, we had many of Mr Jos. Allein's Calls to the Unconverted (Reprinted with the Title of a Sure Guide to Heaven) to give away amongst the poor and ignorant that would be willing to recieve and read them. One of my Friends giving one of these to a boy that served at the Georg Inn it came to the Sight of Sir John Oldfield (a wicked persecutor) who examining the boy where he had it, and thereby finding out him that did distribute them immediately issued out his Warrant and Committed my friend to Prison for dispersing unlicensed Books as he pretended. But fearing that would not warrant what he had done, he got some to read it to see if any thing could be found in the book it Self to ground his persecution upon: but finding nothing (save that the Lawyers that read said it were enough to make one mad) he after a few days released my friend; who put it up, and never presented the Justice for false Imprisonment. But all men inquiring what that book was that Mr Johnson was imprisoned for? it promoted the Spreading of it and made it to be much more read than otherwise it would have been.[265]

[263]William Pendleton became minister of Spalding in 1679. See John Nichols, *Literary Anecdotes of the Eighteenth Century*, 9 vols (London, 1812–1815), VI, pt. 1, p. 57.

[264]William Coldwell, MA (d. 1702), vicar of Wisbech (1651–1702); prebend of Ely cathedral (1699–1702). Venn, I, p. 366.

[265]Rastrick's memory appears to have been in error. The reference is to Joseph Alleine, *An Alarme to Unconverted Sinners* (London, 1672), which was indeed reprinted as *A Sure Guide to Heaven* (London, 1688). The minister of Spalding was Martin Johnson, BD (d. 1678). Venn, II p. 479.

our Meeting that I might go to the Publick in time. But it cannot easily be expressed what a Stirr this made, and how farr it was carryed to my Disgrace; And how it disgusted some rigid Dissenters there, who refused therefore to appear at our Meeting in the afternoon, though <it was>[266] <then> so crouded [267] as it had not been seen; and many Came that could have no Entrance. My Worthy Friend Mr Pell[268] at Boston afterwards talkd to me for this: But when I asked him if he would have me a Renegado? he smiled, and only said, "Nay, I will allow you more than I allow my Self."

But at Spalding as was said this practise of mine was better born, though some could have wished it otherwise, and that I had altogether abandoned the Church of England; about which they were loudest at last (one or two of them) after I had been there some years, and they begun to be divided amongst themselves upon another occasion. They had a pious custom amongst themselves to meet together one Evening in a Week to read some good Book to sing a Psalm together and one of them to pray. I seldom was at it my Self because of the distance of my house from the Town and place of their Meeting. But in time one of them made this a Matter and occasion of ostentation, and omitting reading would exercise of himself calling it a Communicating of experiences and at least half the people were for it and held on his Side till the flame grew hot and their prayers engaged one against another and they offered some of them their own wild fire instead of the calm, cool, and kindly breathings of the Spirit of God. When I understood this I went amongst them; and because they used to read I read the Ius Divinnius Reasons against lay preaching. This much enraged the party concerned I lent him the Book to read and consider But he took the Objections only and pressed them upon the people privately and said they were unanswerable but never acquainted them or himself with the Answer to them. He seemed to be glad that he had met with so much Argument for his practise more than he understood before. So that that should have cured his Mistakes made him worse. &c.——[†]

/fo. 58r/ These with some other things to be mentioned afterward made me very uneasy at Spalding, and disposed me to a Willingness to embrace a Call from thence should Providence offer it; which soon

[†]Marginal note: † And, by the way, this was the reason why Parkhurst Bishop of Norwich did not approve of placing Bishop Jewels works in all churches for the popishly affected would find all Harding in it. &c. See Strypes Life of ArchBishop Parker. page 369r[269]

[266]Replacing *the Meeting was*, above the line.

[267]*the same afternoon* cancelled.

[268]William Pell.

[269]John Strype, *The Life and Acts of Matthew Parker* (London, 1711), p. 369r.

after happened. But before I come to that, I must not forget to give some account of my Exercise of Discipline and the effects of it at Spalding; since a Judgment of discretion in those matters was denyed me in the Church, and that for that cause I left it. I soon found that the Dissenters needed it as well (though not so much) as the Church, and as soon understood that they could as almost as little bear it. I will give an Instance or two,

There was one person for whom I had a great respect, that someway misbehaving himself (at least I thought so) in his Carriage towards some others that belonged to the Meeting, I took an Opportunity to tell him of it betwixt him and me alone. but it put him into a violent and unaccountable rage; and <with>in a week or a fourt'night after he fell sick and dyed. This was improved by the Town against us, as if I had been more severe than I was, and had excluded or debarred him the Sacrament of the Lords Supper, which yet I never did; though I think he once withdrew himself from it upon that occasion a little before he fell sick.

There was another, a rich man, that came out of the Country to live at Spalding, and joyned himself to our meeting <and Communion.> What his ends were we knew not; we hoped well. <For> Sometime he continued with us, and was some help to us by what he Contributed: But afterward he behaved himself so ill, and so much to the offence of many; expressing so much malice against the piousest of the Congregation, that I was forced at last to desire him to keep away from the Meeting; which he bore patiently enough, and without passion. and whereas he used to allow three pound per annum to my Maintenance, I told him (before he spoke any thing of it himself) that I would freely discharge him of that, and not expect it from him. Which, though it was to my loss, yet I did it, partly, because I thought it unreasonable to take his money where he recieved no Benefit: and partly because I would Convince him that it was not his money that I sought but himself; and that he might believe I did it not without cause, or out of meer humour when I did it to my Cost: and Partly because that in the Primitive Church, Impenitents in Gross Sin were not only excluded all Church Communion, but (as one cites from Albaspinaeus) even their Oblations were not accepted. He came two or three times after to the Meetings (but not to the Sacrament) while I stayed But I left Spalding soon after; and the next news that I heard of him was, that going home late one night he fell into the River and was drowned; and was found and taken up dead near his own house.

/fo. 58v/ A third instance is this. There was a young woman that by too hasty a Congress with her after husband was found with child by him before Marriage and when her time drew near she went to Stamford and was brought to bed there and telling the Worthy

Non Conformist Minister there[270] that she belonged to the Meeting at Spalding she prevailed with him to Baptise her child But when she came home I went to her and endeavoured to Convince her of her Sin and the Scandall she had occasioned thereby and told her that if she expected to continue in the Meeting and enjoy the Privileges of it she ought to make a Publick Confession of her Sin and profession of the Repentance for it thereby to remove the Scandall she had given &c. She was very averse from this at first but after some little time upon better Consideration she submitted to it. So I drew up a short Form of Confession out of that larger in the Reformed Liturgy: and after I had prepared the Congregation by a short Preceeding Declaration, I pronounced it; and she audibly, seriously and affectionately with tears said it after me: which when she had done, I repeated several Scripture Promises of Pardon and absolution, and applyed them to her: and then prayed as seriously as I could for the Pardon of her Sin, and for Grace and Strength for New Obedience for the time to come &c. And you would not think how serious and affected the whole Congregation was the while as so awfull and solemn and yet (by Absolution and Prayer) so Comfortable an Ordinance No Scoffs or laughter seen or observed but so tender and compassionate and sensible were the people that few Sermons were thought to have done so much good <at the time> as this thing did. Blessed be God. But another Offending long after in the like kind would never be brought to submit to the like Penance.

Of my Removall to Rotheram in Yorkshire.

And now I am come to the point of my leaving of Spalding occasioned partly by the divisions among the people before mentioned. Partly by the Perfidiousness and Failure of some in the matter of the charge; some withholding or subtracting half and some two thirds of their annual Contribution towards my Maintenance which layd me under great discouragements: (Though some did indeed beyond their power almost; whose estates God did afterwards exceedingly bless.) And partly by the distance of my House from the Meeting (so that I and my weak wife could not dine at our own house on the Lords Days to our great trouble) and the Dearness of that which I last lived in; the Rent of which I could not be by them Enabled to pay out of my small Pittance which they allowed me. And withall

[270] This was probably Isaac Modwitt (Maudit) (d. 1718), who succeeded Edward Browne (d. 1682) as nonconformist minister at Stamford. He left Stamford in 1691. See Alexander Gordon (ed.), *Freedom After Ejection: a review (1690–1692) of Presbyterian and Congregational nonconformity in England and Wales* (Manchester, 1917), p. 313.

the Loss of the most Convenient Habitation I could have had in that Town viz the House next the Meeting /fo. 59r/ So carelessly and treacherously occasioned did very much disturb me. The matter was this. The House last mentioned falling to be void, I had a great mind to it saving that there was an Estate in Land belonging to it which I could make no use of But I told my Friends that if any of them or any other could be found to take off their Land and let me have the house and Garden I should be greatly pleased. So while we were demurring, one of them (in communion with us) pretending a Fear that some Stranger should hire it that might be a bad Neighbour to the Meeting (Though the Bayliff that let it was one of us also, and one of the most Emminent of our Communicants) offered this Expedient, Well (saies he to me) I will hire it at present, and if you can get any one at your leisure to take off the Land you shall have the House. So in a little time four of my Friends were willing to take and imploy the Land that I might have the House <accordingly.> But when I went to tell him that pretended to hire it for me that I had come to <a> resolution to remove to <it>[271] , and depended on his Promise, he told me he would go to it himself. And so I was baulkt of my expectation by the grossest Deciet that every [*sic*] I knew in a Professor. And this also much impelled and Conduced to my Removall Could I have been accomodated with that House I believe I should have stayed much longer at Spalding than I did: though I could not well have subsisted there with such small Helps: which when I was gone they doubled to my Successour.

There was another thing that much influenced my Removal, and that was the change of Air. I had been oft sick at Kirkton of many Autumnal Fevers and some other Distempers for which I could long get no other Cure than by riding up into the High=Country, where I was usually better; and could in my Return back sensibly percieve the Return of my (Head) illness by that time that I had entred a mile or two within the Fen. And though (blessed be God) I had enjoyed a much greater Measure of Health at Spalding than I had at Kirkton (Clyff Waters in Northamptonshire helped me here, as Walcot Waters near Falkingham in Lincolnshire had done when I was at Kirkton)[272]

[271] Replacing *the House*, above the line.

[272] There were chalybeate (iron-bearing) springs at King's Cliffe, Northants. and at Walcot, Lincs. That at King's Cliffe, lying a mile to the south of the village, was called the Spa. Its medicinal properties, including its value for treating ulcers and distempers 'arising from obstructions', had been discovered in 1670 by John Boughton. It was evidently still a popular destination in 1703, when it was visited by John Morton, and there is a thorough description of the properties of the waters in his *The Natural History of Northamptonshire* (London, 1712), pp. 274–277. For the spring at Walcot, see Ian Thompson, *Lincolnshire Springs and Wells: a descriptive catalogue* (Scunthorpe, 1999), p. 38.

Yet I had a sickly wife and I had a great mind to see what Change of Air and Country would do for her. And the Truth is I could never Fancy the Low Foggy Flat Fenny Country; but was always Charmed with the very Sight and Prospect of the Inland Parts: and the more mountainous the more wonderfull and pleasant: which much disposed me to remove thither.

So on the 6th of March. 1696/7 I recieved a Letter from my worthy Reverend Friend Mr Mathew Sylvester of London[273] who knew my Uneasiness at Spalding to remove me to Rotherham in Yorkshire. a place that had been noted for Religion but was /fo. 59v/ of late much declined in that respect And there were some pious Gentlemen in the Country near that were much concerned for it and desirous to try whether the Interest of Religion could not be thus retrieved. Such as Mr White oft Parliament man for Nottinghamshire and Mr Taylor Burgess for Retford and they applyed themselves to Mr Sylvester to recommend them a man and he mentioned me, to whom they ordered him to write[274]

So March 16. I kept in private Fasting and Prayer to implore Gods Direction with respect to this Call to clear it if he saw it for the best or to prevent it if otherwise. And the next day I set forward on my Journey, preached there the two next Lords Days was accepted and chosen by them and urged to come and live amongst them and after some time of deliberation I removed thither the 20th May following. Viz. Anno Domini 1697.

Here I went on in the same Method and course of Preaching and expounding <&c.>. that I had done at Spalding save only that (a great part of the Congregation living at a distance in the Country nor could be at leisure from their Rural Employments) I kept no Lecture on the Week day nor was desired so to do. But instead of that I did constantly Repeat my Sermons in my own house and sometimes Catechise the Youth in the Evening of the Lords Days to which such as lived in the Town to the number of twenty or thirty used to resort. and this more constantly than I could do at Spalding where my house was so distant from such as should have frequented it. But here we had those near us that did.

[273]Matthew Sylvester (1636/7–1708), ejected minister. *ODNB*.

[274]John White (1634–1713) of Tuxford, Notts., MP for Nottinghamshire (1679–1681, 1689–1690, 1691–1698); Richard Taylor (*c.*1649–1699) of Wallingwells, Notts., MP for East Retford, Notts. (1690–1698). White was a friend of Oliver Heywood and the patron of Matthew Sylvester. Taylor employed Elizar Heywood, son of Oliver Heywood, as chaplain at Wallingwells for more than twenty years. See Eveline Cruickshanks, Stuart Handley, and D.W. Hayton (eds), *The House of Commons, 1690–1715*, 5 vols (Cambridge, 2002), V, pp. 611–612, 849.

We had little suitable Society in this Town but in the Country we had much I used often to go to the Lecture at Sheffield kept up by Mr Prime and Mr Jolly[275] <with> whom I had much Pleasant and Profitable Conversation and sometimes preached for them both As I did also elsewhere at Wallding Wells Leighton in the morning &c.[276] And the Truth is I never knew in any Country where I had been so many religious Familys amongst the Gentry in so small a Compass of ground as I found there Such as Mr White of Carberton[277] Mr Taylor of Walding Wels[278] Mr Hatfield of Leighton in the morning aforesaid[279] Mr Westby of Ranfield[280] Mr Rich of Bull=house in Penyston Parish[281] Madam Rhodes at Long=Haughton[282] Mr Cotton at the Hague near Barnesly[283] and others as at Norton in Darbyshire whom through my short Stay in the Country I was not acquainted with. But some of these above named I often visited and preached at their Houses and they would send their Coaches for my wife and were very kind to us. It was pleasing to me to observe how they constantly filled up the /fo. 60r/ worship of God in their houses. For (whereas a short and easie prayer morning and evening is all that one shall find in many places) In all the

[275] Timothy Jollie (1656×9–1714), Independent minister and nonconformist tutor. *ODNB*. Edward Prime (*c.*1631–1708) was an assistant to James Fisher, vicar of Sheffield, from 1655, and ejected in 1662. He kept up the fortnightly lecture there for forty-five years from 1662. See Robert Fern, *The Perfection of the Spirits … In a Sermon upon the Death of the Reverend Mr Edward Prime* (London, 1710), pp. 33–35; Venn, III, p. 399.

[276] Wallingwells, home to the Whites of Tuxford.

[277] Thomas White of Carburton, heir to John White of Tuxford (see p. 137, n. 274 above). Through Thomas White's marriage in 1698 to Bridget Taylor of Wallingwells, who was the sole heir of Richard Taylor (see p. 137, n. 274 above), Wallingwells passed to the White family. For the marriage (where White is rendered Whity), see J.H. Turner (ed.), *The Nonconformist Register of Baptisms, Marriages, and Deaths, 1644–1702, 1702–1752, Generally Known as the Northowram or Coley Register; compiled by … Oliver Heywood and T. Dickenson* (Brighouse, 1881), p. 51.

[278] Richard Taylor.

[279] Probably the Hatfield family of Laughton-en-le-Morthen, near Rotherham, whom Oliver Heywood recorded visiting in 1666 and which included the prophet Martha Hatfield (b. 1640). *ODNB*.

[280] Probably Thomas Westby of Ravenfield, Yorks. (b. after 1665–d. 1747), who was educated in part by Oliver Heywood and was MP for East Retford (1710–1711). The Westby family had strong links among the puritan gentry. Thomas Westby's father-in-law was John White, for whom see p. 137, n. 274 above.

[281] Elkanah Rich (*c.*1659–1729), of Bullhouse, near Penistone, Yorks. Rich married, in turn, the daughters of two ejected ministers: Margaret Shaw (daughter of John Shaw) and Martha Thorpe (daughter of Richard Thorpe). He built a Presbyterian chapel at Bullhouse in 1692.

[282] Lady Mary Rodes (1608–1681), widow of Sir Edward Rodes (1601–1666), of Great Houghton, near Barnsley.

[283] Mr Cotton is most likely to be William Cotton (1648/9–1703), from the family of ironmasters, who had close connections to Oliver Heywood and the nonconformist community. *ODNB*.

families I have mentioned there was always Reading the Scriptures with a short Prayer for a Blessing on the Word preceding and a Psalm sung every evening besides prayer and all with great Solemnity and Regularity the Family being called together by the Ring of a Bell for that purpose, and none might be missing.

I took great delight to travail in this Country it was so new and strange to me who had always lived in one of the Greatest Levels in England but here the Prospects by the Hight of the Hills were very pleasant and enterteining And I took several diverting Journeys in it as to Hull to York to Leeds and Halifax. where I see the learned Mr Thoresby and that learned Mathematician Mr Abraham Sharp at little Horton near Bradforth and that Holy and Reverend Divine Mr Oliver Heywood at North Owram and a Village of my own name in the parish of Yeland.[284] And in another Journey to Manchester I passed thro the Peak of Darby and had the opportunity and pleasure to see most of the Wonders there though the Country it Self was its greatest wonder to me of all. When we were past Sheffield we begun to rise which we did by degrees for some miles till we came to an edge or precipice called Stan-edg Top (quasi Stony edge)[285] By the way seeing a Smoke on my left hand hard by where we passed like the burning of some Swine &c. I was surprized to find that it was a Cloud that grew bigger and bigger but we quickly left it behind us and it did not obscure the fair and sunshine Morning in which we travailed. But when we Came to the Top before mentioned!—— what shall I say? I did not at all wonder that ten thousand Edomites should be Slain by being cast down from the top of a Rock. 2 Chronicles 29.12. This is a long high Clyff or Precipice of perpendicular Descent running along North and South for many miles whence if one should fall it were as from the top of one of the Highest Steeples in England the Rocks jutting or hanging over in many places Vast Stones like Pillars piled upon an End in the Fall and bearing up a great part of the Mountain where we stood for this looks like the effect of some vast Shelve, where the parts below open the Darwen[286] subsided or sunk down cloven off from the rest of the Hill left broken like a vast Wall of rugged Stones looking like Ruines. But when you come to ground tis amazing to see the Multitude and vastness of the Stones that cover all /fo. 60v/ the Side or more sloping part of the Hill below the apparent tokens of some former great Convulsion or Concussion of the Earth For the Stones ly dipping in

[284] For Ralph Thoresby (1658–1725); Abraham Sharp (bap. 1653–d. 1742) of Horton Hall, Little Horton, near Bradford; and Oliver Heywood (bap. 1630–d. 1702), see *ODNB*. Rastrick is a village approximately five miles south-east of Halifax.

[285] Stanage Edge, Derbys.

[286] River Derwent.

such a manner that its plain not a mere Fall but a Violent Cast or projection layed them in the places and pastures in which they are now beheld. Tis awful to behold and gives an occasion of more inquisitive thoughts about the Formation of the Earth than any thing one can see in the Plainer Countries. It is here manifest that there has been a great change in it. If I had not observed how the Seams of Rocks ly in these Mountainous Countries shelving and dipping <in> some places one way in some another I had {scarce}[287] had the Curiosity to read as I after upon this occasion did Burnet's Theory of the Earth[288] an ingenious Book though I incline not to his Hypothesis But rather to that of Mr Hooks viz that the Mountainous Hilly parts of the Earth were raised by an Universall Earthquake by protrusion of the lower parts upward, and not by the Fall of upper parts inward.[289] And so the Flood might be caused by raising the parts that were then Sea and so throwing the Sea upon the <in>habited Countries which best solves the difficulty about finding Fish Skeletons and Shells upon the highest Mountains and that the hardest Marble Rocks should ly the Highest: for they might be protruded from below which is otherwise their more natural place. But where wast thou when I laid the Foundations of the Earth &c. saies God to Job. <38.4.> What we cannot understand we must admire.

The Height of these Hills I cannot account for but its very probable the peak hills are about 3 or 400 yards perpendicular height One may Commonly see (as I did on Stanedge top) the Hills covered with the usual white Wooll pack clouds. and the Snow lies long in the Spring before it be dissolved; and is seen White like Clouds from the lower part of the Countrie about Rotheram &c. I oft wondered to find mention in the Scriptures of Snow and Frost in southern Countries but now I see 'tis their Height that is the reason of it. Tis plain the more Northerly these peak hills ran the higher they grew. And though it was a sunshine Morning and warm on the Top of Stanedg when I was there yet these parts are almost all covered with dewey Mists and Clouds. So that there's no judging of the Weather at Rotheram by the Suns setting under a Bank as in other places for here it almost always does so and whereas I always before thought the Highest places the clearest and enjoying most of the Son here I found my Self confuted. Neither were the Rivers of this Country clear like those in the South parts but black or /fo. 61r/ of a deep Brown like Beer ready brewed

[287] Rastrick uses these curly brackets. *never* is written above *scarce*, which has not been cancelled. As in p. 72, n. 93 above, the intention might have been to provide alternatives for a printed edition.

[288] Thomas Burnet, *The Theory of the Earth* (Latin edn, London, 1681/1689; English edn, London, 1684/1690).

[289] Robert Hooke (1635–1703) had expounded his views on this matter from 1668, but Rastrick is probably referring to *The Posthumous Works of Robert Hooke* (London, 1705), p. 291.

tinged by the Moors that <the Surface of> the greatest part of these Hills consist of For the Highest Hills here are like the lowest Fens and so Extreams agree.

I shall say nothing of the wonders there that so many have described so well. One that sees the Great Cave at Castleton (where I found almost a little Village Houses and Hay Cocks underground: I need not mention it by the Vulgar Name) I say one that sees it and that other at Buxton will not wonder that David and his Army should ly hid in a Cave and Saul go in and not discover them. Elden hole[290] made me shrink in my bed that night to think on it. The Lord save us from the Bottomless Pit.

We dined at the Town called Chappel in the Frith, and got that night to Manchester. What pleased us best there was the Library a place of easie access at the due hours and there I spent some time. The Books are many and all chained. There I saw the Skin (stuffed) of an American Snake (I think a Rattle Snake) of a vast length I think about 14 or 16 foot. A pair of large Globes in an Apartment by themselves, (locked up.) and a handsome Barometer.

From hence I returned by another Road by Ashton under line and could see the Mountains before us which we were to pass covered with clouds as if they were all on a Smoke which put me in mind of Mount Sinai. They are more steep and rise more of a sudden on this Western Side than they do on the Yorkshire Side where one ascends more gradually. the like I have observed of all the Ridges of Hills that I have seen in England which ran North and South that the Western Side has the most precipitious Fall as the Cliff and Wolds in Lincolnshire the Chiltern in Buckinghamshire &c. We dined at an inn called Wood head in the extream North East Angle of Cheshire.[291] We had over against our Inn on the other Side of a deep valley wherein the River Mersey runs a vast High stern Hill covered with thick Clouds and Mists that flew along its edg or Brow. After dinner we mounted into them and rode by Lady Cross some miles in the same Clouds that we had seen scowring along the Cliff of the forementioned Hill. As we descended we gained a sudden View of the Country before us which was very surprising as it first appeared through the Edge of the Cloud or Mist which now begun to be thin. We had a Pleasant Evening when we got down but could when we looked behind us see the Black Clouds we had rode through hanging upon the Hills.

/fo. 61v/ But to return to Rotheram and the people there I shall give some short account of them and so leave them. That flourishing

[290] Eldon Hole, a deep pothole in the Peak Forest between Castleton and Chapel-en-le-Frith.

[291] Woodhead, to the east of Manchester, now lost to the Woodhead Reservoir.

State of Religion that had formerly been in this place could not now be retrieved. 'Tis true they were men of moderate principles and Occasional Conformists and never quarrelled with me for going sometimes to the publick, but <would> go with me thither; which was a great Comfort; there being an able preacher Mr Adam Minister of the place.[292] But excepting three or four serious hearty Christians the most fell very short of what they should have been and were far from Laudable they were rather <a> scandalous clubbing drinking Sort of people and knew not how to prize spiritual Privileges. So that all my Friends in the Country thereabouts wished me better placed. And so that for want of Matter (as the Ministers expressed it in their Meetings when I consulted them) we could not have the Lords Supper constantly: I think we had it but once or twice: so that I was fain to go to Sheffield yea and Nottingham for it my Self. After three or four years I began to know them; and when I began to know them, I began to distinguish in my preaching (chusing the Subjects that I thought they most needed) though not to name or describe any any [*sic*] otherwise than as their Sin described them. But I thought I must do more than barely admonish or reprove. Though we had seldom Sacraments to exclude them from, I thought some of them ought to be warned even from the Meeting. I therefore (because it was the Ministers use at their Meetings to Answer Questions) proposed this Question to be by them answered What Ordinance the impudently Scandalous ought to be debarred from Whether the Lord's Supper only or all the rest, and even the place of Meeting? But this Question they never answered at any of their Meetings. At length I proceeded my Self to warn one of the chief of them from the Meeting; and remitted his Contribution; though he was so civil as to continue it. And I advised with that Pious solid and Worthy person Mr Jolly who kept a Private Accademy at Attercliff;[293] and he approved of what I did, and said I had done nothing but what was my Duty to do. The most took this very well and seemed to be affected with it: and the Town's people were silenced and satisfyed when they percieved that it was not Self Interest and Faction that governed us. and I was told that in general it had done more good than any thing else. But one of the chief of the Congregation (next this censured person) took it so ill that he went off upon it to the Church in great indignation at what I had done. But afterwards upon occasion of a Fall he got by which he had like to have been slain, he fell into great remorse and trouble of Conscience for his differing with me, which he said was

[292] Christopher Adam, MA (d. 1706), vicar of Rawmarsh, Yorks. (1667–1700); vicar of Rotherham (1697–1701). Venn, I, p. 4.

[293] Jollie started an academy at Attercliffe Hall, Yorks. in 1691.

more than all his other pain: and he prayed heartily for me; as I was afterward informed. For just at this Juncture in time when this Ferment was beginning Gods Providence called me away from Rotheram; and then they were my Friends. And the person himself whom I had dealt so plainly with when I visited him two years after was very kind to me and complained that there were so few <that> would be faithful to Souls: which I easily percieved he spake with respect to what I had done in order to his Amendment.

/fo. 62r/

Of my Remove to Lyn=Regis in Norfolk.

Just as this hot displeasure was concieved against me by some at Rotheram for my Proceedings there (though God by a severe Stroke brought the chief person to a deep Repentance for it as had been related) it pleased God by his Providence suddenly to call me away from thence upon the occasion following.

My wife was very desirous after now four years absence to visit her Native Country and her Friends and Relations there and being furnished by our worthy Friend Mr Hatfield of Leighton with accommodations for the Carriage of her and our two Eldest Children we took our Journey at the latter End of May 1701. to Gedney in Lincolnshire where my wife's own Mother with her Father in Law dwelt whence at our leisure we visited our Friends at Spalding Wisbich and Lyn designing to make about a Months Stay and so to return into Yorkshire little dreaming of our coming away for altogether as it proved: For my wife never returned thither again nor I save only to pack up my Goods (after Sale of part of them) and to come away to Lyn=Regis in Norfolk whither I was called in manner following.

My dear and kind Friend Mr Williamson Minister to the Dissenting Congregation[294] there had a great esteem and affection for me and long desired that I might be nearer him and if possible joyned with him I remember as his shaking hands with me at our Parting at Swaffham <once,> he going for Lyn and I for Norwich) how heartily he expressed that desire of his of our Living together adding, it will be before we die I hope. He was a man of a most Excellent Spirit and Temper. the greatest distinction of his character may be seen <to be> his disparaging his Judgment in overvaluing me. My first knowledg of him was at Spalding in Lincolnshire when I dwelt there he with one or two more lay a night at that Town in a Journey to Boston; and I and a friend or two went to his Inn to see him. We soon fell into discourse

[294]Anthony Williamson (d. 1704) was the first minister at the nonconformist meeting at Spinner Lane, King's Lynn. Gordon, *Freedom after Ejection*, p. 385, suggests that he was active there from 1690 to 1701.

about Religion and the Church and he spoke the Notions of my own mind and the Sense of my very heart with so much greater aptness of expression and volubility and freedom of language methought than I could do my Self that I was very much taken with him and went with him next day to Boston for more of his Company which begun acquaintance I not long after renewed in a Journey which I made to Lyn on purpose to see and advise with him in a case I thought needed it and by the event and Success I experi= /fo. 62v/ enced the maturity and usefulness of his Counsel. And all the time that I lived at Spalding (for it was the first year of my going thither viz. 1687 that I got this acquaintance with him) he was the man that Visited me the most of any Minister of my Acquaintance at the like distance Which I gladly endeavoured to repay and a great refreshment it was to me to come over to Lyn for such good Company as his and his Fathers was upon which occasions I oft preached there also and that with great Acceptance seldome observing a more Attentive auditory than this was. And I cannot but with gratitude remember and mention the kind Entertainment I met with from Mr Blithe his Father in Law[295] whom I may call the Gains of that church for his free and generous Hospitality.

But Mr Blithe dying and his estate falling to Mr Williamson who marryed his Daughter and he being thereby enabled to live of himself without the Contributions of the people he had now an opportunity of effecting what he had so long desired And some infirmities growing upon Mr Williamson which made his usual labours harder and more difficult for him to perform and moreover a weekly Lecture being desired there he was more resolved to have an Assistant and I being then as is aforesaid occasionally in the Country he pitched upon me called me to Lyn and after he had got me to Preach to the People there he proposed me to them and at his Instance and desire they met and chose me to be his Assistant and Co=Pastor with him. He offered them his Labours freely and what was given by the People he assigned over to me for my Sallary towards my Maintainance. I made no bargain with them demanded nothing of them but <accepted>[296] what they offered me and so removed to Lyn the latter end of this Summer Anno Domini 1701.

Here Mr Williamson and I lived in great Friendship and carryed on our Work in joynt Concurrence and Unanimity without clashing. We took our turns on the Lords Days (for the Lecture I preached constantly my Self) And when Mr Williamson preached I always

[295] Perhaps William Blyth, who was appointed an alderman of King's Lynn in 1688. See Henry J. Hillen, *History of the Borough of King's Lynn*, 2 vols (Norwich, 1907), I, p. 444.

[296] Replacing *took*, which has not been cancelled, above the line.

begun with Prayer, and read two or three Psalms and two Chapters, one in the Old Testament and the other in the New, One of which I expounded and the like I did when I preached my Self; as I had done in other places. He baptized most of the Children especially at first. And in the Administration of the Lords Supper we took our turns as we did in Preaching. Though he sometimes got me to do it when it was his turn; though I could rather have desired to have been his Assistant only and not Co=Pastor. To Repetition of the /fo. 63r/ Sermons on the Evenings of the Lords Days none here would come though I offered to recieve them to my house to that end it was not regarded. After I was a little settled I preached over the whole Body of Divinity on five points of Doctrine as so many Principles raised from John 3.16. Save that now and then I took a new text to give a better or more direct Occasion to speak of some points as I went along as the Attributes and Relations of God &c. which did much Good (blessed be God) as some told me from their own experience. When I had thus explained the Principles of the Christian Religion, I gave them Publick Notice that I would Catechize the Children and Servants from 14 or 16 years old and upwards of such as would consent thereto. And because expounding the Scriptures filled up the Worship of God in Publick, I offered to that end to come to the Houses of all such as would invite me or give me notice when and where. Which I did because I could then also Instruct the Elder people or parents themselves. But notwithstanding this publick notice twice given, none invited me to their houses to any such End. save one in generall expressions thinking or supposing it might have been more generally practised. And indeed the Youth here seemed to be too high and proud to submit to this so it went not on. As to my Expounding of the Scriptures though one did thank me for it and Express his great Satisfaction with it yet there were others and they the chief who as they did not desire it so their constantly coming late to the meeting (rarely untill it was over) showed what little value they had for it: though it being joyned to the Publick Worship they could not put it by. Save that when I came to Expound the Psalms I was desired to wave it because that they haveing put me into Davids Case and Circumstances by their persecuting me thought that Davids Complaints did too much reflect upon them. Of which more by and by. As for my weekly Lecture they frequented it the least that had most desired it not coming to it above twice in a Twelve month or scarce so often.

For now I must Enter upon a tragical Scene in relating the troubles that I met with at Lyn from a turbulent factious proud Self concieted party there. They had attempted against Mr Williamson once, and had got another Minister but that they could not keep him because they could not maintain him. And I had not been long here before they expressed their great dislike of me. For it is these malecontents that you must suppose me now for the future to be speaking of; the Majority of the Congregation being my hearty Friends; though too few of them that had any right Sense of and Zeal for true Religion. While Mr Williamson lived he kept of the mischievous effects of their wrath from sensibly touching me And his friendship was a relief and compensation for want of theirs

/fo. 63v/ But in the Month of August Anno Domini 1704. Mr Williamson dyed. And in him I lost a dear Friend and Companion the prospect of whose Society was one great Motive of my coming to Lyn. And I was left to manage this untoward Congregation by my Self and to Conflict with the Opposition of about half a dozen male contents three of whom were Scotchmen the other Town Tradesmen two of them the richest of all the Meeting.

The first thing I did after Mr Williamson dyed was to enquire out his List of the Communicants if he had any such by him that I might know the Church; but nothing of that kind could be found. So I gave notice to the Congregation that I desired all such as were in Communion and desired to continue so under my Ministry (who by their choice was half, or Co=Pastor before) would give me in their Names. So I obteined a List of betwixt fourty and fifty which was the whole of this small Society the after Male=Contents being of the Number and as yet Excepting or Objecting nothing against me nor expressing their dislike though they had begun to quarrell or express their dissatisfaction about two or three things (but mostly behind my back) in Mr Williamson's time who quieted them and kept them from breaking out into the open rage that flamed so hotly after his death. But I will account briefly for the particulars that happened both before his death and after in the [297] following Instances.

1. The first occasion given me to discover their Temper was this. I observed that in the Administration of the Lords Supper, it was usual with many of them to hold the Bread and Wine long in their hands while they were about their own secret Meditations which made the whole Ordinance much longer than it needed to be, and even in that part of it which was mostly spent in Silence, in which one's affections were most apt to flagg; <and> which if the Congregation had been very numerous would have caused that it could not have been dispatcht in any due or reasonable Time. So I took occasion (not at the Lords Table but) at another time to tell them of this, and direct them to concieve and finish their Meditations sometime immediately before the Elements came to their hands, which would be both less ostentatious, no less useful to themselves, and greatly expedite the

[297] Blank space in the text, presumably to insert a number.

whole performance &c. But at this they were so angry that it made me think who I was got amongst that would not suffer me to be free with them in so small a matter as this much less take my advice in it.

2. Another thing that digusted them was my recommending Tates and Brady's Version of the Psalms to their use; which I had used after their coming out in other places: and which I had been told that the ArchBishop of York (Sharp) so approved of, that instead of contributing to an Organ in a Certein Town in Yorkshire that applyed <to> him about it he offered them Ten Pound to buy those Psalms for the use of the Parishioners there.[298] And which I had the advantage of King William's Priviledg (the same kind of Authority that the old ones had) to recommend them to this people upon: And which I liked above all my Self. At this they were very angry; and sayed /fo. 64r/ that Barton's Psalms[299] which they had ever used were a great deal better: and in some that they were; and yet recieved them at last upon this occasion. Mr Seel P<e>ast (of whom you'll hear more afterward[300]) burying his Daughter Mary, there was a Funeral Sermon for her; And the Psalm being to be set by me I gave them the 39 Psalm of Tate and Brady's New Version.[301] Some Town's people being come to hear that Sermon (preached by Mr Williamson) were greatly affected with the Psalm; admired it, but did not know what it was. So they inquired of one of the chief of the Congregation about it, what it was? expressing a wonderful liking of it; which when he percieved, how taking they were, though he had most opposed the recieving of them, yet he never to my knowledg did it more after. I was amazed that he should come to ask me what I had sung, that he might satisfie such as had asked him. Why sayed I <it was one of>[302] Tate and Brady's Psalms that you were so angry at me for recommending to your use. So I heard no more of opposition; and the New Psalms went very well down; and

[298] John Sharp (1645?–1714), archbishop of York (1691–1714). *ODNB*.

[299] [William Barton], *The Book of Psalms in Metre* (London, 1644, and many later editions).

[300] Seal Peast (d. 1713) was the son of Charles Peast (d. 1707) and father of Charles Peast (d. 1723). See TNA, PRO, PROB 11/495 (Will of Charles Peast, Gentleman of King's Lynn, Norfolk, 1707) and PROB 11/593 (Will of Charles Peast, Gentleman of King's Lynn, Norfolk, 1723). He was a brewer and became a freeman of King's Lynn in 1682–1683: see *A Calendar of the Freemen of Lynn, 1292–1836* (Norwich, 1913). The Peast family had strong links with nonconformity in King's Lynn. It was at the house of the elder Charles Peast and John Kingstead in Black Goose Street that John Horne and Charles Philips were licensed to preach in 1673. The meeting later moved to the disused round glasshouse in Spinner Lane. See Hillen, *History of the Borough of King's Lynn*, I, p. 416.

[301] *A New Version of the Psalms of David, Fitted to the Tunes Used in Churches. By N. Tate and N. Brady* (London, 1696, and many later editions). It is not clear to which edition Rastrick is referring, but see p. 162, n. 328 below.

[302] Replacing *they were*, above the line.

most in Time got Books, and commended and preferred them before all the other.

3. Another thing that greatly offended them was my Occasional Conformity or going (not to the Communion in Publick but) to hear a Sermon now and then at the Church; as on Christmas day, the Mayor's days and the like. Though I had told them my Temper and practise in that respect when they first chose me and they knew Mr Williamson had sometimes gone to Church himself and taken me with him thither before I came to live here yet now it would not do they were nosed[303] by it by the Townsmen and they could not bear it This was a Subject of great Offence Though they were then told that they would find something or other to carp and rage at if this occasion were removed because they would sometimes say (to agravate the thing) how happy they should be in the Gospel as any place whatsoever if that one fault of mine were but amended which was far from proving so in the Sequel when it was amended; as afterwards it was upon an occasion to be mentioned by and by. As by the Act against occasional Conformity afterwards.

4. But that which enraged most of any thing that had happened hitherto was what I preached from Jeremiah 6.16. Stand up in the ways and see where I endeavoured to state the Points of Schism and Church Communion and account for the Principles and reasons of my practise, and of all others of my mind. When I was come to the end of the 16th Rule or Principle relating to a faithful Ministry and the respect that is to be had to it the noyse and Contention was so great that it forced me to change my Text and to take the last words of 2 Corinthians 12 Chapter (– And yet shew I unto you a more Excellent Way) to deliver the 17th Rule from; (about Love and the Reasons of it.) which I introduced with a Plain and somewhat sharp Preface which may save me the labour of accounting any further for that matter here.

5. I had the more reason to be so plain with them then for what had past amongst them about my Notion of the seventh Chapter to the Romans which I had occasionally delivered; and which was another Subject of Complaint and /fo. 64v/ wrath. They sayed, there could not be more rotten Doctrine delivered in a pulpit than that was. And therefore some time after when it came in my course to expound that chapter they believing that I should do it in the same Sense that I had occasionally done before in some Sermon of mine that had so offended them would not be at the hearing of it; but walked in the Street till the exposition was over. However I did afterwards more fully give them my Sense of that Chaper in a Sermon purposely composed

[303] *nosed*: to be led about by the nose. *OED*.

if it might be to Convince them by laying all my thoughts and proofs together from the Parenthesis in the first verse of that Romans 7 (for I speak to them that know the Law.) where, if you have a mind to know what my Opinion is that occasioned so much discontent with the Reasons of it, you may find it; and I need not relate it here.

6. My Doctrine of the Combate betwixt the Flesh and the Spirit had also greatly disturbed them because I held that one cannot judg of his spiritual State and condition meerly by finding such a Combate in himself (as they had been taught by some) but by which party gets the Victory in the Combate which occasioned my more fully stating and cleeving that point in my Sermons on Galatians 5. 16–18. where my judgment of it may be seen.

It was mentioned even now their saying how happy they should be if I would but leave my great fault of occasional going to the Church: Now I come to tell how little it signifyed when I did afterwards discontinue that practise of mine according to, (though not upon) their desire but upon this occasion now briefly to be related.

Mr Williamson and I being invited by his Brother to his Child's Christening Supper the Child being Baptized at the Church his wife being a Church=Woman and prevailingly urging it there we met Dr Littel the Minister at St Margaret's the Great Church and Mr Samuel Taylor (who afterward stood for Burgess against Mr Walpool) and some persons of Note in the Town.[304] Before we parted we fell into discourse about Church Matters and about Schism in particular which occasion the Doctor took to direct his discourse to one in particular after this manner. Said he I observe indeed that you do come sometimes to Church; but I observe (and you may be sure I would strictly mind you) that you never respond when you are there and what is that but to mock God and the Congregation and he told me plainly to my face that he took an Occasional Conformist to be the Worst of Men. In answer to which I told the Dr that when I was at church I kept as strictly to the Rule as he did or any in the Congregation for, said I, you err as much in excess and going beyond the Rule as I do in defect or coming short of it and I instanced in the people's reading each other verses of the Psalms and prose Hymns which they have no Rubrick for and the like particulars of super Conformity; but I told him in what was material, standing up at the Creed &c. I conformed as much as he: and said I, Dr you see I kneel at your Prayers and that's a Sign I do not come to mock at them. I told him the reason of my coming was to take away the occasion of Offence on the Church's

[304]Thomas Littel DD (d. 1731), vicar of St Margaret's, King's Lynn (1702); rector of Tydd St Mary, Lincs. (1704). See William Richards, *The History of Lynn*, 2 vols (Lynn, 1812), II, pp. 1007–1012; Venn, III, p. 91. Samuel Taylor stood against Robert Walpole in 1711. Walpole won the election, despite being imprisoned, and the election was subsequently declared void.

Side. They should not say I was against all Forms of prayer the use of the Creeds the Doctrine of the /fo. 65r/ Liturgy &c. I told him I took my Self bound to depart from the Church of England no further than I needs must; I did not dissent in every thing. But said I Dr if that which I do to avoid offence do give offence I'll come amongst you no more though it be to my loss and disadvantage. (I meant in respect of the profit I owned I recieved from their preaching.) And so accordingly I refrained going for several years. To what I said about super Conformity I must needs say (without Self-partiality) the Doctor replyed nothing but was forced to own it. He asked me then at last the Reasons of my Non Conformity? Said I, Dr that's too large a Subject to enter upon now at this time and before this company; but if he had a mind to know That, I would come at any time to his house and give him the account he desired: So he sayed he would let me know when I should come; (The people took it as a Challenge and urged the Doctor upon it) But from that day to this he never sent for me and at last Dr Calamy's publishing of my Account of my Non-Conformity prevented any further account of my own to the Doctor about that matter.[305] But this Carriage of the Doctor thus to thrust me quite out of the Church was very displeasing to the generality of the people of this Town.

But with our Male Contents in the Meeting this my total withdrawment from the Church had no effect towards the reconciling them to my Ministry, but their Discontents and dissatisfactions grew higher than ever. For, to go on with the Matter of our Broils.[306]

7. The Bottom of all the Grudg so far as I could percieve and as experience taught me lay chiefly in these two things viz first my Plain way of Preaching and Reproving, and backing of it with something of Church=Discipline, which, because it reached and touched them, the Three chief of the discontented party could not bear. And the other was my Baxterian Doctrine, as they called it, especially my opinion about the Universal Sufficiency of Christ's Death &c. which was as ingrateful to the three Scotchmen who accounted it false and pernicious Doctrine, which they always branded with the name of Rotten. But these two parties joyned their Interests and agreed in their Censures and Opposition all of them quarrelling at both these things For though the Scotchmen could have nothing to say against the Exercise of Discipline it being used in their own Country and tho they would sometimes advise me to it with great Zeal promising to stand by me &c. yet when I came to exercise something of that kind

[305] John Rastrick, *An Account of the Nonconformity of John Rastrick, M.A.* For details of its two published versions see above, pp. 14–15.

[306] *broil*: a confused disturbance, tumult, or turmoil; a quarrel. *OED*.

they were as much my Enemies for it as any of the rest. Pretending, when I satisfyed the Congregation of the Repentance of two offenders whom I had discoursed and made friends that it was more than I ought to have done after I had brought them to Repentance and Reconciliation Though when the like was done in the Case of the two poor women there was nothing said against it by any body And when upon Experience of their Tergiversation[307] I proceeded afterwards in a certein case by my Self they then pretended it was because I proceeded by my Self and took not their advice and Concurrence (who were false to me before–) and /fo. 65v/ they said it was Church Tyranny. Though what I had said in Publick of Particular Persons was only in a way of Absolution and Reception of Penitents (according to the Form in the Reformed Liturgy) as may be seen in an additional paper appended in the Appendix at the End (Numb. [308]) Otherwise I sayd nothing to or of Particular Persons in Publick: Save only that I required of all when they first received the Sacrament of the Lord's Supper, (not of others, nor of them afterwards, except Relaps or discontinuance made it afterwards necessary) that they should renew their Baptismal Covenant promise to walk suitably, and submit to Order &c. Which hardly could some of my own Friends be very well satisfyed to do, after all the pains I took to convince them of the necessity of it. But I did not insist on it, in those who had recieved before, that it should have been in a Meeting; if they had recieved it in the Publick or Church of England I took it as satisfactory. Strangers brought Certificates from the Congregations where they had lived in Communion before. However this charge of Church Tyranny, and Censures thereupon, occasioned my Fifth Doctrine on the first verse of Psalm 15. and what I wrote thereupon: for it was never preached, because I knew it would not be born: For I had experienced how enraged the [*sic*] were at my Sermons on 2 Timothy 5.20. and on Joshua 7.19. designed to instruct and inform them about these things. But I quickly saw that these Dissenters would no more bear Church Discipline than the Church of England would do. For most when I was in the Church (all except one) would submit to Advice and keep from Sacraments when I thought them unfit and convinced them of the same; But when I told some of these in Private that I did no more than what I had done in the Church; and left it, because I could not be satisfyed to admit all promiscuously, and yet had no power to repel the obstinate; and that they might see my Principles and Practise in the Printed Account that Dr Calamy published, One of them cryed, Nay, If I were of that

[307] *tergiversation*: the act of 'turning one's back on'; desertion or abandonment of a cause or party. *OED*.

[308] Blank space in the text, to insert a number.

mind still there would be work enough, I should quickly break all in pieces; or to that effect in great Anger. So little did these Dissenters know on what Grounds they dissent; when Want of Discipline in the church is one of the Weightiest Reasons of our withdrawing from their Communion till it can be reformed. It would have amazed one to see how angry they were at my having spoke privately to one that came to the Meeting for some immoralities and scandalous Practises of his that deserved a severe reprimand much more severe than mine was When as yet they themselves soon after called him the Greatest Rogue in Nature with other Reviling Expressions which they broke out into whereas I my Self had never used such an Expression to him or of him for whose person I had a respect: yet what I had said was not to be born. They always called my reproving, scolding and railing; even every Use of Reproof in the pulpit; for they could never bear to have their Morals touched, which made them so mad at my Sermons on the whole 15 Psalm.

/fo. 66r/ 8. The Eighth Gravamen was my Baxterian Doctrine as they called it which they called Arminianism, <and> which they cryed down at a great rate; being also encouraged so to do by a Neighbour Dissenting Minister who concerned himself in these affairs who called it Pelagianism Popery and Heresie. It was my friend Mr Burroughs of Wisbich from whom I might justly have expected other treatment and respect.[309] Never in my life in any place did I know Mr Baxter and his Books so despised as in these Parts. When Mr Williamson came first to Lyn many years before I came the first thing after they came to discourse that Mr Blith (the chief of the Meeting) put to him was I hope you are not a Baxterian; which Mr Williamson turned of as well as he could: for there was not a man of England more of Mr Baxters mind and a greater Reverence of him than he. But it was crime enough in me to declare my Self in the main of his Opinions; or to reverence an Author that had done me as much good as any. The Point that so much displeased was that of the Universal Sufficiency of the death of christ for its Part So as that none that perish do so for want of a sufficient Sacrifice and that all unbelievers that have had the Gospel shall be judged for refusing him &c. My Judgment was the same with that of the Synod of Dort[310] and the French Protestant Divines Amyrald Placeus Dalla &c. and two Synods that cleared Amyrald &c. and of

[309] Ishmael Burroughs had left the Church of England to become the Presbyterian minister of Wisbech by 1694. See p. 117, n. 222 above.

[310] See *The Judgement of the Synode Holden at Dort, Concerning the Five Articles* (London, 1619), p. 19.

ArchBishop Usher and Dr Preston &c. here in England.[311] and many more. beyond these I went not. I owned Particular special Grace and Redemption also. But see my Sermons and Letters.

The Flame that this broke out into was thus occasioned. Mr Burroughs aforesaid being at my house about the Month of August 1707 in Company with two of the Scotchmen Discourse was begun about these matters. I confess I could not forbear giving my Judgment as it is before mentioned, viz that Christ's death is sufficient though not effectual for all: Then sayd Mr Burroughs, How can it be sufficient if it be not Effectual? A saying which I thought could never have proceeded from a man of Sense! I answered, it might be and was sufficient for its part and explained <it> I think as I used to do by Similitudes. But finding it in vain to speak, I let the discourse at that time drop; And being then preaching on Ezra 10.-2. I did the Lords Day following take occasion to enlarge on the 5th Explicatory Proposition which concerneth this point as may be seen in my Notes. And hinc illae lachrymae.[312] Here began the following Winter's Work. Their Embrion rage was now hatched, and ripened into a formall and formed Opposition. They despised and rejected my Ministry and denyed that they ever had chose me to be their Pastor notwithstanding what I have said before to the contrary and one that could not deny but that he had consented to my coming (viz. the richest of them Mr Peast) yet said he did it with half a heart and carryed two faces under one hood that day being perswaded by Mr Williamson However it was plain that they now sorely repented of what they had done They withdrew from the Lords Table and went some of them ten and sometimes thirty miles to recieve the Sacrament. They gave me all the dismission that could be ever plainly to the bidding me be gone Which my Age and numerous /fo. 66v/ Family was a great Barr to else it may be I had not troubled them nor stayed to have born that base Usage that barbarous and inhumane treatment that Wrath Anger Clamour Noyse and Fury that passed this Winter My wife lay sick that same Winter to my great Charge the Apothecary's Bill

[311] Moïse Amyraut (1596–1664), Jean Daillé (1594–1670), and Josué de la Place (Placeus) (*c.*1596–1655 or 1665) were of the Saumur school of Huguenots; James Ussher (1581–1656), Archbishop of Armagh: *ODNB*; John Preston (1587–1628), Church of England clergyman: *ODNB*. In citing these authors together, Rastrick was, like Baxter, using the authority of the Synod of Dort and the divines of the early seventeenth century to affirm the orthodoxy (against the charge of Arminianism) of the doctrine of hypothetical universalism. It is surprising that Rastrick omits reference to Richard Baxter's *Universal Redemption of Mankind* (London, 1694).

[312] *hinc illae lachrymae*: hence those tears. This Latin proverb, derived from Terence, Cicero, and Horace, was also the title of a work of 1692, *Hinc illæ lachrymæ: or, England's miseries set forth in their true light* (London, 1692).

alone (The Doctor taking no fees) amounting to Ten pound in which instead of Assisting me they hindered me in my Promised Income all that ever they could and prevailed to the lessening of it so much that it fell in proportion to the Encrease of my Family (by many children &c.) and of my Labours after Mr Williamson's death which I bless God I intermitted not preaching the whole day Expounding the Scripture and continuing the Lecture weekly notwithstanding.

Having mentioned this their Lessening my Maintainance I shall here in a few words account for that matter. I had a Friend Mr John Money[313] that Collected my Salary and payed it quarterly by Ten pounds per quarter I never was better paid any thing of that kind in all my Life wherever I had been particularly One Quarter when my wife was to ly in he (having enough in his hands) gave me fourty Shillings more than I used to recieve which occasionally mentioning to two of the Male Contents it cannot be thought how much they were disturbed at it for they Poor Souls weary of me saw that this was not the way to weary me out but to touch me in my Stipend might seem more likely to do it So they asked What had he to do to dispose of their Money And I never saw greater and more ungoverned passion which Mr Peast treated my Friend with in my own house though they had trusted him all along to collect it and bring it to me. But when they saw this would not bear but was of odious Sound and too gross a breach of Justice and Fidelity they altered their Tone and pretended it was for my advantage that they quarrelled with Mr Money and pretending to set all to Rights they charged him with wronging me great Summs of Money and called him to make his Account to them What Moneys he had recieved and how he had disposed of it So a Day was appointed on which he was to bring in his Accounts which he had ready and in good order but that day being put by because one of the Malecontents was to be out of Town Mr Money Considering the Temper in which they demanded the Account and forseeing what might be the Consequences of it they demanding not only to see them but as I remember to keep them at least for some longer time than was necessary He refused to give Account to the adverse Party who had with no good minds demanded it but did it to the Majority of the Charge bearers who were my Friends and recieved their Approbation and Discharge as having acted justly and faithfully according to his Trust. At this the rest were in a greater Rage than ever and yet knew not how to help themselves only by their charging Mr Money with Fraud and injustice as aforesaid they wearyed him out from collecting

313 Perhaps the John Money, writing-master, who became a freeman of King's Lynn in 1712–1713. See *A Calendar of the Freemen of Lynn*, p. 220. John Money was a witness to Rastrick's will. See below p. 206.

it any longer and /fo. 67r/ then my promised maintainance of 20^{li} per Quarter could not be made up but fell short considerably in the management of another that they nominated for that purpose and this for many years which you may be sure was no trouble at all to them that occasioned it: and therefore did plainly show with what intention and view they did quarrel with Mr Money and demand his Account I used to ask them if it was Justice and my Interest that they Consulted why they never called Mr Money to account before but just when they were in a rage against me for my Doctrine, and understood how kind[314] he had been to me? &c. but it signifyed nothing.

Moreover it cannot easily be expressed with what eagerness they promoted in this juncture Mistress Williamson's Marriage whose boarding with us a Servant at a moderate rate was a great help towards our Subsistance but they never left till they got her out of my house and got her Marryed to one at St. Ives whom yet they afterwards called one of the greatest Rogues and Cheats upon Earth; though he was in Communion with the Church there whose minister (Mr Harrison (an Excellent Preacher) was the man of their Favour to whom they went to recieve the Sacrament at his hands when they refused it at mine.[315]

Notwithstanding I have great reason to bless the Lord that preserved my mind and Spirit in so much ease peace and quiet in all this Obloquy and Contempt. The goodness of my Cause the Truth of my Doctrine which I studyed over and over my Care to instruct them the best I could was comfort and Satisfaction to me. Besides I knew that I was not singular if I erred it was in the best Company as any one may see that shall read Dallaeus[316] (whom upon the earnest recommendation of my Reverend Worthy Friend Mr John Spademan of London (a person of the same moderate Principles and Temper with my Self) I now read)[317] or shall view a paper of Authoritys that I collected my Self. I proposed the Case and accounted for my Doctrine to a Meeting of sixteen Ministers and they were all of my mind to a little. I wrote

[314] *they* cancelled.

[315] Michael Harrison (d. 1727) had been the conforming vicar of Caversfield, Oxon., but removed to a Dissenting meeting at Potterspury, Northants., probably in 1692. In 1709, he removed once more, to St Ives, Hunts. See Gordon, *Freedom after Ejection*, p. 280.

[316] Jean Daillé.

[317] John Spademan, MA (d. 1708) was the son of Thomas Spademan, the ejected minister of Authorpe, Lincs. Like Rastrick, John Spademan was an after-dissenter who left his Church of England living (he was vicar of Swaton, Lincs. and rector of Llandynam, Montgomery) to become pastor of the English Church at Rotterdam (1681–1698), before moving to London in 1698 to become John Howe's assistant at the Presbyterian congregation that met at Haberdashers' Hall on Staining Lane in Cheapside. For a long account of his life, and a written covenant, see Samuel Rosewell, *A Sermon Preach'd . . . upon Occasion of the Death of the Reverend John Spademan* (London, 1708).

out four remarkable passages of Calvin asserting the same that I had done and sent them to Mr Peast to consider of: but when I after asked him whether he had so done, he told me, no, but when he saw what it was about he threw it (he sayed) into the fire and burnt it. In the mean time the majority of the Congregation by far were highly pleased with my Doctrine And though the Scotchmens proclaiming it to be poysonous might in reason be thought to be a Great hindrance to mens attendance on the Means yet the Meeting never lessened but was as numerous as ever The Anabaptists came amongst us, and were the most of them well pleased to the vexation of my Enemies who one of them once asked what had they to do there though to do him justice he repented of so saying afterwards.

As to my Self I was loath to impose my Self upon them (considering what Mr Baxter saies; True and Only Way of Concord. part 3. page 127.)[318] and therefore when they disclaimed my Ministry at the rate before mentioned I freely gave the Male contents leave to chuse to themselves another Minister and wrot to them under my hand to that purpose Though I could not leave the place I told them nor could the rest of the Congregation who were my Friends maintain me but as to those things I referred all to the Will /fo. 67v/ and Providence of God &c. So upon this The discontented party appointed a General Meeting to chuse another Minister in which they made up their party about as many more though some they had gained on were no Charge bearers. My Friends were not negligent in such a Crisis but went and made a Great Majority. The Great Question Mr Peast put to them was whether the warning I had sent them was not sufficient to proceed upon towards another Minister? My Friends cryed, No, they took it to be no warning to them nor indeed at all to any even themselves but upon Supposition that they were dissatisfyed with my Ministry Tell him say they that you are satisfyed with it and then if he yet warns you to get another we shall say more to you but as for our parts we are satisfyed we desire no other and we take it as no warning to us. And so the rest seeing the Majority clear for me could not carry their point But the rage that Mr Peast expressed at that Meeting was such that it was feared he would have struck Mr Money for he had much ado to hold his hands. The result was that he told my friends that I should preach in this Meeting no longer than till Easter next which was 1708 This meeting being about three weeks or a Month before And so he sent me word by them So at Easter I expected the Meeting would have been shut up. yet I went on and they cooling upon it the Meeting was not shut up as threatned.

[318] Richard Baxter, *The True and Only Way of Concord of All the Christian Churches: the desirableness of it, and the detection of false dividing terms* (London, 1680), pt. 3, p. 127.

At length as the Spring came on The Odium of this Opposition amongst all Sorts of men wrought upon them somewhat And the Pretender's Landing at that time in Scotland somewhat more for Mr Peast sent for me upon it and being alarmed with the danger as they usually are that have much to lose he told me he was resolved that there should be no more Quarrels amongst us So at length a Meeting was appointed with me for Peace At which my Doctrine came into debate the only Scotchman that was there would have disputed it but Mr Peast and the rest would not suffer him to hinder me from speaking and explaining my Self which I did to their seeming great Satisfaction They told me I did not make my Doctrine so plain in the Pulpit. which I had done but they were not willing to understand me as now they seemed to be. So a general Signification was made of a better understanding begot but short of what it should have been For I was (and it may be too sinfully) loath to be the obstructor of the Peace by a disciplinary putting them upon declaring publickly their Repentance for what had past. So without that to the Sacrament (which was about a fourt'night after) they came though Mr Peast had not been there of Five years before a thing too censurable if they would have born it. But it was passed over. At this meeting I proposed no Article, and made no Terms for my Self, for the making up my defaulted Maintainance. No Consideration for my double Labour after Mr Williamsons Death; nor was any thing done or offered that way by them: though my Maintainance was lessened in proportion to the encrease of my charge; as was observed before. It might be well for me that I escaped /fo. 68r/ without Engagements for they would oft have had me to have promised them not to preach so and so and the like. But I told them but it seems then that I must Conform and subscribe again after all: but sure I should be accounted a very fool, and appear so to my Self, to refuse to subscribe <though> against my Conscience for a hundred a year (if I could get it) in the Church of England, if I could subscribe against my Conscience to them for nothing! One would rather chuse the former than the latter.

In the mean time several awful things happned which must not be wholly silenced, though I make no judgment on them. One old man that had withdrawn from the Meeting in a pettish[319] discontent at some other things as at the use of the 100 Psalm tune; and at my speaking against their keeping on their hats in Sermon time without necessity, and the like. On a Lords day on which he kept at home in the Morning Service time about Eleven of the Clock he fell down his own Stairs and broke his Leg which though he went abroad again

[319]*pettish*: subject to fits of offended ill humour; childishly bad-tempered and petulant; peevish, sulky. *OED*.

some time after he yet scarce ever thoroughly recovered. Another of our Scotchmen one of the forementioned Male-Contents had his Son slain outright with a fall from a horse; and at another time his own ankle bone broke which confined him for a considerable while: and ther those that had taken disgust at the Ordinances amongst us could not attend thereon now if they would. What they thought of those things I know not I mentioned them not to them; but one of them sayed it looked as if God would whip us all round if we would not be quiet. And Mr Peast when he buryed his daughter in Mr Williamson's time told him he feared it was for his wrathful Carriage against me which was then Comparatively small and in a manner but begun. But he soon forgot all afterwards.

But the peace last mentioned was very short lived and lasted but for a very few weeks The occasion of a New Breach comes next therefore to be mentioned which I shall relate as briefly as I can.

Mr Peast having marryed his Daughter to a Church Minister a Conformist and a great Living in Suffolk which they made themselves sure of being otherwise disposed of He to please and prefer his discontented Daughter thought to betake himself to his fast Friend his Purse which would open when the Bounty of others was shut. Now this his Design of buying his Son in Law a Living he one time mentioning occasionally to me I freely and plainly told him that he could not lawfully and honestly do it That is Corruption That his Son must swear that no such thing was done and in short I told him that I thought it one of the greatest pieces of Wickedness in the World. His wife hearing this cryed Nay he loves to talk he intends no such thing: though in his reply to her he affirmed he was serious: /fo. 68v/ But at this time it went off without any Shew of anger A little while after Mr White (one of St Ives that had marryed Mr Williamsons Widdow) being come to Town he and I and Mr Peast and Mr Bagg an Brewer an Alderman of Lyn[320] light in Company together: and after some little other Discourse Mr Peast having said upon some occasion that all Church Preferment was but a Trade to which whether I answered a wicked and unlawful Trade and therefore not to be meddled with I know not but the Dispute was there renewed upon the Question about buying his Son a Living Mr Bagg took my part with very good reason and judgment and Mr White took Mr Peast's part with great Eagerness and scornful contempt of all that I sayed tho he was a Dissenter I minded Mr Peast of a Story that I had before told him of the Judgment of God upon that Practise of my own knowledge in

[320]John Bagge, merchant and brewer, was made a freeman of King's Lynn in 1694–1695. He was subsequently an alderman and twice mayor (1711–1712; 1731–1732). See *A Calendar of the Freemen of Lynn*.

the case of Mr Peters mentioned before[321] and Mr Bagg immediately seconded it with another Story of the like nature of His own knowledg. Mr White mainly justified it because it was a thing commonly done Mr Bagg replyed that there was no good reason you must not, added he, follow a Multitude to do Evil &c. As for my Self when the Dispute grew a little warm I could scarce be suffered to speak a word do what I could but Mr Peast's and Mr White's Clamours silenced me. So not being permitted to speak my mind in a day or two after I wrote to Mr Peast and in my Letter which I ordered to be put secretly into his own hand, and it was so, and might have been kept private if he had pleased I gave him above twenty Reasons against the thing I percieved he designed and withall told him plainly that if he was resolved and persisted in it I could not admit him to the Lords Supper &c. He came after to my house upon some <other> occasion the day I sent it so I then mentioned it to him and desired him not to take it ill to which he said little but by some other discourse at the same time about the Non Jurors he saying what a Mischief it was that the Nation was sworn so much when Security taken would be better a Strain he was never used to discourse in before but the quite Contrary I say by this I percieved that the Oath his Son was to take against Simony stuck most in his Stomack Which when I wrote I thought I could not in faithfulness but lay before him in the very words which was therefore best done by writing that he might consider of them And one of my reasons given him in my Letter was drawn from thence. He seemed to be discontented and reserved this time though he yet broke not out into passion which /fo. 69r/ afterwards broke out and flamed to such a height and heat that it made me study the point of Simony more seriously so that my better than twenty hasty reasons against it quickly rose to as many more and for one Author I quoted in it I could now quote twenty For his Charge against me being so high and his wrath so vehement I could not but the more bethink me of the point and I searched both my own and the two Town Librarys that I might not be deceived my Self and might also be better able to manage the Controversy if there should be further occasion. The Substance or Result of my Search may be found in a small Treatise of mine which I have stiled A Disswasive from Church Merchandize which my Son if he ple<a>ses may publish upon advice taken with his Learned Friends who may peruse it and correct what needs it.[322] Now the Wrath that occasioned this thus broke out The Lords day following, after I had wrote the aforesaid Letter, in my Prayer before

[321] See p. 35, marginal note and n. 21 above.

[322] This treatise appears not to have survived.

Sermon I used that expression [323] and prayed that God would Cast the Buyers and Sellers out of his Temple an expression that I had oft used before especially when on Fast days I prayed for the Reformation of the Church; and which should I now have suppressed when it came into my mind and I had such occasion and need to use, omitting it merely that I might not displease; my Conscience would have accused me of culpable Pusillanimity and fear of man. But this was it that fired Mr Peast to that degree that seeing him the week after to pay him some money that I ought him, He then fell out with me in the bitterest manner than co<u>ld be; He called me Blockhead over and over and scornfully cryed You a Minister! He sayed if I had been a younger man he would have demanded Satisfaction He cryed God forbid that the Church should ever be reformed upon my principles or as I desired it should or that men of my Spirit should prevail: hinting that he would venture his Life to oppose it. Added his old expressed that he would never be Priest-ridden while he lived He said I took more upon me than the Pope of Rome did and another while compared me to the Quakers; but in what I have forgot. He said there was no Sense or reason in any one of the 24 that I had given him against his Simony in my Letter mentioned the Church of England's Approbation of Buying Advowsons, which he bore himself much upon He sayed he would nail my Letter up at his Gate for all to see that they might hoot at me for it. When I had or took occasion to blame some other things in him as his sleeping so much at Sermons /fo. 69v/ He sayd my Sermons were such pityfull Stuff they were fit for nothing but to be slept under. And (as might well be expected) he threatened over and over to withdraw his Subscription and Contribute no more to the Meeting while I was in that he was resolved on Urged my Removal and bad me be gone from Lyn: but when I spoke of staying; and asked, whither must I remove? you cannot turn me out of my house &c. this seemed very much to disturb both himself and others that sat by What, (sayed his wife) you'll Pay on purpose to be a Plague to us, will you? In a word it is not to be expressed with what bitter and scornful rage he foamed for about an hour I never heard the Devil speak more <from> out of a man enmity and Scorn at the Discipline of Christ. and for my Self I never was so reviled abused and trampled on by any even in my Juniority; despised and vilifyed as if I had been a Scullion boy; scarce more by my Enemies at Kirkton nor have I ever seen any treated with greater Contempt. Once in his rambling rage he told us how he came to be a Dissenter (and one that shall read what 'fore-goes would be apt to inquire into that.) Why it was only upon

[323] *that* cancelled.

hearing Mr Killingback (formerly minister at Lyn now at Leeds)[324] preach up the Doctrine of Non Resistance and Passive Obedience But (that he might not be thought a false one or an hypochrite) he sayed he had done and expended more for the Cause than I had done.

After this viz in Christmas 1708 in a very snowy Season away goes my Gentleman with a hot head and cool toes to London to get another Minister. We all presumed what he went about because he went from the Meeting a little before in a rage calling me Rogue for something or other that I had sayed in expounding the 15th Psalm and then in the hearing of some he declared his Resolution. At London applying himself to Dr Williams[325] and Dr Calamy he met with no encouragement but the Contrary So away he comes down again re infecta[326] He saw there was no getting another Minister while I was here and therefore his great Care was how to get me out So at the Mart following when Mr Kinderly of Wisbich (one of my best Friends)[327] and Mr Low of Staffordshire another Friend of mine were in Town he Commissioned them to treat with me about my Removall from Lyn the great thing he was now intent upon He bad them tell me that if I would go peaceably away he would be very kind and Civil to me and buy my house to boot and give me what it cost me (though the next day he was off of that) and that he would do otherwise very well for me. (So the purse and buying must still do every thing: but he did not know that I was of opinion that it is Corruption to be bought out of a place or charge as well as to be bought into one.) But if I would not go away at Lady Day he offered Mr Kinderly to take a Shilling to give him 500[li] if he did not shut up the Meeting house at the said term i.e. in six weeks time. So my Friends brought his Message to me and told me that they percieved in him a mortal hatred to me by his very Carriage which they blamed exceedingly for he could not speak of me with patience so as to contein him /fo. 70r/ Self: So they thought it better for me (if I could remove) to be gone. But that I alleged was not likely at my age, near 60; and with my Family of seven small Children; every place would be shy of recieving us. It's true if Providence had called me elsewhere I believe I should have gone but as it did not I was content to stay and weather out the Storm as well as God should enable me. I was not much troubled or disquieted in my mind all this while nor solicitous how I should live. The pleasure I had in searching the Librarys, and composing my Disswasive; Mind

[324]John Killingback, BD (1649–1716), lecturer of St Nicholas's Chapel, King's Lynn (1682–1690); vicar of Leeds, Yorks. (1690–1716).

[325]Daniel Williams (*c.*1643–1716), Presbyterian minister and benefactor. *ODNB.*

[326]*re infecta*: with the matter unfinished.

[327]For Nathaniel Kinderley (1673–1742), see p. 169, n. 344 below.

and Thoughts so employed and engaged kept out all other Trouble. I showed them (with another London Friend <or two>) my enlarged Reasons proving Mr Peasts Design for which I had reproved him to be very sinful, with which they were highly satisfyed; and one said he believed all the world could not answer them: and another would have had me to have printed them &c.

In the mean time I shall relate a Passage here that ought not to be covered in Silence The next Lord's Day (February 6. 1708/9) in the morning Mr Peast comes to the Meeting then full of Londoners it being Mart time But while the Psalm which came in course was singing For being got as far as the Psalms in expounding the Scriptures of the Old Testament since I came to Lyn, having begun with the New Testament before, I usually sung the Psalm that fell to be so read and expounded This day it was the 27th Psalm Now when the 12th verse in Bradys and Tate's Translation (which we used as aforesaid) was just Concluded The words are these

Lord disappoint my cruel Foes
defeat their ill desire
Whose lying lips and bloody hands
against my Peace Conspire[328]

I say when I had just read the last line of this verse Mr Peast rose up in a passion and throws his Seat door open with a noyse that might have been heard into my own house hard by and away he goes with a swift and hasty pace, and comes no more that day nor but little and that uncerteinly and unconstantly ever after. This opened the Londoners eyes especially when they understood that the Psalm was not designed but came in course They saw then the rancour and Guilt discovered that lay at the bottom /fo. 70v/ In the evening the other male Contents that in all these confusions sided with him went to Mr Peast's to see him and discourse with him upon this his Carriage but to what purpose I know not 'tis said to Comfort him. On Tuesday morning next after this his darling Grand child dyed very suddenly who was well and in the Mart the day before but dead that night. This seemed to have wrought on and humbled Mr Peast a little; for he was twice at the Meeting the next Lords Day, and sat Patiently, and looked very much down and melancholy: And his Son Charles sayd that Nothing (no not his Grandfathers death) went so near him as the Death of this Child. But it quickly wore off. His way was to drown his Sorrows in a Glass of wine to keep his Spirits from sinking as he would say himself So he soon returned to and settled in the same furious disorder and distemper of mind that he was wont to be in towards

[328] *A New Version of the Psalms of David, Fitted to the Tunes Used in Churches. By N. Tate and N. Brady* (London, 1698), p. 49.

me He came to the Meeting indeed once a day or so but he always either slept out the time or heard with the utmost prejudice. He would make the most monstrous misconstructions and misinterpretations of what I sayed in Prayer and Preaching that ever was heard To give an Instance When I prayed against the Enemies of the Church of God I sometimes in allusion to what God did to the Egyptians in the Red Sea prayed that God would take off their Chariot Wheels that they might drive heavily &c. having used this one day he was enraged and berogued me and sayed I prayed that his Chariot Wheels might fly off For he had been at West Winch[329] in his Chariot the Lords Day before which yet I knew nothing of till it came to my ears upon occasion of this rout about it which his misinterpretation and outcrys caused.

He was easily brought to believe by the malecontents that it was a good work to turn me out for when it was represented to them how inhumane and barbarous it was in them to banish or turn me away at this age and with this Family they sayed Gods Glory is more to be sought than the Interest of one Family. (This was in them upon account of my principles.) And therefore when one represented to Mr Peast the Sin of silencing a Minister of Christ he sayed it was no Sin to silence such a one as I. No wonder then if what he had so oft threatened he at last attempted. A Relation of the occasion and Circumstances of which here follows as I wrote it at the time

/fo. 71r/

Of Mr Peast's shutting up the Meeting House against me.

Mr Peast being enraged against me for the Letter I sent him for his simoniacal purpose went to London in Christmas 1708 and applyed him Self to Mr Williams and Mr Calamy in order to get another Minister but they would not meddle in that affair and so he comes down again re infecta[330] But his Discontents rather encreasing than abating he first left the Meeting in part and then altogether and continues his Resolution to trie to get another Minister with whom about half a dozen Concurred who were disgusted at my Baxterian Doctrine as they called it and especially as I have reason to believe at my Pastoral Exercise of Discipline which had touched some of themselves.<*> So applying themselves to some of Mr Hussies Congregation at Cambridg[331] One of them had a Son Who had been

*Marginal note: * all which has been related before.

[329] A village three miles south of King's Lynn.

[330] *re infecta*: with the matter unfinished.

[331] Joseph Hussey (1660–1726) was the minister of Emmanuel Congregational Church, Cambridge. For a brief sketch of his life and extracts from his diary, see A.G. Matthews, *Diary of a Cambridge Minister* (Cambridge, 1937).

brought up under Mr Thomas Goodwin[332] who was now Chaplin to Mr Ottley at Norton in Darbyshire To him his Friends write from Cambridg to come to Lyn and to Mr Peast's house in particular So on Saturday the 14 of May 1709 he Comes and Mr Ottley and his wife comeing also <to> their Sister Marryed here a hearer and very good Friend of mine I went to Invite him to preach the next day and he told me he thought I had been gone from Lyn and so came upon a mistake which now understanding he assured me he would do nothing in the least to my Prejudice and that we might all be easie and that he would rather beg his bread than turn me out So he was willingly heard two Lords Days and on Monday the 23^d^ of May went away to Cambridg But returning again on Friday the 28 and some of the Male contents giving out that they did believe this to be the Man that was to be their Minister and pitying me that I should be so deluded by my seaming Friends who they said were ready to come over to Mr Watsons interest (for that was the young mans name) and subscribe for his coming and bringing me a Message from Mr Peast and Mr Tayler[333] demanding the Pulpit for the next day for Mr Watson I first yielded them all my Interest in the Pulpit not only for the morrow but for the future for Continuance from henceforth and told them I would not oppose Mr Watson and then gave an account thereof to my Friends who being alarmed /fo. 71v/ at it went immediately to gather hands for me that they might know (and we also) who were my Friends and who were my Foes and of about 40 Contributers or charge bearers (which were all that did any thing to this Meeting) they got that afternoon and were assured of 30 or 31 that were hearty for me. But <one> of my Friends signifying to one of them that they would find that <ther> would be those that would oppose them if Mr Watson intended to supplant me this was Carryed to Mr Peast and put him into a new rage. And tho we were all satisfyed that Mr Watson had no such design (upon our discourse with him) and my friends (as <well as> I who had desired it of him) were well content he should preach the next day yet upon the aforesaid Misreport away comes the credulous and jealous man Mr Peast to the house of one of my best Friends (who was then with me and Mr Watson peacably and friendly at Supper together at another Friends and so not at home) and there did he fall into such a rage against us, and against me in particular calling me a blockhead

[332]This was presumably the Independent minister Thomas Goodwin (*c.*1650–1708?), who kept an Academy at Pinner, Middx., rather than the nonconformist minister Thomas Goodwin (1600–1680). *ODNB*.

[333]Stephen Tayler was appointed common councilman of King's Lynn in 1688 (alongside Seal Peast). See Hillen, *History of the Borough of King's Lynn*, I, p. 444. He was also a witness to the will of the elder Charles Peast (d. 1707). TNA, PRO, PROB 11/495 (Will of Charles Peast, Gentleman of King's Lynn, Norfolk, 1707).

and Lying rascally fellow and the like; and this so often and with so foul a mouth that some there said Billingsgate is a fool to it. and thence he went to my house demanded the keys of the Meeting went and locked it up or saw it lockd and carryed them home with him. The next morning Lords Day May 29. 1709. he comes about 9 of the clock to open them but whatever the matter was he could not do it So he comes to my door and sent for me to Come to him and let him and his Friends charge me and mine with haveing taken off the old Lock and set on a new one since he had been there the night before We all denyed it said we knew nothing of it neither I nor my wife &c. He answered we were nothing but our Lyes and Equivocations I only asked him what need he had to lock up the door against us to get Mr Watson in whose preaching no body opposed and told him that he was in a dreadful Temper to attend upon Ordinances in!—— But suspecting the Matter I sent my Servant to trie to open the Door, She went and did it immediately with the same key; and divers (it being a rainy morning) pressing into the Meeting when the Doors were so open Mr Peast made them all go out again and locked up the Doors again and went his way; a Stranger a Yorkshire man of Leeds (being here on his Journey to Norwich) earnestly entreating him to open them but in vain. Upon this One steps in at a Casement that was open and by and by [334] lifting up the Barr of the half door opens them both. This done we sent to Mr Watson who was at Mr Peast's to come and preach but he would not Come; and so I preached. In the afternoon I sent to him again to preach but he refused then also /fo. 72r/ so I performed the Duty the whole day as usually. In the evening we sent for the keys to lock the Doors He sent them but not without a Promise of returning them to him again. which was done.

Now here it is to be observed that though these two things were plain 1. That no body opposed Mr Watsons preaching and 2. That the Lock was not altered to that end: yet did Mr Peast and them with him persist to affirm the Contrary.

And now it is time to mention the State of the Meeting house and what Authority he pretended to do all this. The Meeting house in Spinner Lane in Lyn was given by Deed from Mr Blith and Mr Goddard[335] purchasers and principal Repairers for a Presbyterian Meeting if it may be; if not, then <for> an Independent <Meeting> if not that for a School. And <the> Feofees appointed in the Deed to take care that it be repaired from time to time and put to the mentioned Uses. Three of the Feofees were now dead and four

[334] Illegible word cancelled.

[335] Probably Guybon Goddard (1612–1671), recorder of King's Lynn from 1650, and antiquarian. See *ODNB*; Richards, *The History of Lynn*, II, pp. 1003–1004.

survived whereof Mr Peast is one: Another of them firmly for me: and another indifferent: and the 4th not so hot in the matter as Mr Peast would have him; for he would not accompany him in it on Lords Day Morning as he had done the evening before not knowing as he said whether and about what Mr Peast was carrying him: Though he be one of the Male Contents.

But to return. When the person that locked up the Meeting house doors in course went back with the Keys to Mr Peasts on the evening of the Lords Day aforementioned (May 29.) He found Mr Peast and those that were with him in such a Rant as may justly amaze the Reader as it does the Writer and make his ears to tingle For so provoked and vexed were they that we had had the Liberty of the Meeting house that day, that Mr Peast said, rather than I should preach there he would pull down the Pulpit and Cut up the Seats and Carry them away; and one Peter Brad a Scotchman[336] there in Company Cryed Burn the Pulpit:[337] but young Charles Peast[338] saying he could not do that without burning the House and endangering more, he answered, Bring it out into the Lane and set a Fire on it!—— The Lord forgive them for they know not what they do. Had it been from the bloody Papists such Treatment might have been expected.

On the next day Munday (May 30) Madam Rolf Sister to Madam Ottley beforementioned and my very good Friend went on purpose to see and discourse with Mr Peast upon all this and there did she for five or six hours together plead with him on my behalf with all the force of Argument and Rhetorick that she could use, which was not small, but could prevail nothing. He fell into such Passions against me as did exceedingly astonish and affright her in which he would go out and breath a little and then begin /fo. 72v/ again. She argued with him [339] upon the greatness of the Sin of silencing Christs Ministers: and the Absurdity of the thing that when Dissenters seperate from the Church because there is no Discipline in it but all are admitted to the Lords Table &c. that yet they should not endure the least offer at it or lowest degree of it themselves And that upon Supposition that [340] I were in errour Can there said she be no forgiveness? and what if God should deal with us all as we deal with one another, and as hardly forgive us as we do one another? and the like—— But all this

[336] Possibly Peter Bread, cooper, who became a freeman of King's Lynn in 1718–1719. See *A Calendar of the Freemen of Lynn*, p. 224.

[337] This exclamation and the following one are underlined in the text, presumably for emphasis.

[338] Charles Peast was the son of Seal Peast. He became a freeman of King's Lynn in 1709–1710. See *A Calendar of the Freemen of Lynn*, p. 218; Will, 1723: TNA, PRO, PROB 11/593.

[339] *but* cancelled.

[340] *then* cancelled.

prevailing nothing she brings us that evening this Message from Mr Peast that if I would not desist quietly from preaching there he would certeinly destroy all within the Meeting house both Pulpit and Seats as before was mentioned. But I said rather than any such violence should be used I would desist.

I had been informed that Mr Rolfe Town=Clerk and Father in Law to my worthy Friend[341] now mentioned a person learned in the Law had been reteined by Mr Peast and had advised him upon Sight of the Deed (beforementioned) to do all that he had done And having also but a little before recieved five Briefs which I had signed the Receipt of as Minister of this Meeting according to Law; I considered with my Self, How must I read them if I be shut out? and on whom must the 100^{li} (viz 20^{li} a brief) fall if they be not read and Collected as by Law they ought. So upon a Friends advise I ventured to go to Mr Rolfe with my Case. When I came there I found all that I had heard was false He had not seen the Deed nor had he given Mr Peast any advise or Counsell upon it But as to the thing, said, that it was unreasonable and what Mr Peast had no power to do for at that rate if another should leave a place of advantage to come hither upon their Invitation he might be liable to be turned out again at the Month or two's end upon Mr Peast's humour which is not to be. and as to the Briefs he said that the 100^{li} penalty for default must fall upon Mr Peast if by his means [342] I were disabled from reading them. and as to the main Case before related and one's getting in at a Casement to open the Meeting house one of the Feofees commending it he said we had done no more than what we might justifie, and might do the like again if occasion were: and in the whole gave me his advise with the greatest freedom Candour and Civility that could be. Said Mr Peast was a hot man but he would speak with him and moderate him. And so as the Town Clark of Ephessus had appeased the people in Confusion there by his reason and Law (Acts 19.) Such was the nature and tendency of this Gentleman's Counsel here.

/fo. 73r/ But this Exclusion did not continue long. It's true, Mr Peast would not deliver the keys to me, but to Madam Rolfe he did within a week: So we were deprived but of one Lecture on Thursday that week. which could not be preached.

Mr Watson whom Mr Peast had taken out of his place in Darbyshire he sent with his Son Charles as his Tutor or Companion at least

[341] Edmund Rolfe (1649–1726), town clerk of King's Lynn for thirty-five years; later an alderman and twice mayor (1713–1714; 1720–1721). See R.T. and A. Gunther, *Rolfe Family Records: volume II* (London and Aylesbury, 1914), pp. 50–62; A.E. Gunther, *Rolfe Family Records: volumes I and III* (Heacham, Norfolk, 1962), pp. 4–5.

[342] Illegible word cancelled.

into Holland I wrote a Letter to my friend Mr Loftus preacher at Rotterdam[343] to bring them acquainted with the Country &c. which Mr Peast Senior took extream kindly in so much as Mr Waters seemed afraid it would have brought a Closure and was greatly vexed. But in three of four months time Mr Peast recalls his Son and Mr Watson to the latter's great trouble and vexation For they had newly entred themselves Students at Utrecht and brought the proper Habits But away they must come and Mr Peast sent me word of it beforehand that Mr Watson might enter this pulpit peaceably. So I wrote to Mr Williams (since Dr) for his advice how to carry my Self in this juncture and recieved his Answer. and his advice I followed in every thing but one and that was about yielding the Pastoral Office he was against it but I was for it because it was the exercise of that that was the cause of most of our Quarrels. So Mr Watson comes. but instead of Rivalling me I could not get him to preach of some time and that not above once or twice at most. For the buisness was this he was fallen under Mr Peast's Frown as much as I was He accused him for having debauched his Son Charles was so wicked as to accuse him and the Father readily believes it, and in a few weeks time lets him go away on foot without any Notice or respect afforded him. This greatly disgusted our other Male contents who hoped that Mr Peast would have settled Mr Watson which was the thing that made them abandon Mr Peasts Case and take against him and excuse and favour me which they most did save Mr Waters. and so things begun to take another turn with us.

As to Mr Peast he ordered a woman one Lords Day to take home his Cushions out of his Seat in the Meeting and resolves totally to forsake us (having withdrawn his contribution as he threatened) which for the main he did though now and then once in a Month or two he would come dropping in. So he sometimes went to his Son Charles's to Elm sometimes when there to Mr Burroughs at Wisbich but in Winter time especially he mostly stayed at home I did not hear that he was above once at the Church in Lyn; and then his behaviour was such as was matter of Sport to every body. So at the mentioned rate for three years till in February 1712/3 he dyed of a Palsy that first took away the Use of his hands and then of his reason and then his Speech I went to see him but was not admitted So I saw him no more In

[343]Bartholomew Loftus (1679–1751) was educated at Jollie's Academy at Attercliffe Hall. After posts in Colchester and Amsterdam, he was the minister of the English Presbyterian Church at Rotterdam (first in concert with Joseph Hill (1667–1729)) between 1707 and 1751. See Benjamin Snowden, *The Mourner's Consolation: a funeral sermon preached at the English church in Rotterdam, Octob. 24. 1751. on occasion of the lamented death of the late Reverend Bartholomew Loftus* (The Hague, 1751).

three or four Months time Mr Waters followed him: but him I saw oft in his Sickness, who seemed to be in a good Temper and under great Concern.

In the mean time Gods good providence towards me was very wonderful In my Straits when my maintainance here fell off I had sent me from other places above three Score pound within the space of little more than a Twelve month without any seeking of mine the Circumstances of which were most amazing.* And God at this time a few Months before Mr Peast dyed brought to dwell at Lyn my dear worthy and wealthy Friend Mr Kinderley of Wisbich[344] who a youth at 16 years old had been my constant hearer at Spalding and to whom I hope God made me /fo. 73v/ a spiritual Father as he made him an Earthly Father to me now. For besides that he greatly adorned our Meeting house (which had been threatned to be rifled) He did the first Summer of his coming lay water to my house which cost him fifteen pound and saved us thirty or forty Shillings a year or more carriage. The next Spring after he at his own proper cost and charge (requiring no Mortgage or Security of me, but all his own free gift) Built us up a New Kitchin and Office of Brewing, giving us also all our malt, and so saving us Eight pound a year at least that Mr Peast used to have of us for drink This cost him (with a little Chamber and two convenient rooms under it which he at the same time added to my small house) no less than fourty pound He got up my Sallary by his Interest and Dilligence to what it was at first i.e. Ten pound a Quarter: And was our Friend in every thing, and studyed our Interest upon all occasions. The Lord grant unto him that he may find mercy of the Lord in that day.

It may easily be imagined what an Effect this wonderful change had upon our people; that God had sent us such a one to strengthen our hands. And especially upon our Male contents who seeing all

*Marginal note: And so for the Twenty pound per annum that Mr Peast boasted he had hindred me of God gave me three Twentys.

[344]Nathaniel Kinderley (1673–1742) was born in Spalding, and was a civil engineer who became a key figure in fen drainage projects of the eighteenth century. He was the author of *The Present State of the Navigation of the Towns of Lyn, Wisbeach, Spalding, and Boston* (Bury St Edmunds, 1721), which is mistakenly attributed by the ESTC to Charles Kinderley. Nathaniel is frequently mistaken for his son, also Nathaniel, who published an extended version of his father's tract in 1751. See Mike Chrimes et al (eds), *Biographical Dictionary of Civil Engineers in Great Britain and Ireland: volume 1 – 1500 to 1830* (London, 2002), pp. 286–288. Rastrick's account provides the earliest evidence of Kinderley's whereabouts, his work, and (presumably) his religious sympathies. Rastrick's will and his correspondence with Mr William Steevens, corn factor in Queenhithe, London (Dr Williams's Library, MS 24.115 fo. 46) suggest that Kinderley lived in King's Lynn until 1725, when he moved to Setchey Bridge, about four miles south of King's Lynn.

this, became perfectly reconciled to me and to my Ministry, and very friendly in their Carriage and deportment. So that (except my worthy patron just mentioned) I believe I have no better friends than they who seemed before such bitter Enemies.

/fo. 74r/

Of my Studies

I took my Degree of Master of Arts before I was so much as a Smatterer in any one of them;* not understanding when I was at the University the Logick and Philosophy which was read to me there; (as I partly hinted before:) and therefore sold or swaped several of my philosophy Books which I thought would be of no use to me in the Country. But after I was settled at Kirkton some little time I fell into the reading and Study of the Works of Dr Henry More occasioned by my Acquaintance with Mr Brocklesby (now) of Folkingham. (often mentioned; but not to be mentioned without Honour and respect) In these Studies I soon saw my Defect, in not understanding something of the Philosophy of Des Cartes wherfore I now borrowed him (having parted with my own at Cambridg) and read his Principles over more carefully; and by the advantage of what I had learnt in Dr More I began to understand him; especially his Doctrine of the Vortex's, of which before I had no Notion[345] And with this (upon occasion also of frequent converse with a Neighbour of mine, a plain man, but deeply versed in such kind of Studies) I took in something of Astronomy and some other parts of the Mathematicks. This gave my Mind a large Scope I soon became wedded to the Copernican Hypothesis or the Pythagorick Scheme and System of the World unable to resist the Evidence I saw for it. The Thoughts I had of the Frame of the World and Order of the Creation the Multiplicity of habitable Earths like this of ours (which I thought most highly probable) and especially of the vast Extent of the Universe were thoughts that at once surprised, enterteined, and amazed me! I often tryed in my mind to think or suppose that there were or should be nothing, no World, and I could not. I tryed to limit the Universe, or if I could suppose or believe that

*Marginal note: Which was Anno Domini 1674.
At which time I thought I should have lost my Degree and all my Money I had payd; not dareing to appear at my Call at the Passing of it, because I understood not, and was not satisfyed about the Oath that was put upon such as went up before me. When all was over I spoke to the Procter about it not knowing but that all was lost. But upon better Satisfaction, I passed next morning. God (I thank him) had not abandoned me to a seared profligate Conscience.

[345]On this see Henry More, *The Immortality of the Soul* (London, 1659); René Descartes, *Principia philosophiae* (Amsterdam, 1644, and many later editions).

it has limits, and I could not: for let me travail never so far in my thoughts into the Universe and above the starry Firmament and I was constrained to think and believe that there must be something thick or thin i.e. Space empty or full beyond it; and this also into what Quarter soever my mind or Fancy darted it Self! To help our Conceptions of this matter let us suppose six bodies in motion from some certein Center into so many parts or Quarters of the Universe Ex. Gr. One moving East a second West a third North a fourth South a fifth upward a sixth downward: (Or we may suppose them so many Spirits (if we will) able to /fo. 74v/ penetrate through thick and thin.) And let us suppose them all flying straight forwards towards their several Quarters (and not in a Circular or returning Course) and that with a rapidity many thousand times swifter than the Shot out of any gun (or if you will as swift as the Light, which is demonstrated to move 9000 miles in a Second of time i.e. the 60th part of a minute) And yet, (O amazingly wonderful!) there is Room enough in the Universe for all these eternally, to move onwards <at that rate> and never come at any Stop!—!——! So Comets march up into the Ethereal Expanse, and quickly get out of our Sight; (though the Heads of them be probably as <big as> the Earth we live upon.) And its probable that all the Comets that ever appeared to this Earth are at this present in being in one part of the Universe or other at Unconcievable Distance from us. O then methought how wonderfully Great is God, and how incomprehensible the Divine Immensity! And how much more proper is it to say that the World is in God, than that God is in the World! I soon was assured that all our Conceptions of him as a Person (circumscribed) are false; and that God is rather a Nature (a Divine Nature) than a person. And it made me admire at the Condescension of God in the Mystery of Christianity who by personating himself in the Lord Jesus Christ doth at once relieve our Conceptions and direct our Services.

Nor did I believe that the Opake Spots of the Universe in our own or any other Vortex* were all the Habitable part of it; but that the Ethereall Interspaces were the Noblest Part of it, and inhabited with blessed Spirits, and conteined the Mansions of the Noblest Beings. And though it seem to be a mere Vacuum and the Matter of it Escape all our Senses (as Mr Boyle has demonstrated in his Contin. Exper. of the Air part 1 Exper. 38.39. page 127–128.[346]) yet so dos Spirits themselves. And I thought that seperated Souls acquired new Senses by which

*Marginal note: * Or Systeme

[346] Robert Boyle, *A Continuation of New Experiments Physico-mechanical, Touching the Spring and Weight of the Air and their Effects* (Oxford, 1669).

the invisible world they go into and the things of it are known and discerned. And that therefore it is impossible in the Nature of the thing that a Man should see God and live. I thought their Light different from ours as well as the Sense by which it is to be discerned. And that there is no need to take care what the inhabitants of those Regions shall do for light when the Sun shall be Extinct: as Dr. More doth; (Immort. Soul props finem[347]) which I once suggested to him at his own Chamber at Christs College see Revelation 21.23. And I thought if there were but one Sense as much exceeding ours as our Ey Sight is above all the rest the acquisition of it would make a wonderfull change! And though it may seem impossible to us now that any Being or Spirit should penetrate the most solid Matter, and we know not how to concieve of it; yet so it would seem to a man born blind, if (to instruct /fo. 75r/ in the Nature of Light) you should put a Ball of solid Christal into his hand and tell him that the Light is such a thing that it can pierce that Body through and through and yet make no holes in it, nor cause any Separation of its Parts.

Geometry <in general> (though I went but a little way into it) I much admired. And Trigonometry in particular[348] (into which I went somewhat further) I admired much more, and greatly delighted in the practice of it; having occasion to use it more frequently in Horological Conclusions and Performances, with which I sometimes diverted my Self. And the strange Effect of the Logarithmeticall Tables in Calculation I could not but take notice of with a pleasing kind of Astonishment

Geography, and Travails; Natural Philosophy, (not the systematical, but the experimental kind) The Philosophical Transactions of the Virtuosi: The Works of Mr Boyle, Mr Hook, Mr Ray,[349] <&c.> These and others of the like kind, as many of them as I could get (buy or borrow) I read with much pleasure and profit. Dioptricks[350] I <afterward> got only so much as might help me in some measure to understand a Tellescope; and make some few common Experiments for my own diversion and the Enterteinment of my Friends. My great trouble all this while was, that (as in the Studies of Divinity and my sacred Function, so here,) I was not able (morally speaking) to buy so

[347] More, *The Immortality of the Soul*, pp. 543–544.

[348] *in particular* inserted in the margin.

[349] For Robert Boyle (1627–1691), Robert Hooke (1635–1703), and John Ray (1627–1705), see *ODNB*.

[350] *dioptrics*: that part of the science of optics which treats of the refraction of light. *OED*.

many Books as I desired, and after which I had so great <a> thirst: Nor had I any Acquaintance or Correspondence with many persons of that learning and Furniture of this kind as were able to supply me. And therefore O what Valuing Thoughts had I now of the Advantages of an Academical Life, in comparison of what I had when I was there! And I often wished that all Churches or Parishes were endowed or furnished with well chosen Librarys. (according to the project of Dr Bray in his Bibliotheca Parochialis: or Essay for Promoting necessary and useful Knowledg printed Anno Domini 1697.[351']) as is in many Market Towns in England already; But with the Addition of some Competent annual Sum for the encreasing of the same from time to time for the buying of New Books or changing Old ones for better editions. Many a Minister might by this means be drawn to study, that now having little to read falls to other courses. But to return

In the midst of these Studies I fell into a Profound Admiration of the Works of God who hath made all things in Number and Measure and Weight.* Nothing I could see or Converse with but upon an intentive consideration gave occasion thereof. The Laws of Proportion, The Mysteries of Numbers, the Properties of Figures Geometrical, and Bodies Physical I /fo. 75v/ thought exceedingly wonderfull. The Order and Frame of the World, and even of this Earth is very taking to a thoughtfull Spectator and free inquirer All Gods Works are Beautifull and Good, and it is only the Works of Men and Devils that are so bad. And when I Considered the Eternity and Immutability of the Properties of things in Geometry and Natural philosophy &c it seemed to me to adumbrate and illustrate the like Eternity and Immutability of the Reasons of Good and Evil. (For Vertue is nothing else but Moral Pulchritude, and Proportion; and Vice the Contrary.) And it led me to see the Necessity and Eternity of Law and Right; and the natural and indispensable Obligation we are under to Moral Duties. And who will not from hence infer an Eternal God who is Infinite and Universall Power Wisdom Goodness Justice Mercy Truth &c in the Abstract?

Tis true I might spend too much time in Studies and Practises Mathematical, and they sometimes took up too much of <my> thoughts, when they should have been free for better work: But then they were a great relief to me under my Afflictions, and when I was

*Marginal note: * Wisdom 11.20.

351'Thomas Bray, *Bibliotheca Parochialis: or, a scheme of such theological heads both general and particular, as are more peculiarly requisite to be well studied by every pastor of a parish* (London, 1697).

discomposed and Melancholy; I could fall to them when I could mind nothing else; and so they used me to study and prevented Idleness. And (not only in themselves, but) as they occasioned the Reflections before=mentioned they very much pleased my mind: And I would not for a great Treasure [352] have wanted that little Knowledg that I gained in them But one of the greatest advantages I reaped by these Studies was, that they (though as it were insensibly) tended to make me more exact in the Composing of my Sermons, and to preach with more Evidence and Demonstration: which they did by giving my mind and thoughts a certein ply[353] usefull in other Studies as well as these. For I (that never had a Metaphysical head) could better understand the Trigonometrical Syllogism (as I may call it) than the Logical one. For which reason I cannot but commend those Studies to all young Students that can fancy them whatever profession they Design.

Anno Domini 1679 I added the study of Musick to all the rest upon this occasion. Being desired by the Minister of Spalding to preach in that Church in his absence I found there in the Vestry and elsewhere Playfords Psalms and Hymns in Solemn Musick in four parts in folio which their late Minister Mr Martin Johnson had directed and encouraged the people to use for their improvement in Psalmody.[354] One of these I borrowed of a Friend onely for the Sake of the Hymns which I saw in it, and which I greatly liked. When I had read and transcribed the Hymns I had a great mind to understand the Musick also /fo. 76r/ which though I thought difficult to attain, yet (being naturally a great Lover of it) I resolved to attempt it: So I ventured to send for Playford's Introduction;[355] and (that <though it entred me, yet> not fully, satisfying me) I afterwards procured Simpson's also;[356] which I found to be much the better of the two: So by the Study of these (the latter being clear where the former was obscure) I did (by God's blessing) attain so much Skill as to be able to sing any Psalm tune, and any of the Parts in Playfords or any other Psalm Book; and that in consort with others, when I had the advantage of Musical Company: which was of great Use to me afterwards in directing and

[352] Illegible word cancelled.

[353] *ply*: a bias, inclination, or tendency of mind or character. *OED*.

[354] William Pendleton, who succeeded Martin Johnson at Spalding (see above, p. 98, n. 172). John Playford, *Psalms & Hymns in Solemn Musick of Foure Parts* (London, 1671).

[355] John Playford, *An Introduction to the Skill of Musick* (London, 1655, and later editions).

[356] Christopher Simpson, *The Principles of Practical Musick* (London, 1665).

managing that part of the Worship of God in the Congregation where I preached.[357]

Of my Divinity Studies and Preaching.

Our tutors did not read Divinity to their Pupils in the University, but they were left (so for all I could percieve) to form their Theological Studies of their own heads: and so was I. Catechisms therefore, and Compendious Methods of Divinity I read and digested as well as I could, and they gave me the Scheme Order and Contexture of the Principles of Religion which was of great Use to me: But larger Systems I read none throughout, howsoever I might Consult them occasionally: But having got the Method or Scheme now mentioned pretty well into my Head, I found that (as in Medicine the best Books in that faculty are those that treat of particular Diseases, so) these Divines that have wrote of Particular Heads, Parts, or Subjects in Divinity have done better, and given more light to them (generally speaking) than the systematical writers have done on the same Points.

[357] Rastrick's musical ingenuity around this time was recalled in the preface to his old friend William Scoffin's *An Help To the Singing Psalm-Tunes, By The Book. In a method more easy than is generally taught. With directions for making an instrument with one string, by which any tune may be easily learn'd* (London, 1725), p. iv:

> As to the Instrument with one String, and the Directions given for the making such an Instrument, I have been obliged to my dear and honoured Friend, the Reverend Mr. John Rastrick, Minister of the Gospel at Lyn-Regis in Norfolk; who about thirty years ago, made and sent me an Instrument with One String, which was the first that ever I had seen or heard of.
>
> He made it only of one single Board of Slit-Deal, about Thirty Three Inches in length and Two Inches broad, in the Form of a long Rule: The Thickness of the Board was about a Quarter of an Inch. On this Board from the Nut at the lowermost G, and so upward towards the Bridge he drew parallel Lines for all the Half Notes, at their proper Distance one from another, &c. The length of the String from the Nut to the Bridge was exactly Thirty Inches. My good Friend likewise gave me some short Directions for the making this Instrument with a Table of the Distances of all the Notes, as divided by the Frets on a Viol; from whence (as I remember, he told me) he took them off. And about the Same Time, he gave me also the Book afore-mentioned: For then it was, that I first began to learn to sing by the Notes; and my kind Friend was ready to furnish me with such Helps as might further me therein. These are some few of the very many Kindnesses, which I have receiv'd from my honour'd Friend, since the first Time that I had the Happiness to be acquainted with him; which is now above Forty Years ago. And throughout this long Space of Time, I have always found his Friendship to be real and constant, sincere and very hearty; and was therefore glad of such an Opportunity, for the making this publick Acknowledgment of my great Obligations to him.

This book is not listed in ESTC and is erroneously attributed to William Sherwin in the British Library catalogue. For Scoffin's authorship, see Calamy, *The Nonconformist's Memorial*, II, p. 439.

(as Grotius de Veritate Christ. Rel.[358] Dr Preston, and Charnock on the Attributes of God.[359] Bulkley on the Covenant.[360] Gibbons on Justice.[361] Truman on the Satisfaction of Christ[362] Cudworth, Mede, Patrick, and Virel on the Sacrament.[363] and the like) For he that has bestowed as much or more Study and pains on some one particular (which it may be he has had some special Advantage to illustrate) may be presumed to clear it better than he that with less Study and advantage has grasped the whole. And the Scheme of Truths once well mastered tis easie to reduce all those Authors and their Subjects to their particular places, and so form a Compleat Body of Theology out of them.

The Fathers (Chrysostom Augustine &c.) I had noted down in a paper even when young with a resolution if I lived to procure them (though I knew them only by their being cited in the English Books I read; as Dykes decietfulness of mans heart,[364] which my father had) but when I grew up I found them too costly for my purse: So I never had or read them /fo. 76v/ being never able indeed to read a Greek Author with understanding in his own language, and much less after so great disuse; save only what might enable me to make use of the Greek Testament or of a Greek Concordance for comparing of places, &c. yet even that (Schmidius or Stephanus) I was never owner of, though I could profitably have used them if I had had them.*[365] So all our Juvenile pains of learning the Tongues seems to be in vain, if the Authors cannot be purchased which we should thereby be enabled to understand.

As to a Method of Study, Experience taught me to lay aside that unprofitable one which had foundred me at the University, viz. of assigning particular Studies to particular parts of the Day. So when I

*Marginal note: At last Anno 1714 at 64 years of age I got Stephanus's Greek Conc.

[358] Hugo Grotius, *De veritate religionis christianae* (Paris, 1627).

[359] John Preston, *Life Eternall or, A treatise of the knowledge of the divine essence and attributes* (London, 1631); Stephen Charnock, *Several Discourses upon the Existence and Attributes of God* (London, 1682).

[360] Peter Bulkeley, *The Gospel-Covenant; or the covenant of grace opened* (London, 1646).

[361] Perhaps Nicholas Gibbon (1605–1697), *Theology Real, and Truly Scientifical in Overture for the Conciliation of All Christians* (London, ?1687).

[362] Joseph Truman, *The Great Propriation: or, Christs satisfaction* (London, 1669).

[363] Ralph Cudworth, *A Discourse Concerning the True Notion of the Lords Supper* (London, 1642); Joseph Mede, *The Works of that Reverend, Judicious, and Learned Divine, Mr Joseph Mede* (London, 1648); perhaps Simon Patrick's *Aqua genitalis* (London, 1659) or his *Mensa mystica* (London, 1660); Virel, *A Learned and Excellent Treatise Containing All the Principall Grounds of Christian Religion.*

[364] Dyke, *The Mystery of Selfe-deceiving.*

[365] *Novi Testamenti Jesu Christi Græci, hoc est, originalis linguæ,* Ταμειον, *aliis Concordantiæ . . . Erasmi Schmidii* (Wittenberg, 1638); Henri Estienne, Θησαυρος της Ελληνικης γλωσσης: *thesaurus Græcæ linguæ*, 5 vols ([Geneva], 1572).

begun a Book I seldome took any other in hand till I had read it quite through; if it were such as I designed to read through at all. Except my Morning and Evening Part of the Scriptures: which yet alas for some years I was too Careless and Negligent in; till I was convinced of the Necessity and Usefulness and tasted the sweetness of Scriptural Knowledg. Though when I first got Pool's English Notes on the Bible[366] I did with it as I did with other Books, left it not, after I had begun it, till I had got it quite through; the Profit of which I found to be greater than any Course I had before taken.

When I begun to preach at Fosdike I wrote every word of my Sermons at large and so read them when I [367] preached them, and thought it very difficult to do otherwise: But when I came to Wiberton and was obliged to preach twice a day I was forced to write shorter Notes than I had done before which was a reall help and advantage to me though I might possibly at first make some blunders in my Extempore Enlargements I call them Extempore because they were not wrote, nor thought of before: for whatever I purposed to speak beforehand if I wrote it not I commonly forgot it. So at last I seldome wrote any thing save the Heads of the Scriptures and some particular Notion or Illustration that I would not have forgotten. Though at Kirkton when I had time for preparations of that kind I sometimes wrote all or very largely especially if my mind was much in a Subject Other whiles only the Heads: as was said and sometimes nothing at all; as in preaching over the 12th Psalm: in which I was after beholding to one that wrote after me for my own Notes. And this, (after I was used to some readiness of Extempore Speaking) I found (whatever most people may think to the Contrary to be the Easyest and Idlest way of all; and I commonly took the most pains when I wrote the largelyest

/fo. 77r/ But it irketh me to review most of the Sermons that I composed the half dozen first years of my Ministry (or thereabouts) such is the injudiciousness and Confusion that appears in them (discovering the shallow and unfurnished Head they came from) And so little is the Use I can make of them. Its plain I had but small Skill in the Art of Preaching; though I studyed it, and greatly desired it. When I was at Wiberton I wrote to my worthy friend Mr Brocklesby, for directions, and advice about Books, &c. but he answered me not. But Bishop Wilkins's Ecclesiastes,[368] Bernards Faithful Shepheard,[369]

[366] Matthew Poole, *Annotations upon the Holy Bible* (London, 1685).

[367] Illegible word, perhaps *had*, cancelled.

[368] John Wilkins, *Ecclesiastes, or, a discourse concerning the gift of preaching as it fals under the rules of art* (London, 1646, and many later editions).

[369] Richard Bernard, *The Faithfull Shepheard* (London, 1607).

The Directions in the Assemblies Directory,[370] and in Mr Baxters Saints Rest (part 4. cap. 10. D. 2. p. 745)[371] I read;[372] And I took Mr Baxter for my Pattern. (whose Discourses yet were rather Treatises than Sermons.) So a Method I got: but I tyed my Self too much to that Method, and made all my Subjects conform to it whether they would or no. I thought I must have every thing in every Sermon. I thought (ex: gr.) that it was not a Sermon if it had not a large preface which commonly was either needless and impertinent, or else it did anticipate the Subject Matter of the Sermon that was to follow: and the true and clear coherence of the text with the Context I commonly omitted, or was very short and Careless in. (My Ignorance in the Scriptures being indeed a great cause of that; and my too great Neglect of reading them constantly and diligently with commentary and Analyses.) I thought I could never raise Doctrines enow; from a single verse or text, sometimes half a Score: though most of them would have come in in handling the main Doctrine into which I commonly reduced them all: but so long would it be sometimes as to take up a great part of the page. This commonly followed a Division of the text into the minutest parts that I could crumble it into; and the more sorts of them I thought the better: as also a pretty large exposition of the terms of the text, whether it needed it or no; with the Criticisms and Notes of Commentators in their own language; whether there was any thing of Notion remarkable in them or no; or whether there was any thing in the text doubtfull disputable or difficult or no, that needed their Suffrage or Testimony. And then for handling the Doctrine I commonly multiplyed Heads excessively: For I almost always made those particulars a part of them, which should have been spoke to in the explication of the Text it Self, and not of the Doctrine though even those which related to the Doctrine were oft too many. And in speaking to any Head, or Principal Enquiry, I always strove more to have many particulars than to explain 3 or 4 well; (being always straitned and at a loss to enlarge upon a head) and yet many of those /fo. 77v/ particulars were so much the same with those that went before, or followed after, that they might and ought to have been cast one into another two or three of them together. In the Applicatory part I thought I must have all Uses in every Subject: Inf. Reproof Comt. Exhort. particularly, Infrences; though it may be I inferred nothing but what I had said before. All this proceeded from

[370] *A Directory for the Publike Worship of God, Throughout the Three Kingdoms of England, Scotland, and Ireland* (London, 1645).

[371] Baxter, *The Saints Everlasting Rest*. Rastrick's reference corresponds to the editions printed in 1658, 1659, 1662, 1669 (×2), and 1676.

[372] *I read* inserted in the margin.

want of Judgment; and my Stiffness to my unalterable Method. Yet I oft thought of many things that I knew not where to dispose of in that Method, but crouded them in inconveniently, and drew them by Head and Shoulders. Logic I understood not, so it did me no Service a long time: though afterwards I did sometimes make use of the Topicks in the investigation of Heads, as of Reasons <and the same might be done for> Inferences;) and I oft thought they might be enlarged to a great many more for that purpose. (as in Mr Baxters Arguments for Universall Redemption for example.[373]) but this was not till many years after I begun. And for enlargements upon any of the particular heads, if I would have my Sermon compleat, I commonly studyed more for Sentences and Sayings of Poets Philosophers or Fathers if I could light of them, than for pertinent Scriptures for that purpose.

But after I had been some few times a hearer of my pious and judicious friend Mr Richardson (who had been cast out at Stamford by the Bartholomew Act, and afterwards more oft of Mr Pell at Boston,[374] in the tolerated Congregation there; (who was one of the greatest Textuarys I had ever met with; and would back and illustrate his Heads with such Scriptures as I could scarce have thought had been in the Bible, and would explain and clear such difficult (and one would almost think barren) passages in the Prophets &c. as he went along in his Sermons, as could not but both greatly affect and profit his hearers; having such great acquaintance with the Oriental languages as made him one of the greatest Expositors of the age:) I say after I had been used to his Preaching and Converse; and had read the Sermons of such as Mr Stephen Marshal:[375] (whom I take to be one of the best Patterns for a Preacher that we have.) And after I had begun better to relish the Works of Dr Preston Mr Hildersham, Dr Manton,[376] and such as they, which the Converse of Mr Richardson before mentioned brought me to: All these things together altered the fashion of my Preaching, gave me another Cue, and put me into a more scriptural way than I had used before; So that I studyed more to cite the Prophets and Apostles, than I did before to quote Fathers Poets and Philosophers, for which I searched Indexes and Polyantheas[377] to make out a Garnish. Though both do well in their places; especially if the humane Citations and Authoritys have something of peculiar and uncommon notion in

[373] Baxter, *Universal Redemption of Mankind*.

[374] John Richardson and William Pell (see above p. 95, n. 166, and p. 118, n. 225).

[375] Stephen Marshall (1594/5?–1655), Church of England clergyman. *ODNB*. Marshall published many sermons and Rastrick appears to be referring to them as a whole.

[376] For John Preston (1587–1628), Arthur Hildersham (1563–1632), and Thomas Manton (bap. 1620–d. 1677), see *ODNB*. Rastrick's reference is not specific.

[377] *polyanthea*: a collection of quotations or extracts from literature, esp. poetry; a commonplace book; an anthology. *OED*.

them, and be not bald, or what any body might have thought of. And besides /fo. 78r/ another thing I learnt of Mr Pell which I used not before and that was the Explaining Clearing and stating of the Point by such Propositions Conclusions or Considerations Explicatory as are necessary and proper to that purpose. (which also I oft found used by Dr Manton; much like the Theses of a Disputation.) This I found a Copious way of handling a point; under which I could say or Observe whatsoever I could not well digest under other Heads; and prevent many an Objection that might be made against the Doctrine; and let people clearly see without danger of mistaking what it was I designed to prove. And in a word, for the more successfull management of my Theological and Concionatory studies; Converse and Experience (with the Divine direction) wrought me to the Observation of the Rules following.

1. I was more thoroughly convinced of the Necessity and important Usefulness of studying the Scriptures with all the Care and Diligence I could, and getting the clearest and fullest Knowledge in them possible: and that whatsoever is neglected that should not be so. Which made me take the more notice of that passage of Mr Brand, who said in his latter days, If he had his Time again, he would spend it in reading the Holy Scriptures, with two or three good Commentaries; in Prayer, Meditation, and labouring in Publick (Life of Mr Brand. page 6.[378])

2. I began therfore to read over my Commentarys as I did other Books: i.e. quite through from the beginning to the end; and did not let them stand (as I had done before) only to be consulted occasionally. This lended much to profit. For rare Scriptures and Notes would occur that I should never have found by occasional Search. These I referred to some Sermon head or other; which by this meant I kept filling up: or else to some Plainer Scripture, (not so likely to be overlooked or forgotten, if at any time I should have occasion to preach upon the Subject.) Which I did in my Clarks Bible,[379] in a small hand.

3. I began (when I understood the Usefulness of it) to enter all the various readings I met with, either in my Commentarys or any other valuable Book or Sermon into my Concordance in their Alphabetical places. Or if there be not room in or near its true place it may be set at the bottom of the page referring or pointing thereto by some letter. Or if this cannot be done in a small hand, a Concordance may be got interleaved with fair paper for this purpose. And I have oft and long desired that an English Concordance were made, that, together

[378] Samuel Annesley, *The Life and Funeral Sermon of the Reverend Mr. Thomas Brand* (London, 1692).

[379] *The Holy Bible, Containing the Old Testament and the New: with annotations and parallel Scriptures ... by Samuel Clark* (London, 1690).

with the readings of our English Common Bibles, should also take in all the various readings that are in the Polyglot Bible, or any other Commentator, or Treatiser whatsoever; Englished and Alphabetically disposed and printed with the Sentence they stand in <in> a different character: or with a Mark before them; as our marginal readings are in Newman's Concordance.[380] /fo. 78v/ as also some letter or letters shewing whose Reading it is. One cannot easily, or at first think of what advantage this would be to a Preacher to have them meet him, and to find them when he thinks not of them. If the different reading may be thought to be true, it will Confirm, if not, it will at least Amplify and illustrate his point.

4. Whereas when I went to Cambridg I got a paperbook in folio for a Common placebook I was soon wearyed out of the Use of it: for (1.) I had not judgment to chuse the best things; but some pretty Similes and the like. (2.) Many of the best things I could not reduce to one particular Word called the Common place. (3.) The Transcripts I made were commonly very large and so tedious and took much time to enter. (4.) and commonly the Books were my own from whence I took them and (5.) had it may be Alphabetical Tables of their own in them: or if I liked a Notion that was not in the Table, I entred it there my Self. (6.) When I had preached some time and had got a Competent Number of Sermon Notes by me of mine own (of which I made an Alphabetical Table) there were few things I liked which I met with in my Reading, but I could refer them to some Head or other, in some or other of my own Sermons: (for the Sake and Use of which a Commonplace book is supposed to be made.) But after some years of experience I made Wilsons Christian Dictionary (last Edition)[381] my Common place book for things that is the Void Margent of it: for it has most Common place heads in it with the different senses and respects of them: or if it wanted I could add in the Alphabetical place. And I only in a small hand referred to the Books, (rarely otherwise;) and made it in the Nature of an Alphabetical Index. And this chiefly for such Books as had no Alphabetical Tables or Indexes of their own. And I made Clark's Bible my Common place-book for Scriptures; and wrote down in the Void Margent thereof the Authors of all the Comments Sermons and Treatises of Divinity that I had (or knew where readily to procure) against their respective Books Chapters and Texts. And the like I did with every Scripture that I found well explained in any Book I read, which I had not a mind to lose, viz entered a reference to the Book and page. (And one might add (Tr.) for Treatise. (Ser.) for

[380] Samuel Newman, *A Large and Complete Concordance to the Bible in English* (London, 1643, and many later editions).

[381] Thomas Wilson, *Complete Christian Dictionary* (London, 1678).

Sermon and (cit. or quot.) for such Scripture as occurs in any book by way of proof or citation.) And this Method I found better (using a small hand) than if it had been done in a paper book on purpose: for thus Things met me without my searching, when I thought not of them, and could not remember I had them; and therefore had no Motive or inducement to seek for them especially I using that same Bible when I studyed my Sermons.

/fo. 79r/ 5. As I studied my Sermons and searched my Concordance or other Book I took a piece of loose paper and divided it sometimes into two or three Columns And I wrote down every particular Head as I thought of it or met with it in that loose paper in the place or Column where abouts I thought it might fall As if it were an Use I first thought of I put it towards the End in the third Column a Reason in the middle, and the Doctrine and Explicatory Notes in the beginning in the first Column.* And so as I read over my Concordance on the Words I sought I referred all the particulars occurrent or thence suggested as I met with them to their places as to their several Boxes and then I wrote out all fair afterwards in the best Order I could. And I could not compose one Sermon otherwise for if, (as Dr Harris commonly made the Uses first[382]) I had also thought of an Use first I should have forgot it before I had come at it if I had not set it down; but that could not be, but in some loose paper as I have now related.

6. In this loose paper I set down first all that I could think on of my own Head, before I searched any Books: and then if in searching them I met with any thing pertinent and useful for a Note or Reason or an Use I did not therefore refuse it (if I needed it) because it was written in some Book before. For then what must we say on some Common Subjects? and what are our Books for? We had better have none. And why should Dr Hammond[383] Use himself and command to his Friends, after every Sermon to resolve upon the ensueing Subject; because in the Common course of Study somewhat would infallibly fall in conducible to that Subject, and Materials unawares, be gained for it? But by such a Course as I have described, All the Method, and most of the Matter will be ones own.

7. I wrote all my Sermon Notes with void Margent; and sufficient Competent Interspaces betwixt the Heads; that I might have room to add at pleasure afterwards as I thought of things, and as they Occurred

*Marginal note: Or if it was on a wast paper not divided into Columns I put the Doctrine and Explication at the top the Reasons about the middle and the Uses at the bottom of the paper leaving room enough for the Heads of each.

[382] W[illiam]. D[urham]., *Life and Death of . . . Robert Harris*.

[383] Henry Hammond (1605–1660), Church of England clergyman and theologian. *ODNB*.

in my Reading; and room to make references to other Books, and the like.

8. When I came to use my Concordance I first set down in the rough draught of my Sermon before mentioned all the Terms or Expressions synonymous to the chief Term or Subject of the text that I could Excogitate and then I searched my Concordance not only on the Word or Subject of my text but on all those Synonymas[384] also; with the Relatives, Contrarys, &c. And then I entred those Synonymas I had gathered into the Margent of my Concordance it Self. And by the way I thought it greatly desirable yea highly necessary, that a Concordance should have all the Synonymas printed at the head of every word or term: and it might be done in that that should also include the various Readings as abovesaid.

/fo. 79v/ With the English Concordance (which was that of Cambridg[385]) I sometimes used to very good purpose the large Latin one; and might have done the Greek and Hebrew ones if I had had them. (For the Hebrew one of Marius Calasio in four folios having the Latin Column Concurrent I could have used.[386]) The benefit of Concordances in other languages was, that they would help one to Scriptures, <of> the same Sense, import, and Subject matter though in different words and expressions; Our Translators not always using the same English word to translate the Original by.

But the Principal Use of the Greek and Hebrew Concordances is this that every considerable word of Scripture being there presented to the eye in one view of all those places where it occures; it will be easily gathered, by Considering the Nature, Circumstances, and Sense of those several Places what are the different Senses it will bear, and what it most properly signifies in any of those which by an ill rendring are made either doubtful or obscure. (as Dr Bray saies; Biblioth. parochia page 47.[387]) And so they supply the place of many large Critical Comments which are but the setting the Sense in one place by Compareing the Originals in others, which an industrious Student may do of himself; and that for more places than his Commentators had done.

And I always chose to use Clarks Bible with my Concordance to turn to the Scriptures in; for it was ten to one but his Parallel Scriptures

[384] *synonymas*: synonyms. *OED*.

[385] Samuel Newman, *A Concordance to the Holy Scriptures* (Cambridge, 1662), which was originally published as *A Large and Complete Concordance to the Bible in English* (London, 1643), became known as the Cambridge Concordance, a title that was printed vertically on the page facing the title-page.

[386] Mario di Calasio (1550–1620), *Concordantiæ Bibliorum Hebraicorum*, 4 vols (Rome, 1621).

[387] Bray, *Bibliotheca Parochialis*.

would help me to more, (proper for my purpose,) than that which my Concordance sent me to.

9. I searched my Commentators not only on my Text but on all the Parallel Scriptures, and proofs also that were not very plain For I had oft found (especially when I begun,) that the Concordance would oft direct to places seemingly suitable which when the Sense was regarded were not so. The Use of Clarks Bible in studying and turning to Scriptures (as was said) was a kind and ready help to me in this.

All this while I was very sensible that an Index Materiarum or Concordance of things was very desireable: But I had not such an one that pleased me. The best I had was Ravanellus's Bibliotheca Sacra (in two folios Edition Geneva 1660[388]) which Mr Pell recommended to me and bought for me: which, (though not just suiting the purpose mentioned, though it may be it suited a better;) is so exact in its kind and so exceeding usefull (beyond Wilsons Dictionary in English[389]) that I look upon it as one of the best Technical Books for a Preacher that he can have. But for the Design directly, I took the Indexes at the End of Commentators as of Beza[390] Piscator[391] &c. as good Concordances of scriptural Matter or things (and not of words only) and such as might upon occasion be not unprofitably searched accordingly

10. But I must here lastly advertize, that I did not take all this pains upon every Subject that I preached on; but as the matter was less fruitfull; Or I had a mind to be large, and full in the handling of it.
/fo. 80r/

An Account of my Conjugal Relations, Temptations, Sins, Afflictions, &c.

The Occasion of my Marrying the person above mentioned was this Being upon a Visit at Newton near Folkingham at Mr Seagrave's who marryed my Mother in Law's Sister The Day that I should have come away proved a very stormy Rainy day so that I could not stir. (It was about the 12 of September 1671. when the Sea overflowed the Banks and ran a great way into the Country.) And there being then at the Hall at Mr Savile's this Maid in a very dolefull melancholy condition My Aunt said since Providence stayed me she would send for her to see if I could do her any good or administer by discourse and Advice any Comfort and Satisfaction to her. So she came and opened her grief and I gave her the best Instructions I could and concieved

[388] Petrus Ravanellus, *Bibliotheca Sacra*, 2 parts (Geneva, 1660).
[389] Wilson, *Complete Christian Dictionary*.
[390] Theodore Beza (1519–1605).
[391] Johannes Piscator (1546–1625), co-author of the Heidelberg catechism (1563).

a great pity and Compassion for her and hearing her express with great affection how much she would give or Loose or undergo that she might assuredly be Gods Child &c. it begat in me a good Opinion of her And I (as many others did) took her Melancholy for her Vertue and thought if she had but a Friend near her frequently to advise her, her fears and troubles would all vanish And being from my youth exceedingly delighted with the Company of good people (as appears in my letter to my Aunt beforementioned of May 28. 1670.) and desirous to marry with such a one whenever I did marry if such a one could be found And (so far as I could possibly know my own heart) preferring Piety before Portion, which Comparatively I regarded not. I thought she (who was a Minister's Daughter and highly descended on the Mother's Side) might make me a good and suitable Wife And this I told my Aunt who thought so also and it seems of her own head told Mistress Wilson all that I said of that kind. Which it was feared begat such an Affection in her that had I not proceeded in that way or having proceeded had drawn back it might have proved very predjudicial to one in her Case and Temper So I made some Journeys to see her and being at Newton one Lords Day I preachd two Consolotory Sermons on Psalm 94.19. with a more particular respect to her Case which how far she understood and was satisfyed by I then knew not. But this went on till she removed to live with Mr Mellish near Lincoln[392] and I /fo. 80v/ removed from Fosdike to Wiberton when (for the reasons before mentioned) I renewed my Acquaintance in a direct Suit: telling her instead of Portion I desired but a double Share of Love &c. And so (my Fathers Consent before obteined) I marryed her as before was said.*

A few days after, discoursing with my wife about spiritual things I found her Shortness of Understanding such and her Capacity so weak and shallow unfit to fathom things or to Discourse about them &c. that I was exceedingly dejected and troubled at the Surprisall: to loose my Ends for which I forsook the World and parted with all Portion (for I had but about 9[li] with her.) To look before me and think of that Strangeness in spiritual Converse that we must live &c.! O how it troubled me! We were invited to dinner that Day, but Alas my Dinner was bitter to me.

*Marginal note: On our Marriage Night our Friends and Relations had unexpectedly got my wife to Bed (I not knowing) before we had gone to prayers: This troubled me I made her rise again to prayer, which I after found I had no need to do.

[392] Probably William Mellish, gent. of Bullington, Lincs. For Mellish's will (1690), see TNA, PRO, PROB 11/403.

But yet notwithstanding for a year or two her Conversation in other respects was in the main pretty Loving placid and cheerfull Till one time not long after we went to Kirkton She came down Stairs in such a dreadfull bitter Crying fit and that without any previous occasion given by any person or (outward) thing that it exceedingly affrighted me. After a little while it went off for that time: but this was not the only Paroxysm She grew exceedingly Melancholly The returns were speedy and it abode long upon her Many a time have I been awaked with her Sobs and Cryes as she arose in the morning and sometimes been forced to walk till 4 of the Clock in the morning in the Garden to be out of the hear of them they were so terrible to me In this case no persuasions signified any thing She grew worse and worse though not without the Intervals of a somewhat better Temper The Cause lay all within and the State of her Soul was mainly that which her mind ran upon But yet I began now to see it was no vertue in her as I and others before thought This dark and black humour made her very cross and unquiet Unthankfull and (as Dr Harris saith in his advice to his children[393]) unnaturall in all her Relations Her own Mother (who sojourned with us Summer Anno Domini 1676 as she had done a Summer or two before) would Correct my wife's height of Spirit and undue /fo. 81r/ Carriage towards me She would often tell her Jane, thou canst never do amiss with a Religious man (as she was pleased it seems to account me) for though they be of never so hasty and passionate a temper their Spirits will not suffer them to be long angry or out of the way but they are restless till they be reconcild. But my wife did not greatly Care for her Company at our house.

In the mean time sad and Afflicted was my Life; and being of too melancholized a temper my Self I knew not how to Carry it: and a very great hindrance it was to me in my Ministerial work. In the beginning of the year 1678 I being extreamly busy in Studies of Divinity of great intricacy than ordinary, and my wife being extreamly Melancholy I was fain to send her out to her Brothers for two or three weeks (designed) that I might be free from that heavy disturbance it gave me; though her Trouble was not then changed from spiritual things: She went freely but staid but about a week.

In this Case suitable Christian Society was when I could have it a great relief and refreshment to me and through the gracious Providence of God it came to pass that I was not altogether without it. For at May day 1676 my wife got us a very excellent religious Servant whose name was Martha Wray a pious and sincere hearted Christian and of a good spiritual Sense Understanding and Judgment who stayed with us till a little before she dyed which was above 8 years And about

[393] W[illiam]. D[urham]., *Life and Death of . . . Robert Harris*, p. 111.

that time Mr Sooley Sir Richard Custs Servant[394] marrying Miss Sarah Richardson niece to Mr John Richardson Non Conformist Minister at Stamford came to live in my Parish with whom her Sister Mris Mary Richardson therfore oft sojourned both Excellent serious and Understanding Christians And Mris Mary Richardson in particular came so oft to see us and so loved our Family that she desired to board with us and did so in the Winter 1679 And the Summer before the same year Mr William Scoffin came to live in Mr Shaws Family at Wiberton[395] near us as Tutor to his only daughter with whom my intimate acquaintance and Friendship was now begun For he came to see us often and would stay a Night with us at /fo. 81v/ a time and much heavenly Communion we had many a Night a good part of which we spent in Reading and singing Psalms and Hymns. But the Inconvenience of Womens Company was this as to Mistris Mary Richardson particularly I could not Forbear thinking O if I had but such a wife as she &c. Though I chid my heart for it with all my might at the rising of such thoughts Yet they too much infested and troubled me and were no doubt my great Sin, which I beseech the God of mercy to forgive I was afraid I loved her too much But my heart leaping for joy when I see Mr Scoffin Coming to see us made me hope that it was not as a Woman but as a Christian that I loved her Since Mr Scoffin was as welcome as shee tho she was of a woman as Understanding and heavenly a Christian as ever I had (till that time) Conversed with having known her then about 3, or 4 years But her Father in Laws Death occasioning her being called home to Stamford the Loss of her Company troubled me to such a Degree that I saw my Distemper and therefore applyed my Self to the Throne of Grace in earnest Prayer for deliverance from the same and the subduing all undue affection, and prevailed: Blessed be the Lord that so plainly heard my prayer in that particular.

The next Summer 1680 There was a poor lame Girl in the Town whose name was Alice Hargate that was in danger to be seduced by the Anabaptists and drawn in amongst them which was first occasioned by the earnest desires she had to live in a Family that worshiped God I was desired to discourse this Girl and did and she being earnestly desirous to read I (with my wife's consent) took her and put her to School to learn to read after which our children encreasing she was continued as an Under Servant in our Family and very usefull she

[394] Sir Richard Cust (bap. 1622–d. 1700), politician. Cust had an estate at Kirton in Holland through his marriage to Beatrice, daughter and heir of William Pury of Kirton, in 1644, but his main residence (after 1654) was the Blackfriars in Stamford. *ODNB*.

[395] Probably John Shaw of Wyberton (d. 1686). For the family, see *Lincolnshire Pedigrees*, pp. 868–889.

was in her place and would have been more had she not been so sickly and Hysterical. (in her fits she would sing Psalms and pray and discourse so spiritually and fluently as was to the admiration of all Ministers and others that know and heard her and yet senseless all the while of any thing about her and as in a perfect extasie.) She proved a very serious Religious Girl and betwixt her and Martha there was a very dear Affection. /fo. 82r/ And they managed their buisness with great Faithfulness and Diligence And all our Pious Friends that visited us thought us so heavenly a Family that they almost envyed our Hapiness and wished themselves amoungst us Mr Scoffin particularly did sojourn with us about a Quarter of a Year after he left Mr Shaw. And a great Comfort (blessed be the Lord) was all this to me

But it did my wife no good: nor did it now last long: For the Devil had a Spight at us; And now began my Wife's trouble and Melancholy to change from a Religious one to that of another kind and to turn to Envy and Jealousy about my Maid Servants or at least now more manifestly to discover its Self in words and actions and especially after my Fathers Death at Heckington Anno 1681. And at the latter End of February 1682/3 the Difference betwixt my wife and me about our Servants grew very high and bitter and they both Martha and Alice went away and were away two Months a Girl of quite a different Character was brought in by my wife in their Stead All this was a very great trouble to me and provoked me to such an undue degree of passion as I had cause greatly to lament Soon after I fell into a fit of Sickness the Yellow Jaundice* occasioned as was thought by this Affliction which I took as God's Correcting Rod and I hope it was sanctifyed to a further Repentance and my many earnest prayers for pardon I hope he has heard. And I bless him for that Victory over my passions and that greater Meekness of Temper and Carriage which from that time he has given me. when the provocation was as great.

The true Reason of her distast of these Maid=Servants was I think this that when I used to read any thing in my Family I usually (but indiscreetly) directed my Self and my Speech to them more than to her looking upon them to be more Capable to understand and reply than my wife was which she could not bear In that single respect

*Marginal note: In this distemper being one night very weary sick and restless I went earlyer than ordinary to prayers in my family with much affection devolving my Self upon God: I was suddenly from that very hour better, rode to Stamford next morning with great ease, dined at Sir Richard Custs by the way where the first Recovery of my Appetite begun and by God's blessing on the Means Mr Richardson prescribed I grew soon well and healthfull. Blessed be God.

only (and not in any other) I was too familiar with them for her to digest it For I read where I had encouragement to read and where I saw an Attractive and Receptive disposition in things of that nature. And had I had a religious understanding Scholler in my house to have discoursed with and read to, much of my Family troubles from my Wife's Jealousy upon my too free discourse with the Servants might have been prevented at least the occasion thereof or pretence thereto removed.

But otherwise I may truly say that /fo. 82v/ I bore no undue respect to them And I bless God I was under no Temptation to love them otherwise than as pious faithfull Servants that I thought ought to be prized And my Love to my wife increased and was greater in Conjugall respects at the latter end than at the beginning And as for the Servants they made no undue use of my fore mentioned familiarity but carryed it towards my wife with as much honour and respect as ever they had done, nor could they be charged as faulty in it

At May day after viz 1683 they were permitted to come again and things went on, if not as they ought yet as they could Family reading was much laid aside that there might be no Offence. If it be wondered at why my wife might not be Conversed with as well as others, take this account, Her head was so made that though she could understand Sentences independent one upon another and of short Conception yet an Historical or Chained discourse where a great many reasons or other particulars were to be remembered and laid together she could not Comprehend And therefore when she wrote once to Mr Baxter for Comfort and he referred her to his Method for Peace I knew she could not understand it.[396] And one time before this my Reverend and Worthy Friend Mr Brocklesby of Folkingham besides what physick he ordered her enjoyned that no manner of Religious action or exercise either Reading or Praying though never so short should be used in our Family for some Considerable time because he knew she could not bear <it>. and this when her trouble was all about her own Soul. So in one respect or other or upon one account or other Family Religion was much in the Wain And indeed in all these troubles and after when the change of her Melancholy <begat> great Differences and Unquietness I did observe the Stream to run all along so exceedingly strongly against a Holy Life through Satan's Temptations, as was much to my Amazement: For Commonly when

[396] Richard Baxter, *The Right Method for a Settled Peace of Conscience* (London, 1653, and later editions); the letter is not listed in N.H. Keeble and Geoffrey. F. Nuttall (eds), *Calendar of the Correspondence of Richard Baxter*, 2 vols (Oxford, 1991).

I was in the best Frame, or had some special Work in hand, or on a Satturday our domestick branglings[397] happned.*

But then again (this year 1683) did Gods Wonderfull Providence send me some more good Company. For this Summer my good Friend Mr Ishmael Burroughs (a young man that had been Tutor to Sir Richard Earl) came and sojourned with me for a Quarter of a year. And Mr Richardson's daughter of Stamford Marrying into my Parish it /fo. 83r/ brought her Father, first to make her long Visits, and then to sojourn with her for three or four of the last years of his life and he was a man of such Piety Wisdom and Worth that he was as a spiritual Father to me.[398] He searched into the bottom of our Family troubles with all the prudence and Care that could be, and did what he could to heal them And about this time one Mistress Mary Harrison of Boston who had been Converted from a loose life to a very great Seriousness in Religion desired (by a Friend) the Benefit of our acquaintance. But she being a young woman and Concieving a great respect and esteem for me, and compassion for our Afflictions, and comeing often to see us, (though her Company proved useful to my wife, who had a love for her, yet) it proved a Snare and Temptation to me. For I had much ado to forbear thinking of her as I had done of Mistress Mary Richardson before Though I repelled these thoughts as oft as they arose, or that I observed them; and by mental ejaculations, &c made what opposition against them I could. And about Christmas (this year 1683) I set a Day apart for secret Prayer and Fasting to beg of God deliverance from the Snare and the Mortification of irregular Affections and Desires that might perplex my mind or disturb my peace. and for contentment with true Love to my own wife while we lived together: and that I might love the other onely as a Christian and a Friend, and improve her Society accordingly: and <I> spread my Case and Troubles before the Lord with much enlargement. But after this finding these thoughts to arise and haunt me again, I thought with my Self, In the Strength of the Lord I must get this rebellious Humour subdued: and so I set another Day apart for Fasting and secret Prayer to the same purpose as before and for some weeks had (as I remember) tolerable Satisfaction Content and Peace both in my mind and with my wife.

*Marginal note: Upon which accounts Mr Brocklesby said it would be best for me that she were boarded out and named her Brother Wilson's as a fit place. but this Course was not taken.

[397] *brangling*: noisy and turbulent disputing; squabbling. *OED*.

[398] Ishmael Burroughs married Mary Richardson (b. 1659), daughter of John and Mary Richardson, at Frampton, on 29 April 1684.

But the Spring following (1684) my wife's Melancholy grew to as great or greater an height than ever before. <She> looked wildish with her eyes and much altered in her Carriage and ever and anon expressed extream dissatisfaction with these old Servants still as she had done before. In this exigence Three things were advised and resolved on. 1. That the best means should be used for the Health of her body over and above what she had formerly used and had been prescribed /fo. 83v/ her: and that was that she should drink Walcot Waters this approaching Summer as long as might be thought necessary.[399] The 2^{d} was that the Servants should be put away. Though this went hard with me, who now thought Martha especially as needfull for a Stay of our distracted Family as upon other accounts; yet having read Mr Baxter's Sermon about Melancholy in the Morning Exercise[400] wherein he adviseth that such persons should by all means be pleased, I saw it was a thing that must be yielded to. The 3^{d} was that I should Commit the Case to God in Earnest prayer with Fasting and Humiliation. So I resolved in divine Strength to set one day in a week apart for that Purpose; or after sometimes as my occasions would allow, and my troubled mind prompted and required; for that was a ease to me. And I advised with my worthy Reverend Friend Mr Richardson in what Method I should proceed, and what I should pray for; he answered, That you may be delivered from your Burthen; Adding, it is not your wife that is the Burthen, it is her Melancholy. I was sorry that he was going away to see his Friends in the High Country, whose Assistance else I should have desired and hoped for on those Fast days when I called in the help of other my Friends.

So in pursuance of the first of these resolves May 14 was appointed for my wife to go to the Waters. But <in> the night before, about one of the Clock in the morning she went out and wandered about the Country on foot as far as beyond Sutterton on the High way that was exceeding dirty by the new fallen rain. She took a bundle of clothes as if she designed to come no more. Exceeding Melancholy and discontented she was. But was tyred and after she had got her clothes Washed at a certein house in the further part of Sutterton and layen a while upon a Bed Now says she would I was even at Kirkton again. Till now the woman of the house knew not whence she was for the first word my wife had said to her was I know not where I am nor how I came hither, where am I? So the woman offered to come to Kirkton with her, and did, and Carryed her Bundle as far as the Town

[399] For the spring at Walcot, see p. 136, n. 272 above.

[400] Baxter's sermon, 'The cure of melancholy and overmuch-sorrow by faith and physick', was first published anonymously in Samuel Annesley's compilation, *A Continuation of Morning-Exercise Questions and Cases of Conscience* (London, 1683).

End, if not near our own house. It was observed that she took a Mask to keep her Self from being known /fo. 84r/ as having some Shame of what she did. I thought it was the more strange that she should now go away when she was that day by appointment to be carryed on Horse back to the Waters there to stay as long as would be needfull. I sent out a man and Horse to seek and inquire after her (though none knew which way she went) who found her not: But a little after he was come back she returned, and came into the house alone by her Self, About 11 of the clock. And after Dinner she took horse, and went to Newton to Madam Savile's to drink Walcot Waters.

Soon after she was thus gone thither I gave the Maids Notice and Liberty to go away at Martinmass and sent my wife word so, that her mind might be free and pleased while she drunk the Waters: (For nothing else would satisfie her.) But they hired a little house to live in both together by themselves and prepared to be gone as soon as my wife should return home.

It may be easily be imagined what a noyse all this would make in the Town and Country and what a hindrance it must be to me in my Work. One would say to his wife The parsons wife is runed away and you may run after her. Many of my Enemies and the looser sort believed that my wife would not have Carryed it thus without cause given her by me; and I was talked of as a Whoremaster that lived in Adultery with these Servants and the like.

So I knew not what to do but (in the third place) to betake my Self to God in a Course of Fasting and Prayer and therein to Commit my Case to him which I did with much fervency and enlargement at first by my Self <for two or three daies> and after with the Assistance of my Christian Friends Sometimes at my house and sometimes (on the same days) at their own.

The first day I set apart for this purpose alone by my Self in my Study was the 21 of May this year 1684. I prayed that God would relieve my distempered Family and ease me of my heavy Burthen and that he would not let me loose by parting with all the world for the Sake of his Kingdome and Righteousness and denying Portion and Estate that I might have a suitable companion in the way to Heaven That others might not be scandalized that knew and heard of all this /fo. 84v/ exercise and Affliction which they saw I had with my wife saying "God deliver me from such exercises" and that also knew and heard what I meerly took her for and say "There's nothing to be got by the Preference of Piety a little of something else does better, the Caution of a good Portion lest she prove not well Fat Sorrow's better than lean" &c I argued Lord with what Face shall I advise any in their Marriage to chuse for Piety and make sure of Grace though with less of Earthly Portion and Estate when they shall cast this in my teeth and say yes, as you did! I pleaded the Honour of his Name and Goodness to such as chuse for piety as concerned in this thing Lord what will they do for thy Great Name and I mentioned the Case of Solomon's preferring Wisdom in his Regal Office as encouraging in my Case. I mentioned the Sincerity of my heart and Simplicity (so far as I could know it) in my proceedings unto Marriage: not as Meriting deliverance at God's hands but in all Humility to plead my Cause and strengthen my Faith from that Method of his providence I recounted his dealings with me in other cases before when I was in Straits (as in my Removalls to Wiberton and Kirkton) The Impressions the Lord had made on my mind when I was young. I said I did verily believe I had taken the most Effectual Course to prevent all contention and the sad effect of Shrewishness (that I had beheld others lamentably perplexed with) that could be in the world And I hoped that if the Lord had not seen that my Miscarriage was not Remedyless surely he would not have suffered me to have proceeded but would have put some Barr to have stopped it. and I concluded God would never have let things have risen so high if he had not meant me full relief and Deliverance in some convenient time and way<*>. I begged that God would not suffer Hell to prevail against Heaven in my Family I pleaded that promise Psalm 37.4, &c. and I thought if I delighted my Self in his Image and People I delighted my Self in Him He that loves the Candle loves the Sun. I represented what a Comfort and Advantage or Support I should want in my present circumstances were I to be turned out of my Living. This troubled me more than all the threats I met with at the /fo. 85r/ Visitation that I should have so little Solace at home in my Affliction but I remembered and urged Isaiah 24.8— God doth not use to lay two heavy Afflictions on his people at once. Lord! I'd fain have had a little Comfort, and done Thee some Service, and brought Thee some Honour in my Generation if I could.

For my wife I prayed that God would free her from her Melancholy Enlarge her Capacity Suit and reconcile her with my just desires. And especially I prayed earnestly for the Pardon of her Sins and Salvation of her Soul.

I was commonly very much enlarged and sometimes very much affected even unto tears and I endeavoured to work and compose my Soul to the greatest Sincerity that I was able. But yet I must Confess I could not (or did not) in this long course always refrain from very undue Passions and impatient Complaints nor always suppress undue Motions and Desires and I oft used expressions which (though I met

*Marginal note: * as should seem best to his Godly Wisdom.

with them in Dr Manton Luther and others),* I have been since afraid were too bold and irreverent to be said to God.

And though I oft despaired, yet I was oft supported with stedfast Hopes springing up in my heart that God would some way or other deliver me and make me Glad according to the dayes wherein he had afflicted me. And so thought others of my friends also One saying at [401] that Fast day when I had their help with me (viz. June 10.) when we rose from Prayers the first time I would not have you think of putting Martha and Alice away for I am hugely satisfied that God will send Deliverance some way or other, and it may be in a Way you think not on. But this Advice was not taken nor to be taken for reasons above mentioned.

One solemn Transaction betwixt God and my own Soul I will her [*sic*] Record because it may be of Use to me while I live to awaken me to my Duty by minding me what I Covenanted and Promised in the Strength of Grace It was July 8. I did that Day write down the Grounds of my Trust and particulars of my plea in those branches /fo. 85v/ of the Name of God which I after digested in my Sermon of the life of Faith on Hebrews 10. 38. (in the 2[d] Generall Head page 6–13.) and which I applyed to this Affliction and then added as followeth

[402]Now that I may not loose the Blessing of which here is such rich Assurance given me. I do seriously and sincerely This day as followeth

I. I do solemnly Renew ratifie and confirm my christian Covenant which is this, Renouncing the World, the Flesh and the Devil I do unfeignedly Give up my whole Self to God the Father Son and Holy Ghost as my God and Father my Redeemer and Saviour and my Sanctifier and Comforter: that I may be his Devoted Redeemed and sanctifyed Child and Servant.

II. I do solemnly profess (being Convinced of the Certeinty of all the preceding Grounds) that I do stedfastly Believe that God will ere long to my full Satisfaction and Comfort in some seasonable manner effectually and fundamentally Hear my Prayers Remove these Afflictions Answer my chief Ends in my Matrimonial Relation for which I forsook earthly Riches and Portion.

*Marginal note: For I then read Dr Manton on the 119 Psalm and Dr Spurstow on the Promises &c. for my direction and Assistance in this Duty.[403]

[401] *the* and an illegible word cancelled.

[402] Rastrick's hand resembles printed italics in this passage. The three roman numerals are highlighted in bold.

[403] Thomas Manton, *One Hundred and Ninety Sermons on the Hundred and Nineteenth Psalm, preached by the late reverend and learned Thomas Manton* (London, 1681); William Spurstowe, *The Wels of Salvation Opened: or, a treatise discovering the nature, preciousnesse, usefulness of Gospel-promises, and rules for the right application of them* (London, 1655).

III. Which if my God will Vouchsafe to do, (and for which I now firmly trust in him) I do solemnly Promise that (by His Grace) I will make a Holy Use and Improvement of the Mercy. I will set up some other stated Exercises of his solemn Worship in my House. And I will serve Him and His Interest in his Church with all the Vigour and Alacrity that such a Favour will bring along with it In Testimony whereof (Offering this to Thee my Dear Lord I have hereto set my hand this 8th day of July in the year of my Redeemer, 1684.

John Rastrick[404]

This was signed ratified and Confirmed in the Presence of my God.

Memorandum. When by after Providences and Events I saw cause to suspect the Manner of Management and Temper attending it, and to Repent of the same upon a Review I did and do now at this Transcribing it thus subscribe. This Covenant (abstracted from the Sin that attended it) I desire upon the best Grounds to Continue. John Rastrick.

/fo. 86r/ After this manner I made my Complaint and Prayer to the Lord many days. And on Satturday July 12. (1684) in the afternoon my wife unexpectedly came home from the Waters of her own will without her Friends or physician's knowledg or advice and that in the prime of the Water=drinking Season. And after some rough words given by her to the Servants (who, (we not expecting her so soon) were not yet gone) they presently packed away to their new hired house that night.

When she was thus come home and the Servants gone, I confess I could not forbear now and then reasoning with her upon the Case: I urged her to be charitable to them, and to be often sending them something: but she persisted in her Opinion that they had no more Goodness than any Common silly wenches in the Town, and therefore deserved no such kindness: (Contrary to the Sense of all my Christian Friends that knew them;) She thought it was all nothing but my conciet I sometimes talked seriously and Convincingly with her upon her Souls account and to bring her to Repentance. Asked, How if Christ took them for children, whom she turned out of doors as Dogs I urged that of Mark 18.6. Whoso shall offend &c. (And Philemon verse 16. Not now as a Servant, but &c I had observed to her before:) but nothing moved her She would say all was but my conciet of them. So I resolved to say no more, or as little as I could. Her Carriage was sometimes very terrible and frightfull, and somewhat distractedly she would look; and sometimes would be set upon talking to my great trouble. But I continued my Prayers as had done before.

[404] End of passage in style of printed italics.

About the Middle of September (1684) Martha Wray our ancient Servant fell sick, and dyed on Friday the 26 following at her own house. And on September 21 Lords Day my Wife fell sick of an Autumnal intermitting Fever. On Munday (next day) I consulted Mr Richardson (who had long practised physick) about her health; but she would use none of the means that he prescribed. On Wednesday her intermitting day she went to see Martha then sick at her own house. But on Thursday her Fever returning with a Diarrhœa She dyed on Satturday September 27. about midnight. She spoke in her Sickness what a sad wife she had been to me, and how she could never make me amends. Said she, I have been a high spirited Creature; If I had been but humble and meek and as I should be, /fo. 86v/ Things would never have been as they have been. And when I spoke something of Comfort to her, said she I'm naught, I'm naught; I'm undone, I'm undone. After this her Going away ran much in her mind, Oh, that ugly Sin, as she called it. She Sent for Mr Scoffin; (and sent to Mr Richardson who could not come to see her) to pray for her. And crying out an hour or two before she dyed, sweet husband I went to her, and heard her (as I thought) whisper, Have a Care of my Barnes[405] The Pangs and Agonies of Death were very bitter to her: Sure (said she) God is angry indeed, this shows that he is angry! If this be intollerable what is Hell? O that Sinners knew this: and the like: with some more hard and despairing passages with respect to her Self.

Death is a serious thing; and this was an awakening providence: And when my wife was gone the Lord made me more sensible of my Sins and Miscarriages in my late Marriage State So I set a Day apart (October 10.) for Fasting Humiliation and Prayer that God would forgive my former Relational Sins and heal my Soul. A Burthen can hardly ly long upon a place but it will leave some Soreness or Galledness[406] or at least some Cicatrix[407] or print, especially when we bear it not well but fridg[408] under it: That this might be done away and the Joy of God's Salvation restored to my Soul and his Afflicting dispensations sanctifyed I made my serious Addresses to him this day and pleaded his Promises of Pardon with fervency.

In this State of my Solitude and Widdowhood I could not but Cast my thoughts upon my pious Friend and Acquaintance Mris Mary Harrison Daughter of Mr Ralph Harrison Merchant in Boston knowing none like her for that which I thought I most desired in a

[405] *barnes*: a common way of rendering bairns (children), especially in the north of England. *OED*.

[406] *galled*: irritated, vexed, unquiet, distressed; hence galledness: irritation. *OED*.

[407] *cicatrix*: the scar remaining after a wound or sore is healed. *OED*.

[408] *fridge*: to move restlessly; to fidget. *OED*.

wife. And I kept several days (6 or 7) of Fasting and Prayer to seek God's Direction about it that if he saw it would not do but that I should be decieved and mistaken or run into a Snare in fixing there that he would prevent it by dashing all such thoughts and alienating my affections from her: but if otherwise, that he would succeed it and make us Comforts and Blessings to each other

On one of these days I called in the Assistance of two or three of my best Friends /fo. 87r/ Ministers. viz Mr Richardson (once Minister in Stamford, silenced Bartholomew 1662) and my Neighbours Mr Burroughs Minister of Frampton and Mr Scoffin Minister of Brothertoft. Mr Richardson discoursed very well and gravely before we began and insisted much upon the Need and desireableness of a Meek and quiet Spirit in a wife. Said he, Next to Peace in a Mans Conscience is Peace in his Family A little gravel in the reins is more troublesome than all the dirt and gravel in the High way: and a little Wind in the Bowels worse than all the Storms abroad.— And afterwards he summed up the Considerations about the person pro and con and left me to judg which did preponderate.

I mentioned my thoughts to him that day that though we might not expect all outward good things in kind upon our Prayer for them, yet spiritual Mercies we might expect in kind when we Prayed for them. He said, we had no Promise to encourage us to expect absolutely all spiritual Mercies that we shall pray for, although spiritual; nor ground to Conclude that God would hear our Prayers in kind for every such Mercy of that nature; and he instanced in Assurance which though a Soul Blessing, yet God might see fit for divers reasons to deny several of his children in that should pray for it.

On the 26 of March 1685 I was marryed to Mris Mary Harrison of Boston beforementioned. Who, after she had lived with me about six years and 5 months was taken away by Death at the latter end of August 1691. She dyed in childbed having been delivered of a dead child about a fortnight before. Mr Pell of Boston my esteemed Friend preached her Funeral Sermon at Spaulding whether I was then removed. This was a sharp and very afflicting Stroke. and laid me in Grief and Tears.

She was a Woman that read wrote and Prayed much though her Natural temper was none of the very best. But that which I am principally here with Sorrow to remark is that I did not improve the Society of such a person (as before I had her) I promised my Self I should. So I saw plainly the great Decietfulness of my own Heart. And I had opportunity and Occasion while she lived as well as upon her death to make oft and deep reflections on the former passages of my Carriage towards my first wife For after she was dead God gave me more and more every year the Sight of my Sin and his Providences Convinced me /fo. 87v/ that I had heinously offended by my miscarriages towards her. I was now Convinced that I did not love her as I ought to have done. I was tempted under my Afflictions by her to be weary of her and to desire a change and though when such thoughts arose in my mind I frequently and earnestly resisted and repelled them with, Avoid Satan; and, The Lord rebuke thee Satan, yet, they were my Sin nevertheless; and I found it hard to overcome those Temptations and I thought I might pray that God would rather take her away by death than that her Disorder and Melancholy should arise to Distraction and the direfull effects. But now I saw that Concupiscence, or even the first rising of Corruption in the heart is Sin, though resisted and repelled; and I had hence a feeling and experience that helped me in my Sermons on Lamentations 3.40 which I first preached at Spalding. I was too impatient under my Affliction (by my wife's Melancholy) and did not submit as I ought to the Will of God; and I prayed too little comparatively for such Submission and Contentment and Sanctification of the Affliction. I prayed with too great and sinfull an eagerness for a thing of this Nature. (Which Mr Pell in a Sermon of Prayer first convinced me of Instancing in Rachel Genesis 30.1. with 35.18. compared) I think I was acted with a kind of Enthusiasm in all this and methinks nothing has let me more understand the Case of Enthusiasts and their Sin than this thing. And many sad and sinful Circumstances scandalous Offensive and imprudent to a high degree did attend my troubles and Prayers.

For these things I was struck with a deep Sorrow thought all was lost as to any Service I could do or Success I could expect. daunted in my publick work, and for the two or three last years of my Ministry at Kirkton when the Church was the fullest I was tempted to be lowest in my Voice and shortest, and lost most of the awakening earnestness I had been used to preach with. I never loved to see my face in a glass, much less now when my Sins took such hold upon me that I was not able to look up. as Psalm 40. 12. Ashamed of my own name and an abhorring to my Self for my Sin. Many a waking hour in the Night did I spend in Penitential thoughts and fervent mental prayers, in my second wife's dayes. Methought I never so plainly discerned that Temper that drew me down from God in the Common Apostacy of mankind as in these things I saw it was a kind of Jealousy of God as if he envyed /fo. 88r/ us a Considerable part of our felicity when there are so many things denyed us by his Laws or by his Providence which we have much ado to forbear thinking would be good for us if we might but have them. I oft suspected that it was for the Sin of my Conformity that God brought this Affliction upon me; and suffered me to fall into so much Sin. And these were the Sins I meant in that passage in the close of my last Publick Sermon.

But yet I must not Conceal the more Comfortable Consequences of all this. God's Wonderfull Grace altered my Carriage as well as Sense, and he gave me a Considerable Victory over my Passions and Unnaturalness and in time over my Melancholy also. And I had several Servants came afterwards into my Family, Strangers (as to what appeared) unto God at their coming that in a little time became seriously religious and discovered a Work of Grace upon their Souls, and were a great Comfort to us. And for ought I know those in my own Family to whose Conversion the Lord hath made me Instrumental may be more than those that have been Converted by my Ministry in any if not all the Churches where my chiefest Labours have been bestowed. At least proportionably many more.

And God supported my Spirit under all my trouble and preserved me from Despair As may be seen in that Hymn in which I digested my working penitential thoughts and the Frame and Temper of my mind at that time at the End of Playfords Psalms and Hymns in folio beginning, Lord if thou but hide thy Face &c——[409]

And further, After God had taken away my second Wife He gave me an Unvaluable and Unexpected mercy and Blessing in a Third who was Mris Elizabeth Horn the daughter of James Horn deceased of Sutton in Lincolnshire whose Uncle was Mr John Horn of Lynn Regis the Non Conformist Minister.[410] A woman of that Good Breeding Parts Wit Prudence Piety Meekness Modesty Gravity and Solidity Suitableness to my Temper and Diligence in Instructing and Managing our children &c.* that it is hard to say in which she excelled most which I write now after more than Ten years experience I was Marryed to her the 1st of September Anno Domini 1692.

[411]She was born May 2 1672 was married September 1 1692 and Died November 20. 1740. a Quarter before 5 in the Evening. Aged 68 years 7 Months 6 days.

/fo. 88v/
[Blank page]

*Marginal note: And an Excellent Mother in Law to my other children

[409]For the full text of Rastrick's hymn, based on 'The lamentation of a sinner', in Playford, *Psalms & Hymns*, see Lincolnshire Archives, MS 2 Cragg 4/7, fo. 1v (in separate gathering at the end of the manuscript).

[410]John Horne (bap. 1616–d. 1676), clergyman and ejected minister. *ODNB*.

[411]This sentence, which was written after Rastrick's death, has been inserted at the bottom of the page in another hand.

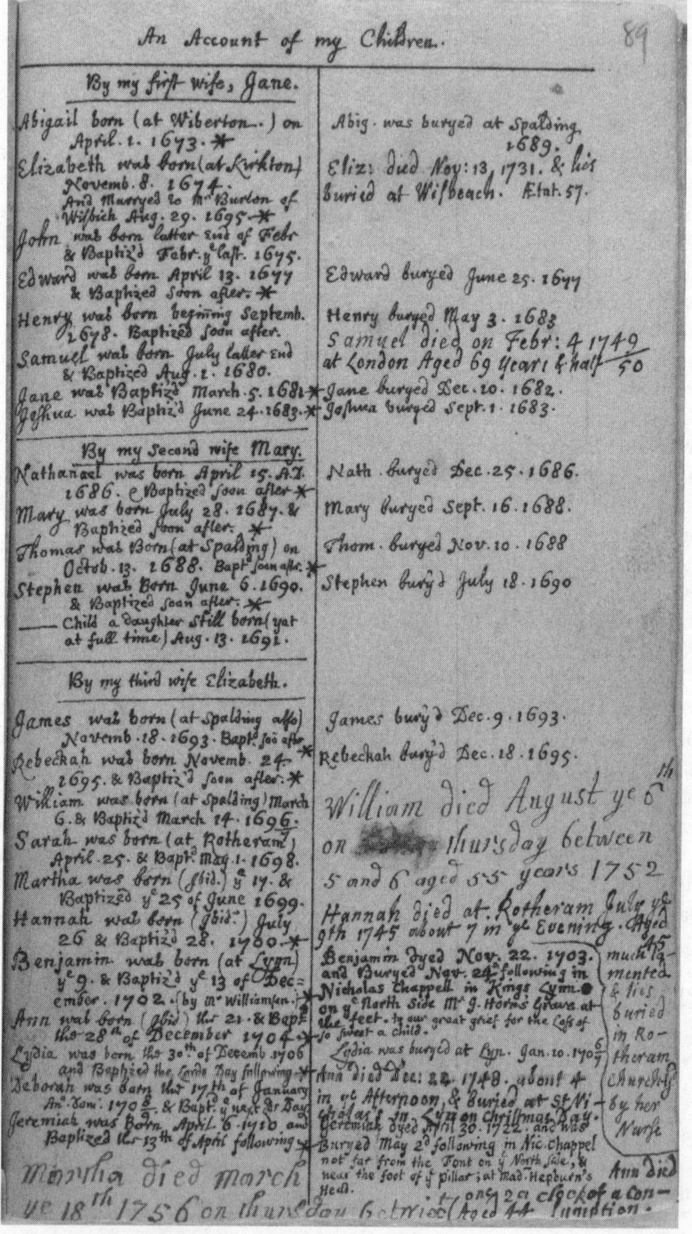

An Account of my Children. 89

By my first wife, Jane.

Abigail born (at Wiberton.) on April. 1. 1673. *
Elizabeth was born (at Kirkton) Novemb. 8. 1674. And Marryed to Mr Burton of Wisbich Aug. 29. 1695. *
John was born latter end of Febr & Baptiz'd Febr. ye last. 1675.
Edward was born April 13. 1677 & Baptized soon after. *
Henry was born beginning Septemb. 1678. Baptized soon after.
Samuel was born July latter end & Baptized Aug. 1. 1680.
Jane was Baptiz'd March. 5. 1681 *
Joshua was Baptiz'd June 24. 1683. *

By my Second wife Mary.

Nathanael was born April 15. A.D. 1686. & Baptized soon after *
Mary was born July 28. 1687. & Baptized soon after. *
Thomas was Born (at Spalding) on Octob. 13. 1688. Bapt. soon after. *
Stephen was Born June 6. 1690. & Baptized soon after. *
—— Child a daughter Still born (yet at full time) Aug. 13. 1691.

By my third wife Elizabeth.

James was born (at Spalding also) Novemb. 18. 1693. Bapt. soo after
Rebeckah was born Novemb. 24 1695. & Baptiz'd soon after. *
William was born (at Spalding) March 6. & Baptiz'd March 14. 1696.
Sarah was born (at Rotheram) April. 25. & Bapt. May 1. 1698.
Martha was born (Ibid.) ye 17. & Baptized ye 25 of June 1699.
Hannah was born (Ibid.) July 26 & Baptiz'd 28. 1700. *
Benjamin was born (at Lynn) ye 9. & Baptiz'd ye 13 of December. 1702. (by Mr Williamson.) *
Ann was born (Ibid) the 21. & Bapt the 28th of December 1704. *
Lydia was born the 30th of Decemb 1706 and Baptized the Lords Day following. *
Deborah was born the 17th of January An. Dom. 1708/9. & Bapt. ye next Ld Day
Jeremiah was Born April 6 1710 and Baptized the 13th of April following *
Martha died March ye 18th 1756 on thursday betwixt 1 and 2 a clock of a consumption.

Abig. was buryed at Spalding 1689.
Eliz: died Nov: 13, 1731. & lies buried at Wisbeach. Ætat. 57.
Edward buryed June 25. 1677
Henry buryed May 3. 1683
Samuel died on Febr: 4 1749/50 at London Aged 69 Years & half
Jane buryed Dec. 10. 1682.
Joshua buryed Sept. 1. 1683.
Nath. buryed Dec. 25. 1686.
Mary buryed Sept. 16. 1688.
Thom. buryed Nov. 10. 1688
Stephen bury'd July 18. 1690
James bury'd Dec. 9. 1693.
Rebeckah bury'd Dec. 18. 1695.
William died August ye 6th on thursday between 5 and 6 aged 55 years 1752
Hannah died at Rotheram July ye 9th 1745 about 7 in ye Evening. Aged 45 much lamented & lies buried in Rotheram Church by her Nurse
Benjamin dyed Nov. 22. 1703. and Buryed Nov. 24. following in Nicholas Chappell in Kings Lynn on ye North Side Mr G. Horn's Grave at the feet. to our great grief for the Loss of so sweet a child.
Lydia was buryed at Lyn. Jan. 10. 1706/7
Ann died Dec: 24 1748. about 4 in ye Afternoon, & buried at St Nicholas's in Lynn on Christmas Day. (Aged 44
Jeremiah dyed April 30. 1722. and was Buryed May 2d following in Nic. Chappel not far from the Font on ye North side, & near the foot of ye Pillar; at Mad. Hepburn's Head.
Ann died

Fig. 2 'A NARRATIVE; OR AN Historicall Account Of The most Materiall passages In the Life of John Rastrick', fo. 89r.

/fo. 89r/

An Account of my Children.[412]

By my first wife, Jane.	
Abigail born (at Wiberton.) on April. 1. 1673. *	Abig. was buryed at Spalding 1689.
Elizabeth was born (at Kirkton) November 8. 1674. And Marryed to Mr Burton of Wisbich Aug. 29. 1695 *[413]	Eliz: died November 13 1731. & lies buried at Wisbeach. Ætat. 57.
John was born latter end of February & Baptized February the last. 1675.	
Edward was born April 13. 1677 & Baptized soon after.*	Edward buryed June 25. 1677
Henry was born beginning September 1678. Baptized soon after.	Henry buryed May 3. 1683
Samuel was born July latter end & Baptized Aug. 1. 1680.[414]	*Samuel died on February 4 1749/50 at London Aged 69 Years & half*
Jane was Baptized March. 5. 1681*	Jane buryed December 20. 1682.
Joshua was Baptized June 24. 1683.*	Joshua buryed September 1. 1683.
By my Second wife Mary.	
Nathanael was born April 15. A.D. 1686. & Baptized soon after*	Nath. buryed December 25. 1686.
Mary was born July 28. 1687. & Baptized soon after.*	Mary buryed September 16. 1688.
Thomas was Born (at Spalding) on October 13. 1688. Baptized soon after.*	Thom. buryed November 10. 1688
Stephen was Born June 6. 1690. & Baptized soon after.*	Stephen buryed July 18. 1690
—— Child a daughter still born (yet at full time) August 13. 1691.	
By my third wife Elizabeth.	
James was born (at Spalding also) November 18. 1693. Baptized soon after*	James buryed December 9. 1693.
Rebeckah was born November 24. 1695. & Baptized soon after*	Rebeckah buryed December 18. 1695.
William was born (at Spalding) March 6. & Baptized March 14. 1696/7.	*William died August the 6th on*[415] *thursday between 5 and 6 aged 55 years 1752*
Sarah was born (at Rotherham) April. 25. & Baptized. May. 1. 1698.	

Martha was born (Ibid.) the 17. & Baptized the 25 of June 1699.		
Hannah was born (Ibid.) July 26 & Baptized 28. 1700.*	*Hannah died at Rotheram July the 9th 1745 about 7 in the Evening. Aged 45*	
Benjamin was born (at Lynn) the 9. & Baptized the 13 of Dec=ember. 1702. (by Mr Williamson.)* Ann was born (Ibid) the 21. & Baptized the 28th of December 1704.*	Benjamin dyed November 22. 1703 and Buryed November 24th following in Nicholas Chappel in Kings Lynn on the North Side. Mr. J. Horns Grave at the feet. to our great grief for the Loss of so sweet a child.	[416]*much lamented. & lies buried in Rotheram Church-yard by her Nurse*
Lydia was born the 30th of December 1706 and Baptized the Lords Day following*	*Lydia was buryed at Lyn. January 10. 1706/7*	
Deborah was born the 17th of January Ano. Dom. 1708/9 & Baptized the next Lds Day.	*Ann died December 22. 1748. about 4 in the Afternoon, & Buried at St. Nicholas's in Lyn on Christmas Day.*	
Jeremiah was Born April. 6. 1710 and Baptized the 13th of April following*	Jeremiah dyed April 30. 1722. and was buryed May 2d following in Nicholas chapel not far from the Font on the North Side, & near the foot of the pillar; at Madam Hepburn's Head.	
Martha died March The 18th 1756 on thursday betwixt one and 2 a clock		*Ann died of a Consumption Aged 44.*

/endpaper/[417]

[412]This section is written in two columns, divided by a solid line. Many of the entries have been written in a different hand to John Rastrick's. They are placed in italics. The asterisks appear in Rastrick's text and indicate children who have died.

[413]Marriage detail in Rastrick's smaller hand beneath.

[414]In his will, William Scoffin (d. 1732) left books to Samuel Rastrick, silk dyer of London and to William Rastrick. *Calamy Revised*, p. 429.

[415]*Friday* cancelled (by rubbing).

[416]This is a continuation of the notice about Hannah's death.

[417]Like the flyleaf, the endpaper is glued to the cover. It appears to be a letter addressed to Rastrick. Although the letter is torn, part of the address is visible: 'To Mr R . . . / his House . . . / Kirkton . . .'.

APPENDIX

Will of John Rastrick, 1727[1]

/82/ IN The Name of God Amen I John Rastrick of Kings Lynn in the County of Norfolk Clerk being mindfull of my mortality and the uncertainty of this present Life and being Sommon'd by age and infirmities to bethink my Self of my Departure out of this world and having thro' Gods mercy the free use of my reason and understanding Do make this my last Will and Testament, written all with my own hand in manner and form following first I Comitt my Soul into the hands of Jesus Christ my Glorified Redeemer and Intercessor and by his mediation into the hands of[2] God my reconciled father with trust and hope of the heavenly felicity and my Body to be decently Interr'd without Unnecessary Expences at the Discretion of my Executrix in hopes of a glorious Resurrection to eternall Life thro' the merits of Jesus Christ my Saviour and as Concerning that Earthly Estate wherewith God hath blessed me which I Shall leave behind me I dispose thereof as followeth Imprimis I doe hereby ratifye and confirm the Joynture that I have given to my dear wife Elizabeth by Indent[3] bearing date the 29th day of May Anno Domini 1696 of my Estate in Heckington and Asgaby[4] in the County of Lincoln willing that it goe according to the Tenor of the said Joynture and Settlement as also that Estate in Sutton St Marys and in Holland in Lincolnshire which Jane the quondam wife of James Horn Enjoyed as her Joynture by her said Husband and unto which my Son William Rastrick is heir at Law this (with the forementioned Estate at Heckington and Asgarby) I do hereby as far as I have power ratifye and confirm to the said my Son William as his Inheritance to be Enjoyed by him after the decease of his mother my present <dear> wife Elizabeth above mentioned Item I give and bequeath my now Dwelling house with the Gardens and appurtenances Situate lying and being in Spinner Lane in Kings Lynn in Norfolk aforesaid which I purchased of my good friend

[1]Norfolk Record Office, Norwich, Will Register, Kirke, 82–84 (Will of John Rastrick of King's Lynn, 1727). Both wills are transcribed keeping original spelling, capitalization, and punctuation. Abbreviations have been expanded.

[2]*Jesus Christ* struck through.

[3]*Indent*: Indenture.

[4]*Asgaby*: Asgarby, Lincs.

Mr John Williamson Deceased as also that Close or pasture conteining by Estimation four acres more or less lying in Kirkton near Boston in Lincolnshire near the gate called Forefen Stow which I bought of Gregory Mapleson late in the tenure of widow Lee of Brother Toft as also that three acres of pasture lying in Sutton St Marys in Holland in Lincolnshire aforesaid Given to my wife Elizabeth by her great uncle Mr John Horne /83/ of Lynn Regis in Norfolk aforesaid Unto my five Daughters Sarah Martha Hannah Ann and Deborah Willing and appointing that the said lands be sold and the money be Divided amongst them for their portions at the Discretion of their Mother my present dear wife Elizabeth aforesaid She having hereby bequeathed to her a power to Live in the said my mansion house in Spinner Lane in Lyn as long as She pleases and to retein or hold the other Lands in this paragraph bequeathed for her and her familys maintenance till her said Daughters Shall marry or be Some other honest way Disposed of by or with her their said Mothers liking and Consent and if any of them Dye before they be soe disposed of I will that the monys raised upon the said Lands be divided amongst the Survivors at her/their mothers Discretion Item my Will is that if my Son William Should Depart this Life having no family or heir of his own that then (after my wife Elizabeth's Decease) all my Estate and lands before mentioned or value of them when Sold (Excepting my four acres in Kirkton) shall be equally Divided amongst my Daughters aforesaid Share and Share like and if any of them die while Single her portion Shall be equally divided amongst her Surviving Sisters and my Will is that in case my Son William Should die without heir of his own Body that then the before Excepted four acres in Kirkton Shall be accounted no part of my Estate so Divided but it Shall be given and I hereby bequeath it in that case only to the Church of Kirkton in Holland aforesaid where I was Sometime Minister as an augmentation to the vicaridge there for Ever according to and by virtue of an act of parliament not Long Since made in such cases provided that is impowering and to make and so Setling such augmentactions and this Conditional provision I make partly in Consideration of a legacy once left me and given to me as minister there and partly also because my Daughters will in the said Case of their Brothers Death have Competent portions without the said pasture Item I give all my Books manuscripts mathematical Instruments Tellescopes Double Barometer and all other things whatsoever of that kind found in my study and parler adjoining Shelves Drawers Cases &c as also my picture done by Deconing[5] To my Son William Rastrick provided

[5]Presumably Daniel de Koninck (1660–after 1720), whose portrait of Lord Chancellor Peter King (1669–1734) is in the National Portrait Gallery, London (NPG 470).

and upon condition that he continue a minister and preacher of the Gospell whether in a Conforming or nonConforming Capacity But if he should not be a minister or Continue a preacher So that he shall have little occasion for them or Should depart this life in a Single State and leave no Son a Scholler to Enjoy them or capable of using them that my will is that if any pious learned Studious minister Conformist or non conformist Shall marry any of my Daughters he Shall have all my Books manuscripts &c before mentioned over and above what her portion as before provided or bequeathed Shall be But if that Should not be then my will is that yet my said Library shall not be auctioned out or Sold to any Booksellers but be disposed of to raise a publick Library for the use of the Dissenting Ministers in the City of Norwich leaving it to their liberty what (by Collection made) to give my Surviving Children for them or my Son William if he live and yet desist from preaching or the Dissenting ministers there for the time being may treat /84/ with the City and upon agreement for their own free use of it add my library to theirs selling the lesser of the Duplicates and with that mony buying Such Books as Shall yet be leanting[6] to the whole and all to be managed at the Discretion of the said Dissenting ministers in Conjunction with an Equall number of the City Clergy whom they the Dissenting ministers shall chuse Item I give to my Son John Rastrick now or late in Carolina if he be yet living the Sum of five pounds of lawfull mony of England to be pay'd him within three months next after his return into England if he so return and also to his Children (if any such be prov'd to be) the Sum of twenty Shillings each to be paid them within the like terme after their arrival in England and if he or they Shall Settle and be diligent he in his Calling (which is that of a Stocking weaver) or they in any honest calling and Shall be of Sober life and Conversation then I hereby recommend to my Executrix to give him or them Such further Encouragement as She according to her ability and at her Discretion Shall think fitt Item I give unto my Son Samuel Rastrick at London Silk dyer the Sum of ten Shillings also to my Daughter Elizabeth the wife of Edmund Burton of Wisbich the Sum of five Shillings to be paid them within Six months after my Decease they having had their portions before Item I give to our maid Servant Susannah Hating (to be paid her within three months after my decease) the Sum of forty Shillings over and above her due wages Item all the rest of my goods and Chattles undisposed of I give and bequeath unto my said dear wife Elizabeth whom I do hereby constitute and appoint Sole Executrix of this my last Will and Testament to see my debts discharged and my legacys or childrens portions paid and my Body decently

[6] *leanting*: leaning, supporting, tending to the character of the whole. *OED*.

Interr'd at the least Expence posable and I do desire my good friend Mr Nathaniel Kinderley of Sechy Bridg[7] to be Supervisor of this my last Will and Testament In witness whereof I have hereunto Set my hand and Seal the Twenty Sixth day of July in the year of our Lord one Thousand Seven Hundred twenty five John Rastrick Published and declared to be the last Will and Testament of John Rastrick the Testator and Signed and Sealed in the presence of us James Hackgill John Money Thomas Wilson

Will of Elizabeth Rastrick, 1733[8]

/289/ In the Name of God Amen I Elizabeth Rastrick of Kings Lynn in the County of Norfolk Widow being mindfull of my mortality and <the> uncertainty of this present Life and being Summon'd by age and Infirmitys to bethink my Self of my departure out of this world and having through Gods <mercy>[9] the free use of my Reason and Understanding do make this my last will and Testament in manner and form following First I commit my Soul into the hands of Jesus Christ my glorifyed Redeemer and Intercession [*sic*] and by his mediation into <the> hands of God my reconciled Father with trust and hope of the Heavenly Felicity and my Body to be decently interred without /290/ unnecessary Expences at the discretion of my Executor in hopes of a Glorious Resurrection to Eternal Life through the merits of Jesus Christ my Saviour and as concerning that part of my Earthly Estate (over and above what is dispos'd of by the will of my late Husband) consisting in money and Houshold Goods I dispose thereof amongst my Children as followeth. Inprimis I give and bequeath unto my five Daughters Sarah Martha Hannah Ann and Deborah that two hundred pounds which was left me by my Cousen John Horn late Schoolmaster at Lyn to be divided equally amongst my said Daughters Share and share alike my son William relinquishing his right or Title to any part or portion of the same Item I give to my Son William the Clock Standing in the Hall Mr Horns Picture my mourning Ring one Silver Spoon and the Drawers wherein my writings are kept To my Eldest Daughter Sarah I give the best Bed in the best Chamber the large oval Table in the Hall and my Silver Tankard To my Daughter Martha I give the best Chest of Drawers in the best Chamber the blue Bed wherein I used to lie in my own Lodging Chamber the Dutch

[7] *Sechy Bridg*: Setchey Bridge, Norfolk, four miles south of King's Lynn.

[8] Norfolk Record Office, Norwich, Will Register, Goats, 289–291 (Will of Elizabeth Rastrick, 1733).

[9] Replacing *grace*, above the line.

painting which hangs in the Hall one of my lesser oval Tables and two Silver Spoons To my Daughter Hannah I give the green Bed in my Lodging Chamber one of the Lesser oval Tables and two Silver Spoons To my Daughter Ann I give the red Bed in the new Room the Table in the best Chamber and two Silver Spoons To my Daughter Deborah I give the Green Bed in the new Room the Table in my /291/ Lodging Chamber two Silver Spoons with all my China Ware and Tea Spoons and the least of the Dressing boxes To my Cousin Mary Buckingham I give my plain gold Ring To my maid Servant Susannah Hatin I give the Bed in the Garret wherein she lies with all that belongs to it as also so much of my wearing apparell as my Daughters shall think fit to Spare her desiring that the best thereof may be divided equally amongst my said Daughters Item I give and bequeath all my Books and Linnen pewter and brass to be divided equally amongst my Daughters aforesaid as they shall agree amongst themselves as also my Cane Chairs willing that each of them have one as likewise the rest of my Chests of Drawers not before disposed of to be divided amongst them willing and appointing that she who has the worst Chest of drawers have also my largest Dressing Box and as to the rest of my houshold goods and furniture my will is they likewise be divided equally <amongst my daughters or else to be sold and the money to be equally divided>[10] amongst them as they themselves shall think fit And I do hereby constitute and appoint my Son William Sole Executor of this my last will and Testament to See my debts discharged and my Body decently Interred at the least Expence possible. In witness whereof I have hereunto Set my hand and Seal this fourth day of June in the Year of our Lord one Thousand Seven Hundred and Thirty Three

Elizabeth Rastrick

Published and declared to be the last will and Testament of Elizabeth Rastrick and Sign'd and Seal'd in the presence of us John Cary Jane Cary John Money. 4th December 1740

Mr William Rastrick Executor within named was legally Sworn before me Thomas Pyle Surrogate

[10] This line has been interlined and is probably a mistake of copying the will into the will register.

INDEX